THE FABRICATION OF THE AUTONOMOUS LEARNER

This book provides a thorough and detailed analysis of how the figure of the 'autonomous learner' shapes educational practices. It unpacks the impact of current educational reform discourse that focuses on the individual pupil as a learner while neglecting the social dimensions of classroom practices. In view of the yet unknown requirements of the knowledge economy, students are demanded to take more responsibility for their learning and to become self-reliant, independent, lifelong learners. In turn, teachers are asked to tailor education to the individual needs of their students and to foster their individual learning trajectories.

Based on in-depth fieldwork and long-term observation of interactions in classrooms and other educational settings, scholars from three European countries – France, Germany, and Switzerland – show how the translation of the figure of the 'autonomous learner' into classrooms is shaped by distinct cultural traditions. Chapters analyse teaching routines and conceptions of self-reliance involved in autonomy-oriented settings and discuss how these change the sociality of the classroom. They scrutinize how autonomy is used to differentiate between students and how it contributes to the reproduction of social inequality. The book brings into dialogue two neighbouring research traditions that study autonomous learning from a sociological and an educational perspective and which have largely ignored each other until now. In so doing, the contributions engage a critical perspective for a careful empirical analysis in order to better understand what is being done in the name of autonomy.

Providing insight into the many facets of developing and nurturing self-standing pupils across various educational contexts, this is ideal reading for scholars in the field of education, as well as teachers and decision-makers across the educational sector.

Judith Hangartner is Professor at Bern University of Teacher Education, Switzerland.

Héloïse Durler is Associate Professor of Sociology at Lausanne University of Teacher Education, Switzerland.

Regula Fankhauser is former Professor at Bern University of Teacher Education, Switzerland.

Crispin Girinshuti is Lecturer and Scientific Collaborator at Lausanne University of Teacher Education, Switzerland.

THE FABRICATION OF THE AUTONOMOUS LEARNER

Ethnographies of Educational Practices in Switzerland, France and Germany

Edited by Judith Hangartner, Héloïse Durler, Regula Fankhauser and Crispin Girinshuti

LONDON AND NEW YORK

Designed cover image: © Getty Images

First published 2024
by Routledge
4 Park Square, Milton Park, Abingdon, Oxon OX14 4RN

and by Routledge
605 Third Avenue, New York, NY 10158

Routledge is an imprint of the Taylor & Francis Group, an informa business

© 2024 selection and editorial matter, Judith Hangartner, Héloïse Durler, Regula Fankhauser and Crispin Girinshuti; individual chapters, the contributors

The right of Judith Hangartner, Héloïse Durler, Regula Fankhauser and Crispin Girinshuti to be identified as the authors of the editorial material, and of the authors for their individual chapters, has been asserted in accordance with sections 77 and 78 of the Copyright, Designs and Patents Act 1988.

The Open Access version of this book, available at www.taylorfrancis.com, has been made available under a Creative Commons [Attribution (CC-BY)] 4.0 license.

Funded by Pädagogische Hochschule Bern, Haute Ecole Pedagogique Vaud and Pädagogische Hochschule Zürich.

Trademark notice: Product or corporate names may be trademarks or registered trademarks, and are used only for identification and explanation without intent to infringe.

British Library Cataloguing-in-Publication Data
A catalogue record for this book is available from the British Library

ISBN: 978-1-032-46007-9 (hbk)
ISBN: 978-1-032-46008-6 (pbk)
ISBN: 978-1-003-37967-6 (ebk)

DOI: 10.4324/9781003379676

Typeset in ITC Galliard Pro
by SPi Technologies India Pvt Ltd (Straive)

CONTENTS

List of illustrations vii
List of contributors viii
Acknowledgements xii

Introduction: The fabrication of the autonomous learner 1
Judith Hangartner, Héloïse Durler, Regula Fankhauser and Crispin Girinshuti

SECTION I
Effects of pedagogical approaches to foster autonomy in preschool (*école maternelle*) and primary school 23

1 Autonomous workshops and individual Montessori-type activities: An analysis of their effects on learning and inequalities 25
 Ariane Richard-Bossez

2 Invented spelling for achieving literacy on one's own: A persistent ideal of autonomy producing inequalities 41
 Fabienne Montmasson-Michel

3 The "pedagogy of autonomy": Similar educational tools for a variety of teaching practices 61
 Julien Netter and Christophe Joigneaux

4 The didactics of autonomy in multigrade classrooms 75
  Laura Weidmann and Ursula Fiechter

5 "Notice how you feel" and "train your brain":
  Mindfulness meditation as a technology of the
  self in education 91
  Jeanne Rey

SECTION II
Teachers' guidance of pupil autonomy in secondary schools 105

6 (Un)supervised autonomy: Getting pupils to "take
  responsibility" for their learning 107
  Héloïse Durler and Crispin Girinshuti

7 Doing reflexivity in a self-directed learning setting 125
  Regula Fankhauser, Judith Hangartner and Ditjola Naço

8 Group pedagogy and the acquisition of autonomy in learning 141
  Marie-Sylvie Claude and Patrick Rayou

9 Practicing social distinction when supervising pupils'
  autonomous projects 158
  Stéphane Vaquero

SECTION III
Autonomy concerns in the context of educational reforms: Inclusion and digitalization 175

10 Inside the "cocoon" of special education classes. When
   autonomy serves as a gold standard for reorienting pupils 177
   Laurent Bovey

11 On the norm of individual autonomy in school 192
   Thorsten Merl

12 The (de)construction of the autonomous learner in a
   digitalized school world 206
   Mario Steinberg and Yannick Schmid

Index 222

ILLUSTRATIONS

Figures

2.1	Tiphaine's writing	52
2.2	Emy's writing	52
2.3	Siméon's writing	53
10.1	Percentage of pupils according to the special education system at the start of the 2019–2020 school year (Canton of Vaud – Switzerland)	179

Tables

7.1	Answers (translated) to the question about typical mistakes and how to avoid them from the "subject-related" block	133
9.1	Socio-academic indicators in relation to pupils' TPE results	164
9.2	Socio-scholastic indicators and pupils' TPE results	170

CONTRIBUTORS

Laurent Bovey, Lausanne University of Teacher Education, Switzerland.
Laurent Bovey holds a doctorate in education sciences and currently works at the University of Teacher Education, in the Canton of Vaud. His doctoral work focused on the special education system in the Canton of Vaud in Switzerland and its effects on the careers of pupils and the reconfiguration of the special education profession.

Marie-Sylvie Claude, Université Grenoble-Alpes, LITT&ARTS, France.
Her research is devoted to the teaching of reading literature and to the reception of other arts in secondary schools. She tries to combine didactical and sociological approaches to analyse the difficulties faced by pupils and teachers.

Héloïse Durler, Lausanne University of Teacher Education, Switzerland.
As Associate Professor of Sociology, Héloïse Durler conducts research and teaches on the themes of teachers' work, school inequalities, and school-family relations. The issue of student autonomy is at the heart of her current research projects. She is involved in the training of future teachers in primary, compulsory, and post-compulsory secondary education and in special education.

Regula Fankhauser, Bern University of Teacher Education, Switzerland.
Regula Fankhauser studied philosophy and literature and did her PhD on German Romanticism. She until recently held a position as a senior researcher at the University of Teacher Education in Bern. Her research projects focused on aesthetic literacy, classroom teaching, and the embodiment of learning. She

is currently investigating how social interaction is framed and performed in individualized learning settings.

Ursula Fiechter, Bern University of Teacher Education, Switzerland.

Ursula Fiechter studied sociology, social and economic history, and pedagogy in Zurich, Switzerland, and wrote her PhD on educational inequality in Darmstadt, Germany. Her main fields of research are teaching and learning in multigrade classes, educational inequality, constructivist perspectives on difference, and ethnographic classroom research, as well as quality management and evaluation.

Crispin Girinshuti, Lausanne University of Teacher Education, Switzerland.

As Lecturer and Scientific Collaborator, Crispin Girinshuti is involved in the management of in-service teacher training. His research focuses on the mechanisms of in-service socialization of trainee or graduate teachers, in the context of teacher education.

Judith Hangartner, Bern University of Teacher Education, Switzerland.

After her PhD in social anthropology, Judith Hangartner turned to the field of education, where she pursues an ethnographic research strategy and is interested in questions of governance and governmentality. Before the project on self-directed learning that she directs together with Regula Fankhauser and Héloïse Durler, she conducted a study on local governance relations in the context of New Public Management reforms. Her recent interest includes how digital platforms are related to approaches of autonomous learning and how these devices shape the classroom and teachers' work.

Christophe Joigneaux, University of Paris Est Créteil, Education and Scolarisation group (ESCOL) of the CIRCEFT-Research Unit, France.

Christophe Joigneaux is Professor of Educational Sciences at the University of Paris-Est-Créteil-Val-de-Marne (UPEC) and a member and co-director of CIRCEFT-ESCOL and the RESEIDA (*Recherches sur la Socialisation, l'Enseignement, les Inégalités et les Différenciations dans les Apprentissages*) network. He is also a member of the editorial board of the *Revue Française de Pédagogie*. He specializes in the sociology of *école maternelle* and early childhood, school literacy and form, and the professional socialization of primary school teachers.

Thorsten Merl, RWTH Aachen University, Germany.

Thorsten Merl is a Visiting Professor of Educational Science with Focus on Diversity at the RWTH Aachen University. He received his PhD from the University of Cologne with an ethnographic study on the creation of dis/ability in inclusive schools. He is currently conducting research on pedagogical authority and the authorization of schools.

Fabienne Montmasson-Michel, University of Poitiers, GRESCO, France.

Fabienne Montmasson-Michel defended a thesis on the language socialization of young children attending the *école maternelle* in 2018. She is currently a Lecturer in Sociology and teaches at the National Institute of Higher Education of Teacher-Training and Education (INSPE) in Poitiers. She conducts research in the fields of sociology of socialization, education, and disability.

Ditjola Naço, Swiss Federal Institute of Technology, Zurich, Switzerland.

Ditjola Naço is a University of Bern graduate in sociology and Eastern European studies. Her master's thesis focused on the governmentality of self-directed learning. She is currently working on research on the improvement of youth labour markets through vocational, technical education, and training.

Julien Netter, University of Paris Est Créteil, CIRCEFT-ESCOL, France.

Julien Netter works on teaching practices and learning inequalities. He is the author of two books (*Culture and Inequalities at School* and *The Fragmented School*) devoted to the transfer of learning between the classroom and activities outside the classroom. He is also involved in primary school teacher training.

Patrick Rayou, Université Paris 8-Vincennes-Saint-Denis, CIRCEFT-ESCOL, France.

His research initially devoted to the sociology of childhood focused on the issue of inequalities in school learning in connection with the injunction to encourage the autonomy of pupils and innovative pedagogies. His approach, inspired by the sociology of the curriculum, attempts to find an articulation with the didactic issues of particular school subjects.

Jeanne Rey, University of Teacher Education Fribourg, Switzerland.

Jeanne Rey is a social anthropologist and teaches at the University of Teacher Education in Fribourg. She studies mobility and professional trajectories in educational and transnational contexts. She has recently coedited a *Critique of Anthropology* special issue entitled "Cosmopolitan Enclaves: Spatial and Cultural (Under) Privilege in Education, Expatriation and Globalization" (2021).

Ariane Richard-Bossez, Aix-Marseille University, MESOPOLHIS, France.

Ariane Richard-Bossez is a Lecturer at the National Institute of Higher Education of Teacher-Training and Education (INSPE) and a member of the Mediterranean Centre of Sociology, Political Science and History (MESOPOLHIS) of Aix-Marseille (France). She conducts research on social inequalities and the process of democratization at several levels of the French education system.

Yannick Schmid, University of Basel, Switzerland.

He completed his BA in primary education at the School of Education, University of Applied Sciences and Art, Northwestern Switzerland, before studying Sociology and History (MA) at the University of Basel. His interest lies in the sociology of conventions and its link to educational institutions.

Mario Steinberg, University of Basel/Zurich University of Teacher Education, Switzerland.

He studied sociology and philosophy at the University of Basel and is a PhD student in Sociology at the University of Basel. In addition, he is engaged in a research project on algorithmic sorting in education at the Zurich University of Teacher Education.

Stéphane Vaquero, University of Limoges, GRESCO, France.

He defended a thesis on the cultural and social domination process in pedagogical *dispositif* in secondary high school in 2019. He is currently a Lecturer in Sociology and teaches at the National Institute of Higher Education of Teacher-Training and Education (INSPE) of Limoges. He published *Les ateliers de la domination scolaire* (Eds., La Dispute) in 2022.

Laura Weidmann, Bern University of Teacher Education, Switzerland.

A geographer and social anthropologist, Laura Weidmann has been working at the PHBern since 2017. Until 2020, she worked on "competence-oriented subject teaching", while completing her PhD at the University of Fribourg, Switzerland. Furthermore, she has been working in the ethnographic research project on the sociality of school settings for self-directed learning, together with Regula Fankhauser, Ditjola Naço, and Judith Hangartner, while teaching social science and methods.

ACKNOWLEDGEMENTS

This book project evolved from a two-day international colloquium which was supported by the Swiss Academy of Social Sciences and the Humanities. We thank Elisabeth Lamothe for translating some of the texts and for her editorial work on the book. The open-access publication was supported by the Universities of Teacher Education Bern, Vaud, and Zürich.

INTRODUCTION

The fabrication of the autonomous learner

Judith Hangartner, Héloïse Durler, Regula Fankhauser and Crispin Girinshuti

The "autonomous learner" is an omnipresent figure in present-day education. It evokes an active, engaged, responsible, and self-reflective individual taking learning into their own hands. The figure lies at the heart of current learning conceptions that are disseminated by the OECD (Dumont, Istance & Benavides, 2010; OECD, 2019; 2006). In consequence, it shapes educational policies, curricula, classroom practices, and far beyond, the way we think about education. Kindergartens, schools, and universities design specific spatial and temporal settings, such as learning studios or hybrid learning environments to foster autonomous learning. Schools can profile themselves as innovative by organizing classrooms into self-directed, self-regulated, or personalized learning environments. Far beyond such particular classroom arrangements, the figure of the autonomous learner influences curricula, teaching practices, and the assessment of pupils in schools.

With the notion of the "autonomous learner", we address an ongoing, profound transformation of education that relocates its focus from classroom teaching to the individual student as a learner. It is accompanied by a discursive shift that discusses education predominantly in terms of "learning" (Biesta, 2015). We claim that this present-day focus on the individual as a learner is shaped by philosophical conceptions of autonomy. Albeit liberal ideas of autonomy have informed our understanding of education for a long time, it is being transformed by the recent learning-centredness. In the present-day learning topography, autonomy amalgamates and intersects with notions of agency, self-direction, self-competence, self-management, self-regulation, etc. Thereby, it is striking that the very term autonomy is, by and large, conspicuously absent in today's discourse on learning. While the *élève autonome* holds some currency in the French discussion (Durler, 2015; Glasman, 2016; Lahire,

2001; Patry, 2018; Périer, 2014), the notion of autonomy is hardly present in the German debate, where the term *Selbstständigkeit* prevails. The term *autonomy* however is widely used in the field of foreign language learning in the literature in English (see later in this chapter). By insisting on the term *autonomy* and coupling it with the notion of learning, we highlight a conceptual relation that often remains implicit. Tackling the self-referentiality of the learning subject by the classical term autonomy, we connect the ostensibly innovative approach with its historical antecedents. It is an invitation to think about the legacies of former understandings of autonomy in education and how these are translated and transformed in present-day learning approaches.

Autonomy-oriented learning settings as a dispositif

The figure of the autonomous learner can only be understood by locating it in the context of the neoliberal political agenda that prefigures discourses on the learning society and lifelong learning (Field, 2006). In view of the unknown future demands of the learning society, students must be able to autonomously organize, plan, and reflect on their own learning. They are expected to "learn how to learn" so that they prepare themselves to become lifelong learners. It is not a question of acting directly on the individual, but of giving them the tools to act by themselves, to make them responsible by "activating" them (Astier, 2007). The autonomous learner corresponds to the entrepreneurial self (Bröckling, 2007), who is eager to actively approach the hitherto unknown challenges of the future. The autonomous learner shows an intrinsic "will to learn" and pursues learning as an investment in her or his human capital (Simons & Masschelein, 2008). While the learning paradigm initially directed learners to deal with economic challenges, now they are to tackle ecological problems, community values, and wellness (OECD, 2019). Thus, the active learning subject is not only imagined as homo economicus but far beyond faces the demand to invest their competences as a socially responsible person.

The policy goal of the autonomous learner is related to inclusive education as the second other major policy trend transforming educational institutions in the present (UNESCO, 2016). The policies of inclusive education and individualized, autonomous learning are united by their recognition of diversity. Inclusive classrooms are accompanied by the demand to individualize teaching to the particular needs of the individual learner and in consequence transfer more autonomy to the learner (Frandji & Rochex, 2011). The joint vision of inclusive education and autonomous learning promises to increase social justice through their attempt to support each student by addressing their particular needs and by advancing their personal interests and talents (Ricken, 2018). They are less concerned with equality and the aim to make people equal, than with equity and to equalize the chances of each individual to fulfil their own life project (Marquis, 2015).

Alongside research that strives to improve students' skills in autonomous learning (e.g. Jansen, van Leeuwen, Janssen, Jak, & Kester, 2019; Reusser, Pauli, & Stebler, 2018; Schunk & Greene, 2018b), there is an urgent need to adopt a sociological perspective to critically analyse the demands and constraints that these efforts place on students and teachers. Taking an interest in the "*fabrication*" of the autonomous learner calls for an understanding of autonomous learning as a *dispositif*: it means to establish an analytical relationship between the "thoroughly heterogeneous ensemble consisting of discourses, institutions, architectural forms, regulatory decisions, laws, administrative measures, scientific statements, philosophical, moral and philanthropic propositions – in short, the said as much as the unsaid" (Foucault, 1980, p. 194). Thus, speaking of a *dispositif* allows one to understand how the principles guiding the use of techniques, discourses, objects, and practices aim at fabricating today the "ideal pupil" (Becker, 1952) as an autonomous learner. The *dispositif* shapes the qualities that learners should demonstrate, their relationship to knowledge, and the power relations in which they must be involved. By focusing on autonomy-oriented learning settings as a *dispositif*, we favour an intermediate scale of conceptualization (Bonnéry, 2009), relating classroom practices and interactions to transformations of the *forme scolaire* (Vincent, 1994) and thus scrutinize the specific mode of present-day school socialization. Due to this anchoring of our perspective in the work of Michel Foucault, we keep the term *dispositif* in French throughout this book. To contextualize the sociological analysis of present-day, autonomy-oriented learning settings, we first summarize a historical systematic reconstruction of philosophical conceptions of autonomy and then reconstruct salient reform approaches of autonomous learning and their transformation during the 20th century.

Autonomy as an "essentially contested concept" in philosophy

While the notion of autonomy is hardly explicitly present in the present-day learning discourse, it is widely discussed within educational and moral philosophy and is considered an "essentially contested concept" (Drerup, 2016b). Deriving from the Greek "autonomous" – self-legislation, it was used in Greek antiquity exclusively in its political sense and referred to the free determination of the internal affairs of a state. As a personal or ethical category, autonomy is only of marginal importance in antiquity (Pohlmann, 2017). Only at the beginning of the early modern era and in connection with the denominational conflicts did autonomy increasingly gain an ethical dimension; in this context, it was understood as freedom of faith or conscience in denominational conflicts and was reinterpreted from a political threat to a positive achievement in a protestant context (ibid.).

In the 18th century, too, the different categorial dimensions of the term – political here, personal there – were discussed and put in relation to each other.

The two conceptual domains have a paradoxical core in common, which was first elaborated by Rousseau in a political context, and by Kant in a moral and pedagogical context. Rousseau's basic figure can be summarized as follows: without lawful order or coercion, there is no freedom (Schweppenhäuser, 2003, p. 102). In Rousseau's concept, political autonomy means voluntary submission to the law one has adopted as a rational being. Self-legislation, critical reason and the sovereignty of the people are mutually related in this figure (ibid.). In the context of Kant's moral theory, autonomy stands for the opportunity of human beings to determine themselves as rational beings. As is well known, Kant defined with the categorical imperative the principle of autonomy as rational self-determination. The autonomous person defines themselves through their ability to reflect on their own motives for action and to judge them in the light of generalizability. To act according to the categorical imperative implies a subject-transcendent obligation as the self-determined commitment to broader principles (Pieper, 2000, p. 31). An autonomous judgement is made when the subject manages to distinguish between their first-order desires – their personal preferences and maxims – and those of the second order – the generalizable ethical principles – and to judge the former from the perspective of the latter (Dworkin, 2015). To be able to judge the desirability of one's own motives, however, implies the possibility of distancing oneself from one's subjective motives. The autonomous subject sensu Kant becomes recognizable and attackable as ahistorical, disembodied, and socially isolated.

The paradoxical figure of voluntary submission has made a career in the history of pedagogy up to the present day, in particular through Kant's pedagogically turned question: "*Wie kultiviere ich die Freiheit bei dem Zwange?*" (Kant, 1983 (1803), p. 711).[1] The paradox that children are to be led to autonomy through more or less imposing force seems to be one of the basic antinomies of pedagogical activity to this day. Some scholars elevate this antinomy to a constitutive feature of the structural conditions of the profession (Helsper, 2004). Other perspectives deconstruct the pedagogical paradox as a consequence of a misunderstood subjectivity and an overstretched concept of autonomy (Ricken, 2007). An idealistic understanding of subjectivity constructs an irreducible opposition between freedom and oppression, which is "pedagogically unsuitable" (ibid., p.163). Autonomy is not only an "illusion" (Meyer-Drawe, 2000); what's more, if autonomy is understood as absolutely freed from external determination, then the pedagogical efforts do not serve liberation, but rather subjugation (Ehrenberg, 1998; Ricken, 2007, p. 165).

The criticism of the concept of autonomy within the field of education is part of a chorus of critical voices within social studies and the humanities that reject or at least relativize liberal autonomy concepts, demands, and impositions. Based on the classic critical approaches of Berlin (1969) and Foucault

(2001), (neo-)liberal autonomy imperatives are revealed to be instruments of power that proclaim a one-sided, individualistic concept of freedom and promote the breaking up of societal solidarity and the economization of all areas of life.

The critique of the concept of autonomy seems to be connectable to almost all contemporary critical debates and thus shows how central autonomy is for modern self-understanding (Drerup, 2016b, p. 128). However, the rather brittle anchoring of the critical debate in theoretical conceptions of autonomy contributed to intensifying the debate on the implications of the concept of autonomy in the philosophy of education.

Ultimately, the autonomy problem raises the question of how pedagogical authority can be legitimized. Within the framework of a pedagogical ethics of autonomy, autonomy is considered a regulative idea that sets the compass in education (Reichenbach, 2017). The ability to reflect critically on one's motives and priorities in the light of their general desirability and to orient one's life accordingly (cf. Dworkin, 2015), is not a prerequisite and starting point, but the goal of education and upbringing. An orientation "thanks to which life may become more dignified and living together more civilized" (Reichenbach, 2017, p. 89; our translation).

Within the more recent discussion about the autonomy-theoretical legitimation of education and upbringing in the philosophy of education, some central lines of difference have emerged. The debate is, firstly, concerned with the understanding of freedom involved in the autonomy regime. If freedom is understood exclusively as negative ("free from"), as in neoliberal argumentation figures, this implies – in pedagogical terms – that one should largely refrain from disciplinary, direct controlling, and regulating measures. If, in contrast, freedom is understood positively as the "ability to" (Nussbaum, 2011), then supportive and accompanying measures come to the fore, which can very well manifest themselves as active intervention and influence. The latter understanding of freedom also takes into account the sociality of autonomy. A socio-relational conception of autonomy considers interpersonal, social, and institutional support as central to leading a self-determined life. This perspective insists on the idea that autonomy is a status that depends on the recognition of others (Mackenzie, 2014, p. 41). It thus distinguishes itself from theories that equate autonomy with individualism and maximum freedom of choice. A socio-relational understanding of autonomy is flanked by the concept of "vulnerability". Unlike idealistic theories of the subject, which conceive the autonomous subject as self-empowering and unassailable, a socio-relational concept of autonomy refers to vulnerability and dependence on others to the danger of acquiring "capability deficits" due to social inequality. Autonomy and vulnerability are not seen as opposites, but the subject is conceived as both autonomous and vulnerable, as "human persons are both" (Mackenzie, Rogers, & Dodds, 2014, p. 16).

A socio-relational understanding of autonomy holds social and institutional institutions accountable for the way and extent to which they promote or impede the autonomy of individuals or groups. This brings two further lines of difference in the current discourse on the philosophy of education into view: firstly, it foregrounds the question of the extent to which educational actors and institutions may be guided by a defined idea of a good and autonomous life, i.e., pursue a perfectionist concept of autonomy. And secondly, it highlights the problem of paternalism, i.e., the controversy as to whether and to what extent those to be educated can be forced to do something they do not want at the moment with regard to their future well-being (cf. Baumann, 2008).

With these two controversial questions, the differences that had already come to light with Kant's paradox are repeated. While the pedagogical classics from Rousseau to Dewey advocate a perfectionist pedagogy and a paternalistic approach, the contemporary pedagogical discourse is rather cautious and reserved towards paternalism and perfectionism (Drerup, 2016a). This places it in the realm of libertarian or neoliberal positions, which conceive of autonomy exclusively in negative terms and are neutral with regard to a positive determination of a good and self-determined life (Christman, 2004). However, such an abstinent position is problematic as it has no instruments at its disposal to evaluate the legitimacy of different autonomy regimes. Following this line of thinking, it disbands an understanding of autonomy as an all-or-nothing issue. Rather, it calls for examining pedagogical arrangements in terms of their degree of appropriation (Drerup, 2015, p. 75) and evaluating them in relation to their objectives. This would have to be based on a concept of autonomy that is not only socio-relationally conceived but integrates both negative and positive dimensions of freedom. It would therefore be a matter of being able to justify theoretically, empirically, and normatively why one particular pedagogical autonomy regime is preferable to another (Drerup, 2016b, p. 137).

Translations of the concepts of autonomy into educational reform approaches

Educational reform approaches that centrally build on the idea of learner autonomy by presupposing the autonomy of the subject (Wrana, 2008, p. 31) are not at all a new phenomenon. Already at the turn of the 20th century, autonomy-oriented educational settings, termed "progressive education" in the USA, *Reformpädagogik* in German, *éducation nouvelle* in France, "child-centred", or "new education" in the UK blossomed (Idel & Ullrich, 2017). These approaches to reform are related to illustrious pedagogues, such as John Dewey, Helen Parkhust, Maria Montessori, Jean Piaget, Ellen Key, Paul Geheeb, Rudolf Steiner, Célestin and Élise Freinet, Alexander Neill, and many others. A popular view romanticizes these founding figures as theoretical and practical innovators who challenged the educational establishment and the autonomy paradox of education (Oelkers, 2010). These rather heterogenous reforms were united by their concerns with the active child and its interests, pupil autonomy and self-government, a less coercive teacher-pupil relationship, and democracy (ibid.; Wagnon & Patry, 2019; Patry, 2018).[2]

In the course of the emancipatory counter-cultural movements of the post-1968 period, child-centred education and alternative, antiauthoritarian, democratic schools and deschooling experienced a new upswing (Hartley, 2009). In addition, new approaches to autonomy-oriented learning settings emerged that also were inspired by the emancipative spirit of the 1970s. Following the earlier reform pedagogy, autonomy-oriented approaches (to this day) take a critical stance towards "traditional" and "authoritarian" pedagogy. Through this stereotyping of diverse and historically changing practices in classrooms, discursive fields of alternative and innovative autonomy-oriented pedagogical approaches are enacted. They are supported by constructivist theories of learning that emphasize learning as an active process in which learners construct new knowledge based on prior experiences and social interaction (Fosnot, 2013). These approaches are not only advanced by alternative private schools but have also been absorbed by public schools. The following brief reconstruction of the recent concepts of autonomy-oriented learning identifies distinct traditions and outlines the inherent understandings of the self and autonomy.

Concepts of autonomy-oriented classroom settings in public schools such as "self-regulated", "self-directed", "autonomous", "self-organized", and "personalized" learning centre on "the ability to take charge of one's own learning" (Holec, 1981, p. 3). Therewith, the autonomy-oriented approaches conceive autonomy not only as a goal but establish it as a central means of classroom practice. This means that autonomy is no longer delegated to the future, as an outcome of education, but is to be achieved and performed during everyday routines in the classroom.

Although the autonomy-oriented learning concepts increasingly show overlapping features, they have different roots and backgrounds: "self-regulated", "self-directed", and "autonomous" learning emerged, along with lifelong learning (Field, 2006), in the field of adult education during the 1970s and were shaped by the emancipative counterculture. In contrast, "personalized" learning was propagated in the early 2000s as a neoliberal political strategy (Mincu, 2012).

The concept of autonomous learning was initiated by the "Council of Europe's Modern Language Project" and enjoys still lively debates on (foreign) language teaching (Benson, 2007). Self-directed learning was propagated as an emancipatory approach in US adult education in the 1970s; it revolved around the idea of a learning contract between teachers and students (Knowles, 1975; Servant-Miklos & Noordegraaf-Eelens, 2021). Approaches to self-regulated learning started with cognitive-behavioural studies in educational psychology in the 1970s and focus on the meta-cognitive, motivational, and behavioural processes to improve learning (Schunk & Greene, 2018a). One major distinction between these approaches is whether their goal is predominantly a technical optimization of the learning process or whether their primary orientation is emancipation. In approaches to self-regulated learning, the implicit autonomy concept is restricted to the control of one's behaviour and the regulation of the learning process (Boekearts, 1999). In contrast, proponents of autonomous learning and self-directed learning weave didactical techniques with empowerment and social transformation: the understanding of autonomy includes setting the agenda and determining the content of learning (Brookfield, 1993; Little, 1991). While models of self-regulated, self-directed, or autonomous learning started with a focus on the individual learner, they gradually included a socio-relational perspective in order to take social embeddedness and cultural differences into account (Benson, 2007; Brookfield, 2009, p. 2620; Candy, 1991; Schunk & Greene, 2018b).

"Personalized learning" was one of the central ideas propagandized by the New Labour Government to restructure English secondary schools in the early 2000s (Mincu, 2012). Personalization policies aimed at raising standards and educational outcomes by focusing on individual aptitudes and interests: the policy demands involved the tracking of students' individual performance data, the adaptation of teaching to individual needs, paces and styles of learning, curricular choices, the improvement of teaching capacities, teacher cooperation and community support (Miliband, 2006). The autonomy concepts inherent in personalized learning are related to "choice" and "voice", turning students into co-producing consumers (Hartley, 2012). Although it is at least questionable how far personalized learning changed classroom practices in English schools (Maguire, Ball, & Braun, 2013), the concept was propagated by the OECD (2006) and has become part of a globalized educational reform discourse (Beach & Dovemark, 2009; Reusser et al., 2018).

With accelerated digitalization and the ubiquity of personal computers, personalized and other autonomy-oriented learning concepts have recently profited from an additional boost (Bingham, Pane, Steiner, & Hamilton, 2018). Digitally enhanced personalized learning settings break the spatial-temporal matrix of the classroom and extend it into an open learning environment (Shemshack & Spector, 2020). Under the digital condition (Stalder, 2018), autonomy-oriented learning is associated with competencies such as collaboration, communication, critical thinking, and creativity (Romero & Barberà, 2014). In digitalized learning environments, the expectations of learner autonomy increase. The "self-organized learning environment" by Mitra & Dangwal (2010), for example, that propagates digitally supported, self-organized learning largely without instruction reaches far beyond the usual autonomy-oriented classroom setting under teacher guidance.

This brief and sketchy overview tried to acknowledge distinct educational and scholarly traditions. In the meantime, the once distinct concepts have largely become detached from their original domains and are often used synonymously. The different terms have merged into a powerful discourse of autonomy-oriented learning, which is globally propagated through educational policies, curricula and teacher education, and which, finally, spreads through the classrooms of public schools. Autonomous learning has become a catch-all concept that can be filled as one sees fit by linking it to ideals of reform pedagogy or liberal concepts of autonomy, to cybernetic processes of self-regulation or the autonomous citizen. The notion might be directed to cognitive aspects of learning or behaviour and might address the goals of education or rather its condition and instruments. Despite these largely positive associations within the current educational debate, the discourse causes fervid criticism.

Critique of autonomy-oriented learning environments

Critical analyses of current autonomy-oriented approaches question their transformative emancipatory potential (Leroy, 2022). Instead of providing a freedom-emphasizing antipode to hierarchical teaching methods, autonomy-oriented learning approaches are adapting pedagogical practices to current governing and economic regimes; thereby, their autonomy concept is shaped by "a permanent oscillation between self- and external control, between freedom and subjugation" (Wrana, 2008, p. 43; our translation). From a poststructuralist perspective, the *dispositif* of the autonomous learner is criticized for its inherent conception of the self-empowered subject as a powerful instrument of government (Simons & Masschelein, 2008). The subject of the autonomous learner "is fabricated not by strategies of surveillance and punishment, but by activating its self-directing potential" (Bröckling, 2007, p. 61; our translation). This perspective exposes autonomous learning as a seductive framework that highlights its emancipatory potential and promises to liberate students from the disciplinary classroom while fostering the self-governing individual as an efficient exercise of power (Peters, 2012; Simons, 2020; Vassallo, 2015). Its conception of autonomy is criticized as being part and parcel of the molecular government of New Public Management (NPM) that transforms control into self-control (Boltanski and Chiapello, 1999). In this vein, the *dispositif* is in line with other NPM policies, such as school autonomy installed as a (self-)governing imperative in many countries around the world (Wermke & Salokangas, 2015).

Current approaches to autonomous learning are suspected of subverting pedagogical ideals of justice. It seems that the promise of equality by adapting education to the individual needs of each learner intensifies competition within the classroom (Beach & Dovemark, 2009). Inclusion then produces the social background against which the individual distinctions between learners – concerning competences and speed – are accentuated. The multiplication of personalized programmes and categories of distinction, such as "special educational needs", results in the fragmentation and hierarchization of the school's social body (Frandji & Rochex, 2011; Garcia, 2019). Rather than fostering equality, personalized learning and individualization of education are blamed for reinforcing inequalities (Beach, 2017). With a concern for the reproduction of inequality by and through education, autonomous learning is accused of corresponding to the cultural codes of the middle class and of supporting their children, while deprived children are further disadvantaged (Sertl, 2007). The Covid-19 pandemic showed drastically to what extent pupil autonomy is structured by social inequality: the sudden school closures during the pandemic with the interrupted, or at least impeded, communication between school and families, and the impossibility of constant teacher control, virtually threw students back on their capacities and resources to act as autonomous learners. However, research showed that access to teachers, internet connection, and learning devices, as well as parental support and the motivation for autonomous learning, have been unequally distributed (Conus & Durler, 2022; Delès, Pirone & Rayou, 2021; Reimers, 2022). The pandemic also made painfully obvious that educational institutions cannot be reduced to spaces of learning, but that they are important locations to feel integrated, to build friendships, and to develop social identities.

From the perspective of a critical pedagogy, the *dispositif* inevitably fails in its emancipatory claims because, unlike e.g., Freire's approach, it does not link learning to visions of social transformation (Servant-Miklos & Noordegraaf-Eelens, 2021). Rather than addressing democratic concerns and wider social questions, autonomous learning reveals its ahistorical and technicist preoccupation with "what works" (Fielding, 2012). More generally, autonomous learning is criticized as part of the "learnification" of education (Biesta, 2015) that empties education of content, purpose, and social relations. The *dispositif* deprives the school of its essential public character – namely, to provide education as a collective good shared publicly in the classroom (Masschelein & Simons, 2013).

The authors of the contributions in this book follow in different ways these critical perspectives. However, they do not enter the chorus of a general critique of the *dispositif*, which itself might be accused of evoking an undifferentiated discourse of autonomous learning. Rather, the contributions engage a critical perspective for a careful empirical analysis in order to better understand what is being done in the name of autonomy. They provide a thorough analysis of how educational institutions in three neighbouring European countries engage with autonomy-oriented learning settings and what challenges they face in their endeavours. They ask what kind of educational practices are generated by the *dispositif* in concrete contexts: how are specific autonomy-oriented settings organized? In what situations is the autonomy of students addressed and challenged? How do teachers engage in fostering the autonomy of different students? How do students deal with the demands of autonomy-oriented settings? What are the intended and unintended consequences of educational devices that strive to enhance the autonomy of students? They also evaluate the legitimacy of the autonomy regimes and scrutinize the forms of autonomy generated and the outcomes that derive from it. Thus, the contributions offer fine-grained analyses of how the autonomous learner is fabricated in particular locations and under specific conditions.

Ignorant neighbours: Francophone and Germanophone research traditions

Even though located in neighbouring countries, research in education in French- and German-speaking countries is conspicuously separated by language differences. Despite the geographical proximity, research exchanges only rarely bridge this boundary. As a consequence, researchers are largely ignorant of the debates, theoretical orientations, and empirical insights of their colleagues across the language barrier. This is even so within Switzerland, where the "*Röstigraben*"[3] (despite its decreasing importance in political questions) still largely divides the research practices between the German-speaking areas and the Romandie, each side being predominantly oriented towards the debates of their own linguistic universes. This mutual disregard of the Francophone and the Germanophone research communities results in a widespread ignorance of the similarities and distinctions of their respective educational practices in classrooms. In both linguistic contexts, there are specific labels for autonomy-oriented settings – such as "self-organized learning" in German-speaking Switzerland, "open(ed) classroom" (*offener/geöffneter Unterricht*) in Germany, and recently, *classes flexibles* in the Francophone areas. Far beyond such labelling employed for profiling schools, autonomy-oriented didactical practices spread through "ordinary" classrooms of public schools in all three countries.

The aim of this book is to bring research on autonomy-promoting learning settings from the Francophone and Germanophone tradition into dialogue. The contributions collected in this volume are based on an international conference held in January 2021 at the University of Teacher Education in Bern. The theme and title of the conference emerged in the context of the editors' joint research project, which was funded by the Swiss National Science Foundation as a cooperation between the Universities of Teacher Education in Bern and Lausanne.[4] The bilingual and thus intercultural orientation of the project was also reflected in the nationality of the conference participants: the conference brought together researchers from Switzerland, France, Austria, and Germany and thus made for exchanges not only across national but also across discursive and cultural borders. To make such dialogue possible, we favoured perspectives that show a certain proximity in their theoretical and methodological orientations. The contributions assembled in the book offer unique insights into the distinctions, similarities, transmissions, and parallel developments in schools and classrooms in the three neighbouring countries.

Besides, they account for the different theoretical concepts, research interests, methodological approaches of two research communities which rarely meet.

Despite their distinct, culture-specific backgrounds, both the Francophone and the Germanophone share a similar research habitus. They all are based on an extensive, ethnographic research strategy. With one exception, the contributions draw on long-term participant observation, which is supplemented by ethnographic interviewing and document analysis. They thus insist on a field approach that distances itself from the dominant reform discourse. Instead of looking for practical conditions for successful autonomous learning, the aim is rather to describe the various manifestations of this form of learning and also to look at the unintended side effects. All contributions are interested in the sociality of learning, i.e., they scrutinize the structures that condition the interactions and the social differentiations resulting from autonomy-oriented learning.

Theoretically and disciplinarily, the contributions are linked to different reference systems. While the Francophone contributions tend to be located in sociology, the majority of the Germanophone contributions are positioned within education, although sociologically-informed. And although both traditions ultimately go back to Bourdieu's praxeology, they accentuate different aspects of his theory. In the context of the Germanophone discourse, a "didactically interested ethnographic classroom research" (Breidenstein, 2009, p. 210) developed, which mostly pursue a practice-theoretical approach. Here – starting with Bourdieu – a variety of theoretical threads have been woven into a theory of social practices (Reckwitz, 2003). Wittgenstein's language game theory, Garfinkel's ethnomethodology, the governmentality of the late Foucault, and Judith Butler's performance theory all function as building blocks for the formation of a theory of social practices. As travelling concepts (Bal, 2002), they migrate into practice theory and shed new light on the objects under investigation.

With regard to the research subjects that have been worked on so far in the Germanophone educational ethnography, we would like to highlight the following topics: dimensions of space and time in individualized settings (Breidenstein & Rademacher, 2013; Reh & Berdelmann, 2012), student self-assessments and feedback practices (Breidenstein, 2018; Rabenstein, 2017), the school class and its meaning for individualization (Rabenstein, Idel, Reh, & Ricken, 2018), practices of doing difference (Rabenstein, 2010), or the shift of power relations in the context of "guidance to self-guidance" (Rose, 2016).

The contributions of the French-speaking authors activate key themes in the tradition of the Francophone sociology of education, focusing on the reproduction of social inequalities (Bourdieu & Passeron, 1964, 1970), on the social aspects of learning and knowledge transmission (Deauvieau & Terrail, 2007), or the articulation between didactics and sociology (Lahire, 2007; Losego, 2014). While the current Germanophone practice-theoretical perspective addressed earlier often discusses the complex relation between social processes and individual autonomy in terms of subjectivation, the Francophone authors in this volume privilege the term *socialisation*: from the sociology of socialization, autonomy is not an individual characteristic but dependent on the individual's social background and thus related to complex socialization processes (Darmon, 2006; Lahire, 1998). Therewith, this perspective is (much more than the Germanophone one) interested in the transfer of dispositions from one context to another (from family to school, for example), and it highlights the tensions, adaptations, and contradictions experienced by the actors of these different socializing experiences. Indeed, if the Francophone focus on inequality largely remains influenced by the thesis of the "reproductive school" on the macro-sociological level, recent research that is influenced by interactionist sociology (cf. Queiroz (de) & Ziolovski, 1994; Payet, 2016) aims to open up the "black box" of the classroom to examine empirically the genesis of these inequalities and the subjects that are produced (Millet & Croizet, 2016). This research perspective is increasingly addressing the subject of autonomy. Specifically, several contributions refer their discussion of learner autonomy to the work of the British socio-linguist Basil Bernstein, whose theoretical perspectives favour the articulation between school, family, language, curricula, pedagogy, and social class. With his "horizontal discourse", Bernstein (2007) addresses a convivial and participatory teaching approach that relates knowledge to the students' everyday world, while his "vertical discourse" refers to a hierarchically and coherently structured knowledge whose access, transmission, and evaluation is governed by explicit rules. Furthermore, Bernstein's theoretical distinctions – between strong and weak forms of classification or framing, as well as between visible and invisible pedagogies – are useful as well to analyse classroom practices and the forms of enacted knowledge. Another orientation of the Francophone contributions is Bernard Lahire's (2001) distinction between cognitive and political autonomy: while the former is limited to school learning and its organization, the latter is oriented towards the autonomous citizen and refers to, e.g., practices of collective negotiation of rules or the setting up of student councils for discussion of life at school.

Beyond their being embedded in different theoretical research traditions, the contributions are united by their focus on social practices and thus on the everyday routines and interactions that emerge in autonomy-promoting educational settings. With this perspective, they elaborate on the orders of knowledge and culturally shaped symbolic structures that underpin these learning arrangements. By juxtaposing the contributions from distinct linguistic and cultural contexts, our ambition is to open up opportunities for dialogue and debate, to examine the kinship and distinctions between conceptual frameworks.

Contributions

In the first section of this volume, we present contributions that examine how pedagogical practices in preschool education, kindergarten, and primary schools promote autonomy and what effects can be observed. Preschool education is called *école maternelle* in France and covers three years for children aged three to six. The following contributions show how preschool education in France, more than in neighbouring countries, advocates academic learning. Informed by Basil Bernstein's sociology of education, *Ariane Richard-Bossez* compares two types of pedagogical arrangements in the last year of the *école maternelle*: the so-called autonomous workshops and individual Montessori-type activities. Her investigation highlights two main processes: firstly, the weak cognitive framing of activities and the limited possibilities of scaffolding that result from it, and secondly, the accentuation of social distinctions in terms of exposure to academic knowledge in the case of Montessori-type activities. She concludes that these processes tend to close off the possibilities of acquiring learning for pupils who have not already mastered it because of their previous school or family learning.

Fabienne Montmasson-Michel also focuses on the connection between social inequality and the autonomy *dispositif* in the *école maternelle*. Her study explores a method used in France since the 1980s to promote literacy in kindergarten (in the third year of the *école maternelle*): by the so-called *écriture inventée*, young children are supposed to learn the alphabetic code from the practice and reflective analysis of their spontaneous writings. By confronting the socio-historical reconstruction of the *dispositif* with her ethnographic observations, she is able to highlight the difficulties and unintended effects of the *dispositif*. Her results also show how the method of *écriture inventée* does not eliminate the existing unequal literacy resources but rather reinforces social inequality.

In their contribution, *Julien Netter* and *Christophe Joigneaux* differentiate Bernard Lahire's distinction between cognitive (related to knowledge) and political (related to discipline and behaviour) autonomy pedagogy. In their comparison of two teachers in the *école maternelle*, who use the same autonomy-promoting instruments in different ways, the authors show the diverse effects on pupils' autonomy that can be attributed to concrete pedagogical practices. They, therefore, argue for increased attention to the influences of concrete teaching practices and to consider different forms of the "pedagogy of autonomy" and its particular links to learning inequalities.

In multigrade primary classes, teachers are confronted with the expectation of using individualizing and autonomy-promoting teaching settings. Much like Julien Netter and Christophe Joigneaux, *Laura Weidmann* and *Ursula Fiechter* compared the autonomy-promoting teaching methods and the underlying autonomy concepts of two teachers in two multigrade classes. In one of the presented cases, autonomy is seen as a working method; in the other case, autonomy is understood as the development of knowledge and skills, which are gradually acquired by the pupils of the multigrade classroom. These different understandings of autonomy by the teachers not only lead to different pedagogical interventions, but they also serve as criteria for their evaluation and assessment.

Finally, *Jeanne Rey* analyses mindfulness practice and training in a Swiss international school in the light of a Foucauldian "technology of the self". Her analysis shows how mindfulness meditation positions the pupils in relation to their thoughts, sensations, and emotions and as self-agents of their learning. This reflective way to frame autonomy echoes the specific microcosm to which the school belongs – namely, an "educational cosmopolitan enclave" where children of diplomats and CEOs mingle with local elites before moving to other destinations across the globe.

The contributions in the second section examine how teachers in secondary schools lead students towards autonomy. The first chapter by Héloïse *Durler* and *Crispin Girinshuti* analyses fieldwork during an autonomy-oriented project in mathematics by two teachers of mathematics in a lower secondary school in Switzerland. The analysis discusses how the two teachers leading the project engage different strategies of "mobilization" through forms of confrontation by which the teachers aim to bring students to take responsibility for their learning. The analysis shows how during the process, the initial freedom granted to students and their empowerment is increasingly restricted and contradicted by pressures and obligations. The authors interpret the emerging contradictions with reference to a conception of autonomy that overlooks the resources (cognitive, behavioural, etc.) needed for autonomous learning in the classroom.

Regula Fankhauser, *Judith Hangartner*, and *Ditjola Naço* examine self-reflection as a pedagogical practice that is highlighted in the context of autonomous learning in a lower secondary school. On the theoretical background of reflexive modernity and with a practice-theoretical perspective they analyse the use of two different reflection tools in an autonomy-oriented secondary school in Switzerland. While one instrument leads to ritualized, formulaic confessions, the second instrument reveals at least the beginnings of authentic self-reflection. In their conclusion, they consider the conditions under which the objective of reflection could emerge.

Group work is considered a promising option to foster the autonomy of students. *Patrick Rayou* and *Marie-Sylvie Claude* put this belief to the test and investigated group work in a French class (nineth grade) in a secondary school in Paris. They base their ethnographic study on the didactical theory of contract pedagogy. It can be concluded from their analysis that group work strengthens the social and the educational contract. In contrast, the didactic contract does not, as intended, enable all students to become autonomous readers, capable of turning the reading of literature into an authentic experience of personal development.

In the last contribution of this section, *Stéphane Vaquero* analyses the distinct forms of autonomy granted to pupils in the context of self-directed projects called *Travaux Personnels Encadrés* in French secondary schools. This setting demands students to find a personal question about a topic of their own choice, to conduct a research process, and to present their findings. Referring to Bernsteins' theory of horizontal and vertical discourses (termed "devices" here), the author points out that students with lower cultural capital are left on their own, while those with higher cultural capital rather attract the interest and support of their supervisors. The contribution discusses how the horizontal devices contribute to establishing distinctive signs of what teachers call "autonomy" and how they tend to reproduce the scholastic and social distribution of cultural capital.

The third section thematizes autonomy in the context of educational reforms such as inclusion and digitalization. *Laurent Bovey*'s contribution is oriented towards the sociology of special education. Applying an interactionist perspective, he shows how in special education classes autonomy works as a criterion in order to gauge whether or not to reorient students. Autonomy is understood in a narrow sense and serves as a "gold standard" for promoting students to return to ordinary classes or to relegate them to separate classes. He concludes that this situation highlights a paradox: while the school advocates student autonomy, it is unable to relinquish its role in controlling and monitoring students.

Thorsten Merl is also dedicated to student autonomy in an inclusive context. In his ethnography, he analyses performed expectations of autonomy in inclusive secondary schools. Based on theoretical perspectives of Disability Studies and Studies in Ableism, he shows three ways by which the ideal of individual autonomy is maintained: by hiding external influences on abilities, by allowing deviation for some students, and by explaining ongoing deviations with disabilities.

Mario Steinberg and *Yannick Schmid* focus on the figure of the autonomous learner in the context of digitalization in education. According to a widespread assumption, digitalization supports and promotes autonomous learning. The chapter examines how different educational actors assess the importance of digitalization for autonomous learning. The analysis, which is theoretically framed by the sociology of conventions, shows the broad spectrum between doubts and utopias that different school actors attribute to technology-based learning in relation to autonomy in classrooms.

Notes

1 "How am I to develop the sense of freedom in spite of the restraint?" (own translation).
2 In contrast to the reform approaches in the neighbouring countries, the German *Reformpädagogik* focused on the notion of community, which was shaped by nationalist influences (Oelkers, 2010).

3 *Rösti* is the Swiss-German name for a dish made of fried, grated potatoes; the term *Röstigraben* is commonly used as a metaphor to highlight not only the linguistic but also the cultural and political distinctions between the Francophone and the Germanphone areas of Switzerland.
4 The conference entitled "The Dispositive of Autonomy in the Learning Society – *Konstruktionen des selbstständigen Bildungssubjekts – La fabrique de l'individu autonome et ses contextes éducatifs*" was held online, January 27/28, 2021. It was part of our joint research project funded by the SNSF, Project Nr 100019_173035, entitled "*Führung zur Selbstführung – Eine ethnografische Studie zu schulischen Settings des selbstständigen Lernens*" (2017–2022).

References

Astier, I. (2007). *Les nouvelles règles du social*. Paris: PUF.
Bal, M. (2002). *Travelling concepts in the humanities. A rough guide*. Toronto: University of Toronto Press.
Baumann, H. (2008). Reconsidering relational autonomy. Personal Autonomy for socially embedded and temporally extended selves. *Analyse und Kritik*, 30, 445–468. https://doi.org/10.1515/auk-2008-0206
Beach, D. (2017). Personalisation and the education commodity: A meta-ethnographic analysis. *Ethnography and Education*, 12(2), 148–164. https://doi.org/10.1080/17457823.2016.1247738
Beach, D., & Dovemark, M. (2009). Making 'right' choices? An ethnographic account of creativity, performativity and personalised learning policy, concepts and practices. *Oxford Review of Education*, 35(6), 689–704. https://doi.org/10.1080/03054980903122267
Becker, H.S. (1952). Social class variations in the teacher-pupil relationship. *American Journal of Educational Sociology*, 25, 451–465. http://dx.doi.org/10.2307/2263957
Benson, P. (2007). State-of-the-art article: Autonomy in language teaching and learning. *Language Teaching*, 40(1), 21–40. https://doi.org/10.1017/S0261444806003958
Berlin, I. (1969). *Four essays on liberty*. Oxford: Oxford University Press.
Bernstein, B. (2007). *Pédagogie, contrôle symbolique et identité: Théorie, recherche, critique*. Sainte-Foy, QC: Presses de l'Université Laval.
Biesta, G. (2015). Freeing teaching from learning: Opening up existential possibilities in educational relationships. *Studies in Philosophy and Education*, 34(3), 229–243. https://doi.org/10.1007/s11217-014-9454-z
Bingham, A.J., Pane, J.F., Steiner, E.D., & Hamilton, L.S. (2018). Ahead of the curve: Implementation challenges in personalized learning school models. *Educational Policy*, 32(3), 454–489. https://doi.org/10.1177%2F0895904816637688
Boekearts, M. (1999). Self-regulated learning: Where we are today. *International Journal of Educational Research*, 31(6), 445–457. https://doi.org/10.1016/S0883-0355(99)00014-2
Boltanski, L., & Chiapello, E. (1999). *Le nouvel esprit du capitalisme*. Paris: Gallimard.
Bonnéry, S. (2009). Scénarisation des dispositifs pédagogiques et inégalités d'apprentissage. *Revue française de pédagogie*, 167, 13–23. https://doi.org/10.4000/rfp.1246
Bourdieu, P., & Passeron, J.-C. (1964). *Les héritiers. Les étudiants et la culture*. Paris: Minuit.
Bourdieu, P., & Passeron, J.-C. (1970). *La reproduction. Eléments pour une théorie du système d'enseignement*. Paris: Minuit.

Breidenstein, G. (2009). Allgemeine Didaktik und praxeologische Unterrichtsforschung. In M.A. Meyer (Ed.), *Perspektiven der Didaktik*. Wiesbaden: Verlag für Sozialwissenschaften. https://doi.org/10.1007/978-3-531-91775-7_14

Breidenstein, G. (2018). Schülerselbsteinschätzungen im individualisierten Unterricht zwischen pädagogischer Ambition und didaktischem Vollzug - eine Fallstudie. In K. Rabenstein, K. Kunze, M. Martens, T.-S. Idel, M. Proske, & S. Strauss (Eds.), *Individualisierung von Unterricht. Transformationen - Wirkungen - Reflexionen* (pp. 103–120). Bad Heilbrunn: Verlag Julius Klinkhardt.

Breidenstein, G., & Rademacher, S. (2013). Vom Nutzen der Zeit. *Zeitschrift für Pädagogik, 3*(59), 336–356. https://doi.org/10.25656/01:11941

Bröckling, U. (2007). *Das unternehmerische Selbst. Soziologie einer Subjektivierungsform*. Frankfurt a. M.: Suhrkamp.

Brookfield, S. (1993). Self-directed learning, political clarity, and the critical practice of adult education. *Adult Education Quarterly, 43*(4), 227–242. doi:10.1177/0741713693043004002

Brookfield, S. (2009). Self-directed learning. In R. Maclean & D. Wilson (Eds.), *International handbook of education for the changing world of work: Bridging academic and vocational learning* (pp. 2615–2627). Dordrecht: Springer Netherlands. https://doi.org/10.1007/978-1-4020-5281-1_172

Candy, P.C. (1991). *Self-direction for lifelong learning*. San Francisco, CA: Jossey-Bass.

Christman, J. (2004). Relational autonomy, liberal individualism, and the social constitution of selves. *Philosophical Studies, 117*, 143–164.

Conus, X., & Durler, H. (2022). L'enseignement à distance en temps de crise en Suisse: révélateur ou renforçateur des inégalités sociales et de genre autour du rôle de parent d'élève? *L'éducation en débat: Analyse comparée, 12*(1), 55–71. http://hdl.handle.net/20.500.12162/5800

Darmon, M. (2006). *La socialisation*. Paris: Colin.

Deauvieau, J., & Terrail, J.-P. (Eds.). (2007). *Les sociologues, l'école et la transmission des savoirs*. Paris: La Dispute.

Delès, R., Pirone, F., & Rayou, P. (2021). L 'accompagnement scolaire pendant le premier confinement de 2020: De la différenciation dans l' "école à la maison". *Administration & Éducation, 169*, 155–161. https://doi.org/10.3917/admed.169.0155

Drerup, J. (2015). Autonomy, perfectionism and the justification of education. *Studies in Philosophy and Education, 34*, 63–87. https://doi.org/10.1007/s11217-014-9426-3

Drerup, J. (2016a). Liberalism without perfection? Autonomy, toleration and education in Nussbaum's capability approach. *Ethical Perspectives, 23*(1), 41–71. https://doi.org/10.2143/EP.23.1.3141834

Drerup, J. (2016b). Soziorelationale Autonomie, liberaler Individualismus und die Haltlosigkeit des modernen Selbst. In N. Ricken, R. Casale, & C. Thompson (Eds.), *Die Sozialität der Individualisierung* (pp. 127–160). Paderborn: Ferdinand Schöningh.

Dumont, H., Istance, D., & Benavides, F. (Eds.). (2010). *The nature of learning. Using research to inspire practice.* Paris: OECD.

Durler, H. (2015). *L'autonomie obligatoire. Sociologie du gouvernement de soi à l'école*, Rennes: PUR.

Dworkin, G. (2015). The nature of autonomy. *Nordic Journal of Studies in Educational Policy, 2015*(2), 28479. doi:10.3402/nstep.v1.28479

Ehrenberg, A. (1998). *La fatigue d'être soi. Dépression et société*. Paris: Odile Jacob.

Field, J. (2006). *Lifelong learning and the new educational order*. Stoke-on-Trent: Trentham Books.

Fielding, M. (2012). Personalisation, education, democracy and the market. In M. Mincu (Ed.), *Personalisation of education in contexts: Policy critique and theories of personal improvement* (pp. 75–88). Rotterdam: Sense Publishers. https://doi.org/10.1007/978-94-6209-028-6_6

Fosnot, C.T. (2013). *Constructivism: Theory, perspectives, and practice*. New York/London: Columbia University Teachers College Press.

Foucault, M. (1980). The confession of the flesh. In C. Gordon (Ed.), *Power/knowledge. Selected interviews and other writings* (pp. 194–228). New York: Pantheon.

Foucault, M. (2001). *L'herméneutique du sujet*. Paris: Hautes Études, Gallimard, Seuil.

Frandji, D., & Rochex, J.-Y. (2011). De la lutte contre les inégalités à l'adaptation aux "besoins spécifiques". *Education & formations, 80*, 95–108.

Garcia, S. (2019). Intensification du travail enseignant et bureaucratisation: L'exemple des PPRE. *Revue Suisse de Sociologie, 45*(3), 409–426.

Glasman, D. (2016). Préface de l'ouvrage de Philippe Foray Devenir autonome. *Apprendre à se diriger soi-même* (pp. 9–10). Paris: ESF.

Hartley, D. (2009). Personalisation: The nostalgic revival of child-centred education? *Journal of Education Policy, 24*(4), 423–434. doi:10.1080/02680930802669318

Hartley, D. (2012). *Education and the culture of consumption: personalisation and the social order*. New York: Routledge.

Helsper, W. (2004). Pädagogisches Handeln in den Antinomien der Moderne. In H.-H. Krüger & W. Helsper (Eds.), *Einführung in Grundbegriffe und Grundfragen der Erziehungswissenschaft* (pp. 15–34). Wiesbaden: Springer Verlag für Sozialwissenschaften.

Holec, H. (1981). *Autonomy in foreign language learning*. Oxford: Pergamon.

Idel, T.-S., & Ullrich, H. (Eds.). (2017). *Handbuch Reformpädagogik*. Weinheim: Beltz.

Jansen, R.S., van Leeuwen, A., Janssen, J., Jak, S., & Kester, L. (2019). Self-regulated learning partially mediates the effect of self-regulated learning interventions on achievement in higher education: A meta-analysis. *Educational Research Review, 28*, 100292. https://doi.org/10.1016/j.edurev.2019.100292

Kant, Immanuel. (1983 [1803]). Über Pädagogik. In W. Weischedel (Ed.), *Immanuel Kant, Werke in 10 Bänden* (Band 10, pp. 691–764). Darmstadt: Wissenschaftliche Buchgesellschaft.

Knowles, M.S. (1975). *Self-directed learning: A guide for learners and teachers*. Chicago, IL: Association Press.

Lahire, B. (1998). *L'homme pluriel. Les ressorts de l'action*. Paris: Nathan.

Lahire, B. (2001). La construction de l'"autonomie" à l'école primaire: entre savoirs et pouvoirs. *Revue française de pédagogie, 134*, 151–161. https://doi.org/10.3406/rfp.2001.2812

Lahire, B. (2007). La sociologie, la didactique et leurs domaines scientifiques. *Education et didactique, 1*, 73–82. https://doi.org/10.4000/educationdidactique.86

Leroy, G. (2022). *Sociologie des pédagogies alternatives*. Paris: La découverte.

Little, D. (1991). *Learner autonomy 1: Definitions, issues and problems*. Dublin: Authentik Language Learning Resources.

Losego, P. (2014). Rapprocher la sociologie et les didactiques. *Revue française de pédagogie, 188*, 5–12. https://doi.org/10.4000/rfp.4528

Mackenzie, C. (2014). The importance of relational autonomy and capabilities for an ethics of vulnerability. In C. Mackenzie, W. Rogers, & S. Dodds (Eds.), *Vulnerability. New essays in ethics and feminist philosophy* (pp. 33–59). Oxford: University Press. https://doi.org/10.1093/acprof:oso/9780199316649.003.0002

Mackenzie, C., Rogers, W., & Dodds, S. (2014). Introduction: What is vulnerability and why does it matter for moral theory? In C. Mackenzie, W. Rogers, & S. Dodds (Eds.), *Vulnerability. New essays in ethics and feminist theory* (pp. 1–30). Oxford: UniversityPress.https://doi.org/10.1093/acprof:oso/9780199316649.003.0001

Maguire, M., Ball, S.J., & Braun, A. (2013). What ever happened to …? 'Personalised learning' as a case of policy dissipation. *Journal of Education Policy, 28*(3), 322–338. https://doi.org/10.1080/02680939.2012.724714

Marquis, N. (2015). III. Le handicap, révélateur des tensions de l'autonomie. *Revue interdisciplinaire d'études juridiques, 74,* 109–130. https://doi.org/10.3917/riej.074.0109

Masschelein, J., & Simons, M. (2013). *In defence of the school. A public issue.* Leuven: Education, Culture and Society.

Meyer-Drawe, K. (2000). *Illusionen von Autonomie. Diesseits von Ohnmacht und Allmacht des Ich.* München: Kirchheim.

Miliband, D. (2006). Choice and voice in personalised learning. In OECD (Ed.), *Personalising Education.* Paris: OECD Publishing.

Millet, M. & Croizet, J.-C. (2016). *L'école des incapables? La maternelle, un apprentissage de la domination.* Paris: La Dispute.

Mincu, M. (2012). Editorial introduction. In M. Mincu (Ed.), *Personalisation of education in contexts: Policy critique and theories of personal improvement* (pp. xiii–xxii). Rotterdam: Sense Publishers.

Mitra, S., & Dangwal, R. (2010). Limits to self-organising systems of learning – the Kalikuppam experiment. *British Journal of Educational Technology, 41*(5), 672–688. https://doi.org/10.1111/j.1467-8535.2010.01077

Nussbaum, M.C. (2011). *Creating capabilities. The human development approach.* Harvard: Harvard University Press.

OECD (Ed.). (2006). *Personalising education.* Paris: OECD Publishing.

OECD. (2019). *Student agency for 2030. OECD future of education and skills 2030 concept note.* Retrieved from http://www.oecd.org/education/2030-project/teaching-and-learning/learning/student-agency/Student_Agency_for_2030_concept_note.pdf (accessed: 25.08.2022)

Oelkers, J. (2010). *Reformpädagogik. Entstehungsgeschichte einer international en Bewegung.* Zug: Klett Kallmeyer.

Patry, D. (2018). L'autonomie: L'incontournable de toutes les pédagogies actuelles? *Tréma, 50,* 1–17. https://doi.org/10.4000/trema.4237

Payet, J.-P. (Ed.), (2016). *Ethnographie de l'école. Les coulisses des institutions scolaires et socio-éducatives.* Rennes: Presses Universitaires de Rennes.

Périer, P. (Ed.). (2014). L'autonomie de l'élève: Émancipation ou normalisation? *Recherches en éducation, 20.* https://doi.org/10.4000/ree.7675

Peters, M.A. (2012). Personalisation, personalised learning and the reform of social policy: Prospect for molecular governance in the digitised society. In M. Mincu (Ed.), *Personalisation of education in contexts: Policy critique and theories of personal improvement* (pp. 89–106). Rotterdam: Sense Publishers.

Pieper, A. (2000). *Einführung in die Ethik.* Tübingen/Basel: Francke.

Pohlmann, R. (2017 [1971]). Autonomie. In J. Ritter, K. Gründer, & G. Gabriel (Eds.), *Historisches Wörterbuch der Philosophie online.* Basel: Schwabe. DOI: 10.24894/HWPh.367

de Queiroz, J.-M. & Ziolovski, M. (1994). *L'interactionnisme symbolique.* Rennes: PUR.

Rabenstein, K. (2010). Förderpraktiken im Wochenplanunterricht: Subjektivationsprozesse von Schülern zwischen Selbstständigkeitsanforderungen und Hilfe-bedürftigkeit. *sozialer sinn*, *1*(11), 53–77. https://doi.org/10.1515/sosi-2010-0104

Rabenstein, K. (2017). Zur Verschiebung schulischer Leistungsbewertung. Ethnographische Beobachtungen zu Rückmeldepraktiken im individualisierenden Unterricht. In C. Bünger, R. Mayer, S. Schröder, & B. Hoffarth (Eds.), *Leistung – Anspruch und Scheitern*. (pp. 41–60). Halle-Wittenberg: Martin-Luther-Universität.

Rabenstein, K., Idel, T.-S., Reh, S., & Ricken, N. (2018). Funktion und Bedeutung der Schulklasse im individualisierten Unterricht. *Zeitschrift für Pädagogik*, *64*(2), 179–197. https://doi.org/10.25656/01:21817

Reckwitz, A. (2003). Grundelemente einer Theorie sozialer Praktiken. Eine sozialtheoretische Perspektive. *Zeitschrift für Soziologie*, *32*(4), 282–301. https://doi.org/10.1515/zfsoz-2003-0401

Reh, S., & Berdelmann, K. (2012). Aspects of time and space in open classroom education. In B. Bergstedt, A. Herbert, A. Kraus, & C. Wulf (Eds.), *Tacit dimensions of pedagogy* (pp. 97–110). Münster: Waxmann.

Reichenbach, R. (2017). *Ethik der Bildung und Erziehung*. Stuttgart: utb.

Reimers, F.M. (Ed.) (2022). *Primary and secondary education during Covid-19. Disruptions to educational opportunity during a pandemic*. Cham: Springer. https://doi.org/10.1007/978-3-030-81500-4

Reusser, K., Pauli, C., & Stebler, R. (2018). Personalisiertes Lernen. *Zeitschrift für Pädagogik*, *64*(2), 150–178. https://doi.org/10.25656/01:21816

Ricken, N. (2007). Von der Kritik der Disziplinarmacht zum Problem der Subjektivation. Zur erziehungswissenschaftlichen Rezeption Michel Foucaults. In C. Kammler & R. Patt (Eds.), *Foucault in den Kulturwissenschaften. Eine Bestandesaufnahme* (pp. 157–176). Heidelberg: Synchron.

Ricken, N. (2018). Die Sozialität des Pädagogischen und das Problem der Individualisierung – Grundlagentheoretische Überlegungen. In M. Proske, T.-S. Idel, K. Rabenstein, K. Kunze, M. Martens, & S. Strauss (Eds.), *Individualisierung von Unterricht: Transformationen–Wirkungen–Reflexionen* (pp. 195–213): Julius Klinkhardt.

Romero, M., & Barberà, E. (2014). *Computer-based creative collaboration in online learning*. Berlin: Heidelberg.

Rose, N. (2016). Paradoxien (in) der Individualisierung. Schulische Programmatik im Horizont moderner Anrufe zur Individualisierung. In N. Ricken, R. Casale, & C. Thompson (Eds.), *Die Sozialität der Individualisierung* (pp. 181–196). Paderborn: Ferdinand Schöningh.

Schunk, D.H., & Greene, J.A. (2018a). Historical, contemporary, and future perspectives on self-regulated learning and performance. In D.H. Schunk & J.A. Greene (Eds.), *Handbook of self-regulation of learning and performance* (pp. 1–15). New York: Routledge.

Schunk, D.H., & Greene, J.A. (Eds.). (2018b). *Handbook of self-regulation of learning and performance*. New York: Routledge.

Schweppenhäuser, G. (2003). *Grundbegriffe der Ethik zur Einführung*. Hamburg: Junius Verlag.

Sertl, M. (2007). Offene Lernformen bevorzugen einseitig Mittelschichtkinder! Eine Warnung im Geiste von Basil Bernstein. In M. Heinrich & U. Prexl-Krausz (Eds.), *Eigene Lernwege - Quo Vadis? Eine Spurensuche nach "neuen Lernformen" in Schulpraxis und LehrerInnenbildung* (pp. 79–97). Wien/Münster: LIT.

Servant-Miklos, V., & Noordegraaf-Eelens, L. (2021). Toward social-transformative education: an ontological critique of self-directed learning. *Critical Studies in Education*, *62*(2), 147–163. https://doi.org/10.1080/17508487.2019.1577284

Shemshack, A., & Spector, J.M. (2020). A systematic literature review of personalized learning terms. *Smart Learning Environments*, *7*(1), 33. https://doi.org/10.1186/s40561-020-00140-9

Simons, M. (2020). The figure of the independent learner: On governing by personalization and debt. *Discourse: Studies in the Cultural Politics of Education*, 1–15. https://doi.org/10.1080/01596306.2020.1732302

Simons, M., & Masschelein, J. (2008). The governmentalization of learning and the assemblage of a learning apparatus. *Educational theory*, *58*(4), 391–415. https://doi.org/10.1111/j.1741-5446.2008.00296.x

Stalder, F. (2018). *The digital condition*. Cambridge; Medford: Polity Press.

UNESCO. (2016). *Education 2030: Incheon declaration and framework for action for the implementation of sustainable development goal 4*. Ensure inclusive and equitable quality education and promote lifelong learning opportunities for all. http://uis.unesco.org/sites/default/files/documents/education-2030-incheon-framework-for-action-implementation-of-sdg4-2016-en_2.pdf (accessed: 19.08.2022).

Vassallo, S. (2015). Using self-regulated learning to reflect on the critical commitments in educational psychology. *Knowledge Cultures*, *3*(2), 49–65.

Vincent, G. (Ed.). (1994). *L'Éducation prisonnière de la forme scolaire? Scolarisation et socialisation dans les sociétés industrielles*. Lyon: PUL.

Wagnon, S., & Patry, D. (2019). Le self-government: L'instauration d'un principe fédérateur de l'Éducation nouvelle (1900-1930)? In V. Castagnet & C. Barrera (Eds.), *Décider en éducation. Entre normes institutionnelles et pratiques des acteurs (du XVe siècle à nos jours)* (pp. 139–154). Lille: Presses Universitaires du Septentrion.

Wermke, W., & Salokangas, M. (2015). Autonomy in education: Theoretical and empirical approaches to a contested concept. *Nordic Journal of Studies in Educational Policy*, *2015*(2), 28841. https://doi.org/10.3402/nstep.v1.28841

Wrana, D. (2008). Autonomie und Struktur in Selbstlernprozessen. Gesellschaftliche, lerntheoretische und empirische Relationierungen. In C. Maier Reinhard & D. Wrana (Eds.), *Autonomie und Struktur in Selbstlernarchitekturen. Empirische Untersuchung zur Dynamik von Selbstlernprozessen* (pp. 31–101). Opladen: Budrich Unipress. https://doi.org/10.25656/01:8524

SECTION I

Effects of pedagogical approaches to foster autonomy in preschool (*école maternelle*) and primary school

1

AUTONOMOUS WORKSHOPS AND INDIVIDUAL MONTESSORI-TYPE ACTIVITIES

An analysis of their effects on learning and inequalities

Ariane Richard-Bossez

As analysed by Bernard Lahire, the ideal-typical figure of the autonomous pupil in school is that of "an active pupil, in search of meaning, a pupil reflecting, discovering for himself, organizing himself, making choices, self-evaluating and sometimes self-correcting, a pupil who has contributed to making common rules and who, as a result, respects them" (2005, p. 158, our translation). This conception of what a pupil is leads to pedagogical arrangements in the classroom which reflect these expectations of autonomy and the intellectual, instrumental, moral, and expressive forms of engagement that underpin them (Durler, 2014). This autonomy is generally considered as being "already there" and its historical, social, or educational conditions are neither explicitly acknowledged nor questioned. It thus contributes to the development of educational inequalities among pupils who are more or less familiar with the attitudes required in these forms of organization (Périer, 2014). This vision of an autonomous pupil can be found in the first years of schooling in many countries. In the case of France, Christophe Joigneaux (2014) has highlighted how, in the ministerial texts dedicated to the *école maternelle*, autonomy constitutes a "pedagogical ideal" whose clout has been growing since the 1970s.

DOI: 10.4324/9781003379676-3
This chapter has been made available under a CC-BY license.

> **THE FRENCH *ÉCOLE MATERNELLE***
>
> The *école maternelle* is the first level of the French education system. Since September 2019, it has become compulsory for all children aged 3–6 (but this was already the case in practice since the 1990s). The *école maternelle*'s teachers have the same level of qualification, training, and status as primary school teachers. It is organized around three levels:
>
> - The *"petite section"* for children aged 3–4 years
> - The *"moyenne section"* for children aged 4–5 years
> - The *"grande section"* for children aged 5–6 years (the equivalent of kindergarten)
>
> Conversely to other countries, particularly those of northern and central Europe, the French *école maternelle* is characterized by an educational approach that is strongly oriented towards the academic aspect and preparation for later schooling (Bertram & Pascal, 2002; Veuthey, Marcoux, & Grange, 2016).

In order to further question the effects of this conception of an autonomous pupil on learning and on school inequalities from the first years of schooling, this chapter analyses the forms of autonomous work that can be observed in French *école maternelle* by comparing two types of situations: "autonomous workshops" and individual Montessori-type activities. The data upon which this chapter is based stems from two studies carried out via observations in *grande section* (kindergarten) classes. The first study is doctoral research (Richard-Bossez, 2015) based upon a field survey carried out in 2010–2011 in six socially contrasted kindergarten classes in a medium-sized town in the South of France (three classes from schools located in priority education zones with pupils from disadvantaged socio-economic backgrounds, three more socially heterogeneous classes). The second study derives from research carried out during a collective project which enabled the observation in 2016–2017 of Montessori-type activities implemented in a kindergarten class located in a priority education area (Richard-Bossez, 2021). The point of view adopted is based on the sociology of pedagogy proposed by Basil Bernstein and his followers (Bernstein, 2007; Frandji & Vitale, 2008; Vitale & Exley, 2015) and on works about the construction of educational inequalities in preschools (Bautier, 2008; Joigneaux, 2009; Laparra & Margolinas, 2016; Millet & Croizet, 2016).

This contribution is divided into three parts. The first part will outline the theoretical and conceptual framework underlying the presented results. The second will put forward the most common situations of autonomous work observable at the kindergarten level called "autonomous workshops". The third one will describe the case of Montessori-type autonomous activities which are developed in certain classes. In a transversal way, the aim is to examine the methods used in these activities, the processes at work, and their effects on pupils' learning.

Analysing autonomous school activities: The contributions of Basil Bernstein's sociology of pedagogy

British sociologist Basil Bernstein laid the foundations of a sociology of pedagogy (Bernstein, 2000) that makes it possible to describe the pedagogical process. In this sense, he wished to set himself apart from theories of reproduction, which he criticized for not questioning the pedagogical discourse itself and for considering it only as a neutral vector of class or power relations that are external to it. In doing so, Bernstein establishes pedagogy as a sociological object. For him, pedagogy is not a simple transmission relationship but, on the contrary, an instrument of symbolic control that regulates consciousness and identity. Several of his theoretical and conceptual propositions allow us to describe what greater autonomy given to the pupil in the pedagogical relationship produces. We will develop two of them: the notion of "invisible pedagogy" and the concept of "framing".

Invisible pedagogy

In 1973, Bernstein published an article entitled "Classes and Pedagogies: Visible and Invisible" in which he analysed the pedagogical model then in place in British preschools, which he named "invisible pedagogy" and which is characterized by:

- Implicit control of the pupil's activity by the teacher
- A teacher's role essentially based on setting up the context in which the pupils are to evolve
- A high degree of apparent autonomy for the child in his or her activities and relationships with others
- Little emphasis put on the transmission-acquisition of knowledge and methods
- Varied and diffuse assessment criteria, based on the pupil's activity and relying on psychological explanations

In this pedagogical model, learning is seen as an invisible and tacit process in which activity and play are central elements.

For Bernstein, this pedagogy is a pedagogy of the "new middle classes" working in the area of cultural or symbolic regulation. It is a form of pedagogy that anticipates a long period of schooling and a mode of communication based on relatively abstract meanings. The family model of socialization that corresponds to the type of pupil in tune with this pedagogy is that of a "nuclear family", with a mother devoted to the education of her children. Because of these assumptions, which are close to a middle-class lifestyle, it has consequences for children from working-class families who are not prepared for these specific requirements. It is also a pedagogy that is less understandable to working-class parents and can create a disconnect between working-class families and school. Another problem raised by Bernstein relates to the break in pedagogical mode between preschool and primary school, which requires a shift in code for the pupil: such a shift is likely to be easier for middle-class children than for working-class ones. Thus, for Bernstein, "in the microcosm of the nursery or infant class, we can see embryonically the new forms of transmission of class relationships" (Bernstein, 1973, p. 24).

This work, which has since become a "classic", therefore emphasizes the risks of social inequalities inherent in invisible pedagogies because of their stronger affinity with the educational practices of middle-class families. In the wake of this work, Bernstein sought to develop more general concepts that could describe all forms of pedagogical relationships.

The concept of framing

The concept of framing is one of Bernstein's central concepts: "it regulates relations within a context, it refers to relations between transmitters and acquirers, where acquirers acquire the principle of legitimate communication" (Bernstein, 2000, p. 12). It allows us to describe "*who* controls *what*" (ibid.). If the framing is strong, then it is the transmitter who controls the different elements of the pedagogical situation: the pedagogy can then be described as visible or explicit. If it is weak, it is, on the contrary, the learner who seems, at least in appearance, to have greater control over the situation: the pedagogy is then considered "invisible". For Bernstein, framing is exercised on two types of interrelated discourses. On the one hand, there is the "regulative discourse", which refers "to the forms that hierarchical relations take in the pedagogic relation and to expectations about conduct, character and manner" (Bernstein, 2000, p. 13). On the other hand, there is the "instructional discourse", which corresponds to apprenticeships themselves (knowledge, specific skills). Regarding instructional discourse, control can be exercised over different elements: the selection of what is transmitted, the sequencing of learning over time, the expected pace of learning, and the criteria defining knowledge. This framing transmits the "rules of achievement". These allow the learner to perceive, within the particular context in which he or she finds himself or herself, the criteria for producing what is expected of him or her.

For Bernstein, framing is always linked to a classification of knowledge, i.e., to the way in which knowledge is more or less strongly delimited. Classification and framing can vary independently of one another, and their combination makes it possible to characterize different pedagogical codes. In Bernstein's theory, these concepts form the link between the micro-sociological and macro-sociological levels: classification conveys the power relations specific to a society and framing the social modalities of control. It should be noted, however, that in the works mobilizing Bernstein's models, these concepts are often used in a more descriptive and independent manner.

Operationalizing the concept of framing to analyse autonomous activities in école maternelle

To analyse the autonomous activities that we observed in kindergarten, I used the concept of framing. Methodologically, the cues used to characterize framing are both verbal and non-verbal. On the verbal level, I focused more particularly on the modes of address to others. Thus, imperative/injunctive forms were considered as strong framing modes. For example, a teacher addressing a pupil by saying "OK, now that's enough, stop talking and sit down" has been analysed as a strong framing of the regulating discourse. Conversely, open-ended questions, such as when a teacher asks the class "What should I do?" about an exercise sheet, were considered as weak framing of the instructional discourse. On the non-verbal level, the cues used were mainly gestures meant to show and summon physical action on others. For example, if a teacher grabbed a student by the shoulders to encourage him or her to sit on a chair, this was considered strong framing of the regulating discourse. In another example, the teacher's pointing out an error on an index card with her finger, without any other comment, was interpreted as a relatively weak framing of the instructional discourse because it was not explicit.

This allowed me to empirically question the effects of practices based on pupil autonomy in the two types of situations observed (autonomous workshops and Montessori-type activities), as I will show in the next two parts.

Autonomous workshops in French *école maternelle*

Traditionally, since at least the 1980s, learning activities in French *écoles maternelles* have been organized around the "workshop-grouping" form, i.e., collective activities when time slots during which all pupils are with the teacher alternate with activities in small groups of pupils, in "workshops", which are carried out successively by the different groups of pupils. These workshops can take different forms: directed workshops which take place under the constant presence of the teacher, semi-directed workshops where the teacher comes and goes, and autonomous workshops where the pupils have a task to carry out alone. In the latter case, the work to be done is presented by the teacher before the pupils do it alone. Once the work has been completed (usually a photocopied exercise sheet to be filled in), the pupils either show it directly to the teacher or put it in a box provided for this purpose so that the teacher can check it and mark it afterwards. This type of organization allows for relatively little framing, if any. Several processes relating to the mode of presentation of the activities, the materials used, and the forms of support can be observed during these autonomous workshops.

A less knowledge-centred way of presenting activities

Firstly, during these autonomous workshops, we can observe that the teacher tends to present the activities that the children will have to carry out later on their own by mobilizing the knowledge involved much less than the global activity in which the exercise is embedded and the tasks to be completed. This is often done by exemplifying and demonstrating the expected result.

The following extract is quite emblematic of this way of doing things. Here, the teacher explains to the pupils that they will have to complete an exercise sheet by classifying word labels in four circles according to the initial cipher they have in common and by noting the letter in question in a box next to each circle ("the label"):

> So the [blue group], I'll show you: this is work with words, word labels that you have to cut out, all these labels, there, we cut on the line, there, straight on. We cut on the line and then there are four bubbles, but there are small labels, but nothing is written on the labels, so you have to look at the first letter of each word, there are words that start with the letter P, words with the letter [she says the names of the letters with the pupils]. [...] In one of the bubbles, I'm going to put all the words that start with the letter P, this one, that one, that one, I'm looking for, there must be 1, 2, 3 [shows the words]. I'm putting them here [...] so listen carefully, I'm explaining. The three that start with P, I put them in the same bubble, and here I write P [...], the three that start with C, I put all three together [...] carrot [...] cauliflower and then cabbage and courgette there, in the little label, I put the letter C. The three that start with R: radish, rice and [...] and grapes ("raisin" in French), I'm going to put them here and I'll put the letter R. And the last ones are those that start with F: strawberry ("fraise" in French), fava bean.

Two characteristic elements of this mode of presentation can be highlighted. First, the degree of abstraction in the teacher's speech is relatively low. This can be seen in the importance given to the description of the material (bubbles, word labels, explanation of tasks to be done, etc.). The mode of presentation is therefore very contextualized and relative to the sheet used. We then observe that the framing of the knowledge to be mobilized is relatively weak. Thus, there is no use of specialized terms, such as "initial" for example. On the other hand, the procedural aspect is much more accentuated, indicating how to cut out the labels and the tasks to be carried out. Here, the demonstration even goes so far as to present the pupils with the whole of the work to be carried out since the words are all indicated by the teacher, thus illustrating what didacticians call the "Topaze effect",[1] i.e., a situation where the expected answer is so suggested that it ends up being given away without the need to resort to other elements.

Other modes of presentation of activities that are much more centred on knowledge can be observed in the classes (cf. Richard-Bossez, 2020b), but these are much more frequent when the teacher is more continuously present with the group of pupils. Thus, the fact of giving pupils a task they have to carry out independently seems to induce a mode of presentation that tends to make the knowledge in question less visible; as a consequence, it risks making access to it more difficult for pupils who have not been made familiar with it in other contexts. Indeed, as Bernstein had already shown in the 1970s, and as other studies have since confirmed (in particular Bautier, 2008), focusing on "doing" more than on "learning", without making the underlying knowledge explicit, can mislead pupils about what is expected of them in school and prevent them from accessing the required knowledge.

Activities more frequently organized around photocopied worksheets

Secondly, we can see that most of the activities in the autonomous workshops are based on photocopied worksheets. Lahire has also emphasized the role that objects play in the desire to build autonomy at school:

> A pedagogy which bypasses the "frontal" strategy of the lecture in order to set up different activities according to the pupils or groups of pupils and to favour "autonomous" (individual) work without direct help cannot do otherwise than to rely upon devices resting on objectified knowledge.
> *(Lahire, 2001, p. 157, our translation)*

Thus, if the teacher is not physically with certain groups of pupils, the sheets constitute a sort of "relay" to make up for this absence. This is not without effects on the knowledge targeted (Richard-Bossez, 2016).

Indeed, an analysis of the worksheets used in the classes in our sample shows that they tend to approach knowledge on the basis of specific tasks that are not very varied. Thus, among the sheets we collected, instructions of four different kinds group together almost all the tasks required of pupils.[2] The most frequent task is "Cut and paste" (in 17 out of 43 sheets). It corresponds to labels representing drawings, words, or letters that the pupils have to cut out and then place in a spot corresponding to the given instructions. Three other instructions are also relatively common, although to a lesser degree than the previous one: "circle", "colour", and "write" (respectively, 8, 9, and 10 times in the 43 sheets examines). In these cases, the aim is to select specific elements from a greater whole or to write or trace words or signs. Four other instructions are also present in our corpus but appear only once in the entire corpus of sheets: "Cross out", "Complete", "Organize in order", "Connect". Thus, while the number of sheets is large, the tasks they propose are relatively limited and repetitive.

Thus, the use of photocopied worksheets places more emphasis on what the pupil must do than on what he or she must know, as other authors have pointed out (Bautier, 2008). This also leads, indirectly, to an emphasis on the type of knowledge necessary to lead to a task that can be carried out through a worksheet. This emphasis on doing leads to a focus on learning that is often more technical. For example, in the area of literacy learning, greater emphasis is placed on certain areas: the "alphabetical principle" (sheets proposing work on words, sentences, or letters), the "sounds of language" (sheets relating to a specific sound, the association of sounds or the place of a sound in a word), and writing (of letters, words or sentences). Activities relating to the social functions of writing or understanding of texts are much less present in the activity sheets. At the same time, this also tends to exclude other types of tasks such as the manipulation of objects, board games based on notions relating to literacy, or activities based solely on language mediation for example.

Joigneaux (2009) has shown that exercise sheets in *école maternelle* are becoming increasingly complex graphically. We can also observe that the graphic elements present on the sheets have the function of implicitly guiding the pupil's actions. This is the case with dots indicating where the writing should begin, or dotted lines, lines, or spaces intended to guide the drawing or pasting of labels. These graphic elements can also have a self-correcting function insofar as the number of spaces provided gives an indication of the number of elements to be placed there. The "labels" meant to be pasted on the sheets have the characteristic of isolating various units on mobile material, which can be drawings, letters, syllables, words, or even sentences. As a result, they allow for greater focus on these units by dissociating them from the other units present on the sheet. However, as Gachet-Delaborde (2009) points out, the fact that these different units are integrated into the same type of medium (a rectangle of paper) can also potentially cause confusion between the different types of units.

Thus, the use of worksheets in autonomous workshops tends to reinforce the technical aspect of learning to the detriment of its more cognitive aspect.

Near absence of support for pupils

Thirdly, as in all activities observable in *école maternelle* classes, we can discern very different forms of appropriation of learning activities by pupils, more or less close to school expectations. The particularity of autonomous workshops is that these differences in appropriation are less likely to be the subject of support. This is due to two interrelated reasons.

On the one hand, because the most frequent exchanges within the autonomous workshops take place among pupils, a very frequent form of exchange among peers during autonomous workshops is copying. Such situations of copying among peers are sometimes a last resort when a pupil doesn't manage to do the exercise alone and doesn't get outside help. This is the case of Fatou who has to colour the drawings of the words containing the O sound.[3] She starts by asking, "'Escargot', do you hear O?" As she does not get any answer, she says thoughtfully, "I don't know anymore" and looks at her neighbour who has coloured the drawing in question. Some pupils are even able to copy from a pupil who is sitting opposite them and whose sheet is therefore "mirrored" onto their own. These copying situations are generally not detected by the teacher who validates these answers as being those of the pupil himself or herself, thus preventing any possibility of feedback on what the pupil has not understood. Forms of mutual help among pupils can also be observed, but these raise several questions. Firstly, because the help requested by a pupil is not always granted, as we have just seen with Fatou's example. Secondly, the cognitive operations underlying such help often don't correspond to the cognitive processes expected in school. For example, Soria starts by asking her group, "What's it called?" by showing the drawing of the gorilla. Elio replies, "Gorilla". She then asks, "Can you hear the O?" Samir replies, "Yes, in 'go'". Elio retorts and says, "Well, no (it's not there)". Samir repeats "go" in disbelief. Soria replies, "Well, no". Samir laughs in an awkward manner. These exchanges among peers, therefore, have relatively weak and sometimes counterproductive effects on targeted school learning.

On the other hand, this form of support is less frequent because exchanges with the teacher are also at their lowest in the autonomous workshops. In some cases, the teacher may not monitor the pupils at all and will only check the work done afterwards (by annotating the sheet, for example). In other cases, the teacher may drop in randomly during or at the end of the workshop. Conversely, in other, more directed forms of workshops, we see that these moments of teacher-pupil interaction are precisely key moments in the possibilities of revision of the pupils' knowledge acquisition (Richard-Bossez, 2020a). During autonomous workshops, when moments of teacher support occur, they are often shorter and faster than in other types of workshops. In these situations, it is almost impossible for the teacher to identify the pupils' difficulties and the operations they have implemented.

In this way, autonomous workshops provide less opportunity than more directed forms of activity to revise pupils' responses when they do not correspond to the intended learning situation. As a result, for pupils who have not yet mastered the knowledge involved, this type of activity does not provide the necessary resources for them to re-examine the knowledge they previously acquired and develop new forms of it.

Individual Montessori-type activities

Since the 2010s in France, there has been a movement to disseminate practices inspired by Montessori pedagogy in state schools (Huard, 2019), whereas they had previously remained quite limited to the more socially selective public schools. The teacher I was able to observe in 2016–2017 is very representative of these new practices (Richard-Bossez, 2021). Every morning in her classroom, the teacher sets up individual Montessori-type activities. Compared to more ordinary workshops, these activities are characterized by:

- A free choice of activities by the child: the material is made available, and the pupil chooses what he or she wants to work on, provided that the teacher has already presented it to him once. Pupils decide for themselves how long they want to work on the activity and may change whenever they want.
- More individual work using material to be handled and designed to be self-correcting. This material is not exclusively Montessori material but also material designed by the teacher or produced by other publishers.

Quantitative and qualitative differentiations

During my observations, two forms of processes likely to induce educational inequalities could be discerned in the Montessori-based activities.

The first form is quantitative. It relates to the quantity of school activities carried out by pupils. Some pupils, namely those who are already best in tune with school expectations, carry out several complete activities during Montessori-inspired activities periods, whereas others, generally those who are not – or not yet – in a school learning logic, do much less and/or do not complete them. The example of two pupils with strongly contrasting kinds of behaviour illustrates this point, which may be observed in varying degrees for other pupils in the class. Léa is one of the "very good" students in the class. The teacher says that she already knows how to do things that she has not yet shown her, which suggests that she is already familiar with many activities at school that she probably does at home. During the workshops, she usually does several activities in succession, which she conscientiously completes. The teacher says of her, "Léa, she doesn't stop". She is also very demanding and will often ask the teacher for specific work to be done. For example, she asks if she can write the date on the board by herself, even though this is not a planned workshop, or asks the teacher to show her how to write her first name in cursive letters because she cannot do it by herself. In contrast, Djamel, a boy from the same class, was described as an "agitated" pupil who "sucks up" the teacher's energy and lives in a complicated family situation. He carries out fewer workshop stints to completion or tends to flit from one activity to another without completing them. He hardly ever asks the teacher for help, and when she encourages him to participate, he generally does not comply. Through these two examples, we can highlight a first process of differentiation linked to a specificity of Montessori-type activities: the fact that each pupil chooses their activity and the duration of it. This results in a strongly differentiated solicitation of the pupils, which leads some to be more exposed to school activities – and therefore to the learning that they convey – than others. Compared to classes where more "classic" workshops are organized around a single activity, Montessori-type workshops tend to reinforce the differences among pupils. For the most "demanding" pupils, who generally do not have the opportunity to carry out several activities in the more traditional workshops, this allows them to increase their exposure to school learning and their practice of the exercises proposed. On the other hand, for pupils with fewer academic demands, who often do not spontaneously go for the activities proposed in the framework of the Montessori-type activities, the more traditional workshops allow for greater attendance of learning activities by the fact that they are "imposed" upon them without any possibility of choice.

Another more qualitative form of differentiation concerning the cognitive nature of the activities chosen can be observed. Indeed, some pupils (who are generally the same as those who follow several autonomous workshops in a row) prefer the most "academic" activities: learning to write words based on the sounds produced by the letters, classifying words according to the sounds or syllables they contain, working on numbers and quantities, etc. This is further reinforced by the fact that the same pupils will sometimes call out to the teacher for a particular task (learning to write a word, asking for a model to do an activity, etc.) when those proposed do not correspond to their expectations. During this time, other pupils choose less academic activities: pouring different types of seeds or liquids into containers, manipulating modelling clay, doing a jigsaw puzzle with a small number of pieces, drawing, etc. Thus, while Léa practices making lines of Js in cursive writing, corrects herself by erasing the letters that do not seem to fit, and imitates her teacher who circles the most successful letters, Djamel, on the other hand, plays with modelling clay, making balls that he throws around the classroom without considering the proposed model cards.

This form of differentiation, relating to the cognitive operations mobilized by the pupils, is further reinforced by the possibilities of "diverting" the material proposed. Thus, certain activities can aim at learning which, in the practices of certain pupils, is subjected to a deviation towards a more playful activity or carried out on a register which is not the one that was intended. This can be observed, for example, when a pupil manipulates geometric shapes and comes to consider them as characters in an imaginary game and makes them speak or when a pupil reproduces letters, but without respecting the conventional sense of the writing. This can also be seen in the use of Montessori materials, which are considered self-correcting. This is the case with the red and blue bars intended to work on the sequence of numbers from 1 to 10, which pupils are supposed to align in a progressive "staircase" starting from the same point and which can be diverted (voluntarily or not) to make a pyramid or be transformed into an imaginary sword. In the same way, lines of pearls that have to be arranged in boxes according to the number of pearls they contain can be arranged loosely by some pupils. As can be seen, for some, the operations mobilized will be essentially procedural, whereas for others they will be more intellectual and more "academically profitable" for the continuation of their schooling. These processes were also observed by G. Leroy (2020) in his work on "Montessori-inspired practices". These forms of diversion can also be observed in the more "traditional" workshops, particularly when they take place outside the constant presence of the teacher but much less frequently in the so-called directed workshops.

The central issue of monitoring and supporting student activity

These differentiating processes are based to a large extent on the fact that these Montessori-inspired activities are subject to little framing and, consequently, little scaffolding. This is because the teacher is usually busy presenting activities to a few pupils and can therefore hardly monitor directly the activities carried out by the others.

To illustrate this point, here is an observed sequence involving Léa and Djamel, whose strongly differentiated school attitudes were seen earlier:

> Léa is placed on a mat with cards showing a picture and the names of different emotions. She has to match word labels with the names of the emotions on them. She compares word for word the name written on the cards and on the labels before placing the label under the corresponding card. Djamel voluntarily passes and moves all of Léa's labels. The teacher asks him to help Léa put them back in place. Djamel first refuses, then when the teacher gets closer to him, starts putting the labels back at random before announcing, "Here we go!" Léa tells him "No, that's not it" and goes to find the teacher. Again, he leaves, but the teacher calls him back, explains what is expected and asks him what he has to do. He replies "look at the model". The teacher then takes a word label and tells him, "You have to put at least that one on". She places the first label under the first card and asks him if it is the right word, he answers "no"; she then makes him compare it to the other words. He thinks he has found the solution but confuses "happy" and "sad" because of the dot over the i and j in those French words. The teacher makes him compare the words letter by letter and he realizes his mistake. He finds the right place. She hands him the next word and then a third, which he places correctly. At this point, the teacher is called up by another student. Djamel starts to get up, the teacher sees him and says "continue, continue" and gives him another label.

He continues to place the labels. At the end of the activity, the teacher asks Djamel to go and get his notebook to write down what he has done. A little later, he goes to get a box containing some material and asks, "teacher, can you explain this to me?"

This long extract allows us to grasp how a pupil like Djamel, whose behaviour is generally quite far from what is implicitly expected during independent workshop time (refusal of activity, flitting about, diversions, etc.), can adopt a very different attitude, much more in line with school expectations, when the teacher exercises a stronger control over his activity and offers support adapted to the difficulties he encounters. This type of observation, revealing moments of learning for pupils *a priori* considered to be in great difficulty in the classroom, was also observed in more ordinary classes. This leads us to emphasize that the support phases constitute real moments of immersion in learning for these pupils. However, they require the teacher to be available to interact with them and to accept a more constraining approach than that generally advocated in Montessori pedagogy, in particular the fact of not waiting for a "sensitive period" in the child. As G. Leroy underlines it, among teachers practicing Montessori pedagogy, "the idea of heterogeneous rhythms [sometimes] opens the way to resignation towards the weakest" (2020, p. 135; our translation).

The strong commitment of the students in autonomous Montessori-based activities

Finally, I would like to emphasize another process observed during the Montessori-type activities in the class surveyed: that of the strong involvement of the pupils in the activities proposed to them. In this area, a significant difference can be noted in comparison with the classes run in a more classical manner. Indeed, it is striking to observe that in this class, the commitment is much more obvious than in the other classes I studied. This can be seen in the calmness that often surrounds these Montessori-type activity periods and in the fact that many pupils do not move when the recess bell rings, preferring to continue their activity rather than go and play outside, or even ask to stay in the classroom to do other activities during recess time. The implementation of these Montessori-inspired activities thus seems to enable many pupils to mobilize their energy and resources towards learning more than other types of organization but does not guarantee that this learning will be systematically achieved.

Thus, in the Montessori-type workshops that I have observed, we can discern processes of openness to learning that are not very frequent in other types of functioning. These openings concern the pupils' commitment to the proposed activities and learning for those pupils who are attracted to and have already mastered the school expectations and for whom the workshops constitute a stimulating and more intensive form of training. On the other hand, we can also observe processes of refusal of learning that are more marked than in more ordinary forms of functioning, particularly for pupils who have not mastered the expected intellectual procedures; they remain in a cognitive register of lesser academic profitability when the organization in an autonomous form allows for less control of the activity by the teacher than in other types of functioning. In these individual activities of the Montessori type, we find, on the one hand, the same difficulties as in the autonomous workshops linked to the weak supervision by the teacher and consequently to the little support offered for the pupils' learning. But on the other hand, there are also forms of differentiation in terms of exposure to school knowledge, which means that some pupils will attend these learning sessions much more than others.

Conclusion

Sociological research has long emphasized the risks of creating inequalities in connection with the development of autonomous educational *dispositifs* (Bernstein, 1973; Lahire, 2005; Joigneaux, 2014; Périer, 2014; Durler, 2015). This is due, in particular, to the socially implicit stakes of "invisible pedagogies", which are closer to the forms of socialization of middle-class children than to those of working-class children and which may consequently prevent the latter from perceiving school expectations when these remain implicit. As Bernard Lahire puts it,

> These pedagogies of autonomy are above all based on an unspoken law that could be formulated as follows: "Let the person who enters the school carry within him the dispositions to act and think in the direction expected at school".
>
> *(2005, p. 346, our translation)*

The comparison of the autonomous workshops traditionally present in *école maternelle* classes and the new forms of individual activities inspired by Montessori pedagogy makes it possible to highlight processes underlying the autonomous school activities which produce school inequalities. A first process, which is found in the types of autonomous activities observed, relates to the weak cognitive framing of activities inherent in autonomous arrangements and the little scaffolding possibilities that result from this. A second process relates to the accentuation of the gaps in exposure to the most academic knowledge in the case of Montessori-type activities, which propose a form of autonomy going as far as the choice of activities and their duration. These processes tend to close off the possibilities of revising learning for pupils who have not already mastered it because of their previous school or family learning experience and thus run the risk of accentuating inequalities within classes from the first years of schooling.

Notes

1 In reference to the eponymous play by French author Marcel Pagnol and its main character, a schoolteacher named Topaze who, in the first scene of the play, gives a dictation to his pupils by inducing the spelling of words through the exaggerated pronuciation of some final silent letters ("the sheepssss").
2 N.B.: Several instructions may be present on the same sheet.
3 All names have been pseudonymized.

References

Bautier, E. (Ed.). (2008). *Apprendre à l'école, apprendre l'école. Des risques de construction d'inégalités dès la maternelle.* Lyon: Chronique Sociale.
Bernstein, B. (1973). *Class and pedagogies: Visible and invisible.* Paris: OECD. (C.E.R.I.).
Bernstein, B. (2000). *Pedagogy, symbolic control and identity. Theory, research, critique.* Lanham: Rawman & Littlefields Publishers.
Bertram, T., & Pascal, C. (2002). *Early years education: An international perspective.* Birmingham: Centre for Research in Early Childhood.
Durler, H. (2014). Les pratiques du gouvernement de soi à l'école: Les dispositifs pédagogiques de l'autonomie et leurs contradictions. *Recherches en éducation, 20,* 76–86. https://doi.org/10.4000/ree.8105
Durler, H. (2015). *L'autonomie obligatoire. Sociologie du gouvernement de soi à l'école.* Rennes: Presses Universitaires de Rennes.
Frandji, D., & Vitale, P. (Eds.). (2008). *Actualité de Basil Bernstein. Savoir, pédagogie et société.* Rennes: Presses Universitaires de Rennes.
Gachet-Delaborde, M. (2009). *Formes et sens de l'univers graphique en maternelle. Etudes de cas et enjeux didactiques.* Thesis defended at Metz University.
Huard, C. (2019). L'entrée en pédagogie Montessori d'enseignant.e.s d'écoles maternelles publiques française depuis 2010. Raisons et modalités. *Spécificités, 12*(1), 14–30. https://doi.org/10.3917/spec.012.0014
Joigneaux, C. (2009). *Des processus de différenciation dès l'école maternelle. Historicités plurielles et inégalités scolaires.* Thesis defended at Paris VIII University.
Joigneaux, C. (2014). L'autonomie à l'école maternelle: Un nouvel idéal pédagogique? *Recherches en éducation, 20.* https://doi.org/10.4000/ree.8103
Lahire, B. (2001). La construction de l'"autonomie" à l'école primaire: Entre savoirs et pouvoirs, *Revue Française de pédagogie, 134,* 151–161. https://doi.org/10.3406/rfp.2001.2812
Lahire, B. (2005). Fabriquer un type d'homme "autonome": Analyse des dispositifs scolaires. In B. Lahire (Ed.), *L'esprit sociologique* (pp. 322–347). Paris: La Découverte.
Laparra, M., & Margolinas, C. (2016). *Les premiers apprentissages scolaires à la loupe.* Louvain-la-Neuve: De Boeck.
Leroy, G. (2020). *L'école maternelle de la performance enfantine.* Bruxelles: Peter Lang.
Millet, M., & Croizet, J.-C. (2016). *L'école des incapables? La maternelle, un apprentissage de la domination.* Paris: La Dispute.
Périer, P. (Ed.). (2014). L'autonomie de l'élève: Émancipation ou normalisation? *Recherches en éducation, 20.* https://doi.org/10.4000/ree.7675
Richard-Bossez, A. (2015). *La construction sociale et cognitive des savoirs à l'école maternelle: Entre processus différenciateurs et moments de démocratisation. Le cas des activités relatives à l'écrit en grande section.* Thesis defended at Aix-Marseille University.

Richard-Bossez, A. (2016). La fiche à l'école maternelle: Un objet littératié paradoxal. *Recherches en Education*, *25*, 46–56. https://doi.org/10.4000/ree.5649

Richard-Bossez, A. (2020a). Les interactions langagières en maternelle: Moment clé pour la révision des savoirs relatifs à l'écrit. *Recherches en Education*, *40*. https://doi.org/10.4000/ree.447

Richard-Bossez, A. (2020b). A l'école maternelle, une entrée différentiée dans l'écrit entre oralité et littératie. *Pratiques*, *183-184*. https://doi.org/10.4000/pratiques.7533

Richard-Bossez, A. (2021). Importer des pratiques alternatives dans une classe "ordinaire": Entre ruptures et continuités. Etude d'activités d'inspiration montessorienne dans une classe de maternelle. *Spécificités*, *16*(2), 10–24. https://doi.org/10.3917/spec.016.0010

Veuthey, C., Marcoux, G., & Grange, T. (Eds.). (2016). *L'école première en question. Analyses et réflexions à partir des pratiques d'évaluation*. Louvain-la-Neuve: EME éditions.

Vitale, P., & Exley, B. (Eds.). (2015). *Pedagogic rights and democratic education. Bernsteinian explorations of curriculum, pedagogy and assessment*. London: Routledge.

2

INVENTED SPELLING FOR ACHIEVING LITERACY ON ONE'S OWN

A persistent ideal of autonomy producing inequalities

Fabienne Montmasson-Michel

The French *école maternelle* is specific in that it offers a collective education to young children from the age of 2 within the framework of the educational institution.[1] It was established in the 19th century with the Ferry laws of 1881–1882 which founded the contemporary elementary school system. This school system designed for early childhood is part and parcel of the educational rationale: it is placed under the supervision of the Ministry of National Education, organized into school age groups, with *curricula* aiming at school-based knowledge and skills and teachers trained at university to teach children from 2 to 11 years of age. Its non-compulsory nature has not prevented it, throughout the 20th century, from conquering the educational monopoly over young children from the age of 3: since the mid-1990s, it has enrolled 100% of the 3–6 age group in metropolitan France[2] (Ministry of National Education, 2012). This process reached a new stage with the introduction of compulsory schooling from the age of three implemented by the last school law[3]: in France, schooling has thus become virtually compulsory from the age of 3.[4]

Nevertheless, the French *école maternelle* has historically built up for itself an identity as a separate school system, drawing its specificity from the very young public it caters to, with particular concerns and its own distinct pedagogy considered as non-academic. This is due to the great attention paid to physical education, sociability, welcoming children and families and the promotion of an "expressive model" (Plaisance, 1986). This pedagogical model, which reached an acme in the 1970s, valued individuality, self-fulfilment, and personal expression; it promoted learning through exploration, playing, and artistic practice. Besides, it privileged oral skills over written techniques (Chamboredon & Prévot, 1973; Plaisance, 1986). It was thus opposed to a "productive model" (Plaisance, 1986), which valued traditional school-based forms of learning: training in writing techniques, repeated exercises, memorization. However, during the second half of the 20th century, a new social demand gradually came to prevail over the preschool and kindergarten system: the prevention of "academic failure", which followed the massification of secondary education and the lengthening of schooling (Isambert-Jamati, 1985), with its focus on academic reading (Chartier, 2007). A "field of professional intervention"[5] was then formed around early literacy to provide knowledge, standards, and recommendations to usher young children into written culture: a practice of oral language shaped by the constraints of writing and an initiation to the concepts, objects, and techniques of writing. Several studies emphasize the fact that this social demand generates a process of schooling in the *école maternelle* around school expectations and rationales (Garnier, 2009; Leroy, 2020). In that movement, at the turn of the 20th and 21st centuries, language becomes a priority in the formal *curriculum*: whether it is channelled through oral or graphic skills, the language in question is embedded within written culture and intended to prepare for further schooling (Montmasson-Michel, 2018). However, the expressive model embodying the identity of the *école maternelle* as specific to early childhood has not disappeared and co-exists with the priority given to language. While it is questioned by those who see the *école maternelle* as a propaedeutic period towards elementary school, the expressive model also benefits from support among educational and political circles, including in the field of professional intervention on early literacy. Indeed, a lexicographical analysis of programmatic texts for *the école maternelle*[6] reveals two simultaneous movements: on the one hand, the continual increase of discourse on language and on the other, the pendulum swing of expressive discourse, moving forward or backward from one programme to the next, without ever vanishing entirely (Montmasson-Michel, 2018, pp. 151–164). This being said, the promotion of a preschool system that distances itself from pedagogical practices traditionally attached to school-based learning (exercises, repetition, organized transmission of knowledge, etc.) does not exclude strong cultural and academic ambitions. On the contrary, sociological studies show that the expressive model of the *école maternelle* is not socially neutral: it is in keeping with the perspectives and educational resources of the culturally dominant social classes that have forged the figure of a young child endowed with language skills who is the recipient of a "legitimate culture". They have founded the pedagogical standards of the massified preschool system (Bernstein, 1975; Chamboredon & Prévot, 1973; Plaisance, 1986). According to these educational perspectives, the young child is prepared for the demands of long, reflexive, and conceptual studies (Bautier & ESCOL, 2008), not only for the more modest demands of an elementary school system focused on the systematized learning of the alphabetic code. The pedagogy of initiation to writing carried out by the expressive model is indissociably invisible (Bernstein, 1975), because it does not come across as the transmission of knowledge and techniques, and non-explicit, because it does not make learners acquire, in a structured and progressive way, the intellectual techniques indispensable to the autonomous acquisition of writing (Garcia, 2021; Garcia & Oller, 2018).

Thus, the "ideal client" (Becker, 1952, p. 451) for that kind of pedagogy is the offspring of culturally dominant social classes, the child who is prepared to read in school at an early age thanks to their family socialization (Renard, 2011). Such a child is endowed with the reflexive linguistic and cognitive resources present in extended literacy[7] (Bautier, 2010), and also with technical acquisitions made at home (Garcia, 2018): thus, they can take advantage of school socialization without being subjected to academic forms of learning through exercise and training. Thereby, they are cognitively autonomous children, to take up sociologist Bernard Lahire's conceptualization (2001a); in other words, children who ideally learn on their own.

This chapter proposes to examine this norm of autonomy in early literacy learning by focusing on the sociological analysis of a pedagogical and didactic *dispositif* originally designed to teach the alphabetical code to young children without any prior explicit learning or specific technical training. This is the paradigm of "invented spelling" (Fayol & Jaffré, 2014), translated as "invented writing" (*écriture inventée*) in French, also referred to as approximate, provisional spelling or writing or even writing by trial and error. Its principle consists in putting children in a situation enticing them to write when they cannot yet read or write, in order to gradually lead them to learn the alphabetical code. The latest preschool syllabi thus recommend to schedule "writing trials" intended to entice children to produce "first independent writing(s)" (Ministry of National Education, 2015; Ministry of National Education, Youth and Sports, 2021). This chapter aims to show that this is indeed a *dispositif* based on the "cognitive autonomy" (Lahire, 2001a) of young children and that as such, it participates to increasing social inequalities in schools.

This analysis is based on the findings of our dissertation dealing with the socialization through language of *école maternelle* pupils (Montmasson-Michel, 2018). It is based on a literature review and documents analysis, as well as ethnographic field research conducted from 2010 to 2015 in preschools and kindergartens and in families living in a rural environment around a medium-sized town located in the north of the area called Nouvelle-Aquitaine. The research target respondents were aged 2 to 6 and were enrolled in 15 classes from 5 public preschools and kindergartens with differing social characteristics. Two of them were the subject of a longitudinal survey conducted over several years: one where lower and working classes predominate, the other where middle classes prevail. The data collection is based on observation sessions, interviews, and documentary collections. A total of 153 children were interviewed, with a focus on 25 of them (via intensive and systematized data collection); there were 270 hours of observation with note-taking, sound recordings, and photographs; the observation of 12 teachers; 62 interviews with 58 children; 34 interviews with 30 school staff (including 22 interviews with 19 teachers); and 35 interviews conducted in the homes of 23 families with varying social conditions. The local pedagogical recommendations were also captured thanks to immersion in the geographical and social environment during the time of the survey: it included access to the pedagogical resources available in the *département*, informal exchanges with various actors, and attendance at pedagogical activities.

The theoretical framework of this study is a sociology of socialization which considers that what individuals are and what they do are the outcome of their social experiences. These are internalized in the form of dispositions that are propensities to perceive, act, think, mobilize language, etc., in a socially situated manner (Darmon, 2016; Lahire, 2001b, 2003). The social configurations founding the social dispositions studied in this research have been characterized by the existing research on autonomy in school (Durler, 2015; Lahire, 2001a) and on learning to read in France (Deauvieau et al., 2015; Deauvieau & Terrail, 2018; Garcia, 2013; Garcia & Oller, 2015). According to the latter, alphabetic techniques have been devalued by the slogan "reading is understanding", which subsumes the social definition of reading required by long studies (Chartier, 2007). They have been replaced by a literary and scholastic conception of reading and the process of learning to read which grants supremacy to reflexivity (Garcia, 2013). This proves detrimental to children from lower and working classes but also to some of those who come from lower-middle classes.

In order to demonstrate the logic and effects of this pedagogical *dispositif* requiring early cognitive autonomy, the first part of our study offers a historical perspective examining its formation in the scientific field and its penetration in France into the field of research on education; then we turn to the formal *curriculum* and official recommendations. Our second part examines its implementation in the actual *curriculum*, by focusing on what the teachers who practice it say and do, and then we turn to the analysis of a session observed in a class involving three children with different literacy backgrounds.

From universal psychogenesis to the *curriculum*: An ideal of cognitive autonomy for early childhood

A psychogenetic theory of ethnocentric reading

As early as the 1960s and 1970s, English-speaking researchers discovered that young children have an understanding of the written word before they reach school age (Durkin, 1966; Goodman, 1986); they collected samples of children's graphic productions bearing witness to this (Chomsky, 1970, 1971a, 1971b; Clay, 1975; Read, 1971, 1986). Positioning them as a set forming a series reveals what appears at first as "emergent literacy" (Joigneaux, 2013), eventually leading to the mastery of writing: they start with scribblings followed by drawings mixed with signs – pseudo letters, numbers, and letters – to finally make room for letters that align and order themselves and then to grapho-phonological combinations, words, sentences, and texts. Much of this work adopts an ethnocentric perspective based on the innate: they aim to capture what could be a self-taught manner of learning to read in the graphic performances of children who are socially situated since they belong to the researchers' social group and are even sometimes their own children (Joigneaux, 2013, p. 121). For instance, Glenda L. Bissex, who was a teacher of English in the United States, published *GNYS AT WRK* ("genius at work") in 1980, whose title faithfully reproduces the message her son Paul posted on his bedroom entrance when he was working on inventing his own writing system at age 5 (Bissex, 1980). He is said to have learned to produce standardized texts in a few years, on his own and as his own teacher (Bissex, 1984). This paradigm, therefore, presupposes the existence of a child genius, able to learn the alphabetical code and techniques all by himself as soon as he is allowed to express himself in writing.

That being said, such early Anglo-Saxon works made very limited inroads into French education circles, and it was in the 1970s, between Geneva and South America, that the theory successfully imported into France was forged in the guise of the work of Argentine psychologist Emilia Ferreiro. Forced into political exile by the military juntas, trained by Jean Piaget in Geneva, rapidly publishing her work in Spanish, English, and French (Ferreiro, 1977, 1979, 1984, 1986, 1988; Ferreiro & Teberosky, 1979, 1983), she thus subsumed several conditions leading to her gaining influence in the *milieu* of the French "pedagogical left" engaged in inventing the "genius young reader" precisely at that time (Garcia, 2013, pp. 23–114). In those circles, the promoters of early literacy who idealized the concept of a reflexive young child found reasons to re-assess the learning of the alphabetical code as well as their so-called low-level techniques and to cultivate social distinction (Bourdieu, 1979), while claiming to be engaged in reducing social inequalities in school.

For Emilia Ferreiro, the child "tries to understand the world around them and develops provisional theories about the world" (Ferreiro, 2001, p. 24) and this is how they learn the alphabetical code. To demonstrate this, she developed a methodological *dispositif* that was to be replicated on a large scale for several decades in different fields and among different populations: each child, before he was a reader and an autonomous writer, was invited – and even prompted – to write, and then was subjected to a Piagetian "clinical interview" of their production, intended to reveal their conceptualization of writing. Emilia Ferreiro elaborated a psychogenetic and universal theory of writing by stages from this broad empirical basis:

Everything seems to indicate that we are in the presence of a real psychogenesis with its own internal logic, which means that the information coming from the environment is incorporated into interpretative systems the succession of which is not random.

(Ferreiro, 2000, p. 59)

The child is said to learn the alphabetical code by asking themselves "epistemological questions" (Ferreiro, 2000, p. 61) and not by learning alphabetic techniques, the teaching of which is forbidden because it would prevent the conceptualization of writing. It is thus a genetic theory which, on the theoretical as well as methodological levels, evacuates the social construction of dispositions. However, as the French historian of education and reading Anne-Marie Chartier points out, what these studies reveal is more

a socially and historically situated experience. (…) Knowledge of letters and of the written language, reconstructed by children before they know how to read and write, shows the extent to which they are immersed, from an early age, in a school-based and "scripted" universe. The fact that this pre-knowledge has been transformed (wrongly) into proof that the child learns by "spontaneous development" and into a tool for teaching reading and writing is not the least of existing paradoxes.

(Chartier, 2011, pp. 8–9)

The French appropriation of Emilia Ferreiro's work and the didactization of the invented spelling paradigm

In 1979, Emilia Ferreiro was invited to Paris to attend the Ministry of National Education's conference on *Apprentissage et pratique de la lecture* (Learning and Practicing Reading), to explain "how the child discovers the writing system" (Ferreiro, 1979). She was welcomed enthusiastically by a group of pioneers working in the professional field of early literacy. All were active in contiguous territories around the same ideology: the child is a being evolving in the very midst of language and capable of creative, demanding cognitive activities such as confronting complexity, making hypotheses, assessing and solving problems as well as interpreting language. Ferreiro's work definitely penetrated French education circles from then on. At the end of the 1980s, she published in French presses recognized in the educational world (Ferreiro, 1988, 2000, 2001; Ferreiro & Gomez Palacio, 1988). Her work was very quickly replicated by teams of researchers in education, supported by action-research initiatives involving teachers and their instructors, thus permeating all initial and continuing education training schemes (Besse, 1990, 1993, 2001; Besse et al., 1988; Brigaudiot, 1998, 2015; Calleja et al., 1998; David & Fraquet, 2011, 2012; David & Morin, 2013; Fijalkow & Fijalkow, 1991;

Fraquet & David, 2013; INRP & Brigaudiot, 2004; Jaffré et al., 1999; Pasa et al. 2006; Rosaz, 2003). In 1992, her publications were referenced in an institutional text presenting a state-of-the-art description of scientific knowledge on the processes involved in learning to write, which was widely distributed by the institutional prescriptive apparatus (Ministry of National Education and Culture, 1992, p. 153, 176–177). From 2002 onwards, the paradigm penetrated the *curriculum* for preschool and kindergarten teaching and the supporting documentation. According to the 2002 *curriculum*, the child "invents successive writing systems", and "it is important to let them build upon their knowledge of the alphabetic principle" (Ministry of National Education, 2002, p. 24). The supporting documentation on language devotes five pages to "writing trials" (Ministry of National Education, 2006, pp. 100–104). The recommendation to have "writing trials" disappeared from the 2008 programme (Ministry of National Education, 2008), but it persisted in the supporting documentation (Ministry of National Education, 2011), then reappeared in the 2015 *curriculum* and in its revised version of 2021, where it is combined with the notion of "independent writing(s)" (Ministry of National Education, 2015; Ministry of National Education, Youth and Sports, 2021). Finally, it is found among a glut of "support resources" available online.[8]

Including the paradigm of invented spelling in official school prescriptions is motivated by research on education. In the 2000s and 2010s, the clinical research protocol formalized by Emilia Ferreiro was reconfigured into a didactic *dispositif* (Fijalkow et al., 2009), prompting students to behave like "word builders" and "discoverers of writing material" (Rosaz, 2003, p. 17) in order to "produce writing through the progressive resolution of linguistic and (ortho)graphic problems" (Fraquet & David, 2013, p. 40). Two elements structure this didactic transposition. The first one appears in the institutional recommendations made from 2006 onwards (Ministry of National Education, 2006): in order to write, children are called upon to mobilize the external resources, and not merely internal ones like Emilia Ferreiro thought, found among the "referents" or written material available in the classroom (displays, posters, tools). But the chronotopic[9] and alphabetical[10] prerequisites necessary for the mobilization of such resources, which young children actually find in their material environment, seem to be overlooked: finding the written materials that work as reference is thought of as obvious and their mere presence in the environment is felt to be sufficient for children to appropriate them successfully. A second element of didactic transposition is the conversion of the clinical interview into a "metagraphic interview" (Fraquet & David, 2013) during which the child is expected to produce a reflexive discourse on their writing. Considered in this literature as the core of teacher expertise for children to conceptualize alphabetic writing, this didactic principle recalls the inscription of the *dispositif* within the reflexive demands of extended literacy.

Those studies belong to a francophone scientific environment, embedded itself within an international scientific environment that has committed much effort to emergent literacy (Joigneaux, 2013). For example, a report produced by a Canadian researcher specializing in the issue for the consensus conference[11] *Écrire et Rédiger* (Writing and Reading) held on March 14 and 15, 2018, by the Cnesco (National Council for School System Evaluation) (Sénéchal, 2018) concluded that "invented spelling (*écriture inventée*), when done with the help of an adult, can become one of the levers that facilitate learning to read" (ibid., p. 8). The note adopts a North American approach, more pragmatic and much less ideological than the one that prevailed in France around the elaboration of the 2002 *école maternelle* programmes for the alphabetization of young children: supported by Anglo-Saxon research on emergent literacy, it considers in particular that a good part of children's skills comes from family socialization (Sénéchal, 2006; Sénéchal & LeFevre, 2002) and clearly distances itself from the original paradigm according to which intervening before children begin school or when they are actually learning impedes their conceptualization of the written word. However, this new paradigm is not devoid of conceptions based on cognitive autonomy, which is not very sensitive to social inequalities, especially when it comes to children who are not very familiar with writing. Indeed, the note is centred on a thoroughly detailed study by the author (Ouellette & Sénéchal, 2008) intent on measuring the effects of an activity based on invented spelling practices to be compared with two control groups. The children in the three groups received instruction in the ten letter-sound correspondences used in the tasks assessed. However, the control groups were then placed in a situation not very or not at all conducive to the alphabetization of children without prerequisites: a purely phonological activity (involving the sound analysis of language based on images)[12] and a non-alphabetic activity (drawing). Thus, this case study does not specifically attempt to show the value of the *dispositif* for teaching literacy to children with little or no prerequisites, nor does it show its potential advantage over more explicit pre-literacy approaches, such as teaching letters and grapho-phonological correspondences through demonstration, practice, and repetition. On the other hand, research on invented spelling, whether it is done internationally or in France, reveals the extreme heterogeneity of children's productions when invented spelling is done on demand, which underlines their unequal character and symbolic violence: a review of contemporary work thus finds an average of 20% of children refusing to write in kindergarten[13] (Fraquet & David, 2013, p. 29). A significant proportion of the children produce nothing, and some productions contain almost no alphabetical signs, while others engage in actual writing. However, since one of the main features of the system is the reflexive discourse that the children produce on their own drawings, we are forced to note that the less the children have acquired what allows them to produce invented spelling, the more disadvantaged they are by the *dispositif*.

These elements confirm the characterization of the invented spelling *dispositif* – both in its original form and, to a lesser extent, in its didactic form – as a *dispositif* based on cognitive autonomy. It is probably appropriate for children with previous knowledge of literacy (especially of chronotopic and alphabetical elements), but it does not seem to be very conducive to the alphabetization of children who know almost nothing about logic, knowledge, and techniques of writing. Let us now examine how the prescriptions of invented or approximate spelling or writing are translated into the actual *curriculum* of the French *école maternelle* in the light of the ethnographic survey carried out between 2010 and 2015.

A transposition into the actual *curriculum* that is difficult for the teachers and unequal for the children

An ideological recommendation, with little concern for concrete practices

What is striking, first of all, in light of the ethnographic survey, is the gap between the infatuation of the prescription apparatus with invented spelling on the one hand, and its weak and difficult transposition into the real *curriculum* on the other hand. While the *dispositif* was greatly promoted locally in the 2000s and 2010s through various modalities (such as conferences, training workshops, canvassing, and the promotion of volunteer teachers), over the course of the entire survey, all the material collected on invented spelling remained limited to the following: six teachers declaring that they practice it a little, mainly in at the kindergarten level; a poster featuring the collective productions of kindergarten children in the school whose enrolment base is predominantly lower and working-class;[14] two yearly individual productions found in the folders of pupils in one kindergarten class, and three productions in the other, in the school whose pupils come predominantly from middle-class families;[15] and a single observed session of about 25 minutes involving three children in the second of those classes.

Analysing the comments made by the teachers who said that they practiced invented spelling reveals three things. First of all, they experience the institutional enthusiasm for the system as a form of pressure, through the manner in which their teaching is assessed and through the comments made by the National Education inspectors[16] (incentives, encouragements, congratulations). Without radically questioning the *dispositif* itself, they distanced themselves from these forms of coercion by various means: for example, by irony ("no, that can't be, I only did one session this year! [...] my, I must have hit the jackpot!" said one teacher, which was congratulated by her inspector) or the expression of reluctance ("she wanted to push further and then do too much. Then too much is too much!"). The second salient aspect is the concern they expressed for the significant difficulties experienced by some children to produce invented spelling, which they say they had to cope with: they speak of "stops", "kids [who] are not well", "dejection", "panic", one of them even declares, "I have the impression that I was being violent towards them". They also noted that only the most advanced students could use the famous "referents", i.e., the written material interspersed in the class which is supposed to constitute a form of support for writing endeavours. The third aspect that emerges is the revelation of arrangements with the ideology of independent writing that they are hardly aware of. Most of them say that they provide "support" to the children, i.e., prior alphabetical and grapho-phonological acquisitions: they teach the children their letters and some grapho-phonological links, or they train them to encode regular syllables during dictation exercises. Two of them even propose explicit teaching through showing, training, and a didactic set-up which has nothing to do with the ideal of a *dispositif* allowing for autonomy. First, a teacher in an ordinary preschool class explains how she "sells out" information to her young students (Bourdieu & Passeron, 1964, p. 111): "well in advance (...) I find a sentence (...) and there, I explain how I do it. So, I pronounce the words, I insist on the beginning and then I say, 'well it's this letter here that makes the noise', at the beginning I SAY everything". The second is a special education teacher, working with children identified as "having learning difficulties" at the end of kindergarten because they are not very literate; she implements a progressive support system, which thoroughly guides the students to encode words. She chooses a restricted set of letters corresponding to simple and univocal graphemes, she resorts to memorization games, and the children manipulate the chosen letters in the form of pre-selected mobile letters and encode them into words chosen by the teacher because they contain one or two regular syllables that can be written with these letters only.

However, at the time the survey was conducted, these explicit pedagogical practices based upon visible learning remain strategies that teachers individually tinker with, without support from the educational institution, which does not provide any opportunity for collective development and sharing among peers. Their pedagogical discoveries do not seem to attract the attention of the pedagogical supervisors working in the district in question. In their respective schools, the colleagues of the two teachers who voiced out their difficulties were not aware of their practices and therefore could not identify them as resources and appropriate them to overcome the difficulties encountered with certain children. In fact, it is striking to note the extent to which the inspectors' encouragement and incentives fail to be accompanied by any concrete pedagogical advice. Their discourse, as it appeared in the survey, can be summarized as follows: kindergarten is not the place for systematic training in alphabetic techniques, it is necessary to practice invented spelling, and if it fails, it is because more of it must be done, earlier and more frequently. Nothing is said about what this practice implies in order to make all pupils improve, neither in terms of the kind of work that can be done upstream nor in terms of situational support for the least prepared students. As far as standards and their diffusion in the real *curriculum* are concerned, when this study was undertaken the practice of invented spelling was mainly an ideal and even an ideology of cognitive autonomy.

The researcher, the tester, and the castaway

The analysis of the only occasion during which invented spelling could be observed in the course of this survey, in a kindergarten class of a predominantly middle-class school, allows us to grasp the way in which this *dispositif*, based on children's cognitive autonomy, can actually generate educational inequalities. The situation is a "writing production" session that took place in first grade in March 2015. The pupils had to respond to the instruction, "Write a sentence that begins with: In the yard, I play…". The session was made up of two parts: the first one where the teacher guided the children to try and write together, "In the yard, I play…", and the second one where they had to try on their own to flesh out the sentence, based on their individual writing intentions.

Three children are involved: Emy, Siméon, and Tiphaine.[17] The family socializations of Emy[18] and Siméon[19] are well-known: reading together is valued, but not early literacy techniques. In fact, both of them have less literacy knowledge than most of their peers, but gender socialization also makes a difference: Emy has reading and graphic practices in female fictional universes that lead her to take an interest in the alphabetical code and to make learning attempts with her sisters, her female friends or to ask her mother. For example, she recognizes many letters, knows how to write them, and knows also some sound values. On the other hand, Siméon constructs language dispositions on the oral and practical levels thanks to his fictional universes and his male peers (Montmasson-Michel, 2016, 2020), which is not very conducive to literacy. Tiphaine's family socialization[20] is not known. However, when she is observed during her kindergarten year, she demonstrates that she is comfortable with school exercises and has well-developed alphabetical knowledge. At the end of kindergarten, for example, she knows the names and sounds of many letters and phonetically encodes short regular words.

During the first part of the group session, Tiphaine and Emy quickly responded to the teacher's questions, as she guided them step by step to write "*Dans la cour je joue*" (In the yard I play) by activating and developing their skills, Tiphaine's skills being more numerous, more confident and also more regular than Emy's. Siméon did not make any suggestions, said that he heard "nothing at all" when he was asked questions, that he could not write certain letters anymore; he copied his classmates' work, often drew letters backwards, and erased his work often. His pencil fell on the floor several times. In a second phase, the children were left on their own to write the rest of their sentence.

52 Fabienne Montmasson-Michel

Tiphaine was very comfortable and quickly managed to write "*o papa é la maman*" (for "I play mom and dad") (Figure 2.1) by resorting to her own skills. Then she began to draw her illustration, with much painstaking care.

On the other hand, Emy then found it impossible to move forward like Siméon since the teacher was no longer there. Their weak cognitive autonomy is thus underscored by a weak "political autonomy", which is the ability to discipline oneself along the lines of expected school behaviour (Lahire, 2001a). Both of them engage in a discussion typical of children (Montmasson-Michel, 2016), which enables them to forego school rules: they start playing with their pencils to amuse themselves and invent stories (their pencils shake, clash, roll, tip over, slide, fall to the ground, then become swords, etc.). They immediately stop when the teacher returns. She then helps Emy, who wants to write "*louveteaux*" (cubs) and writes /OOUVOT/ (Figure 2.2).

Then it was Siméon's turn to write "*chasseurs de Pokémon*" (Pokemon hunters), and he began by writing /O UO E/ for "*aux chasseurs de*" (to the hunters of). The teacher asks him to "read again" by pointing out what he has written,

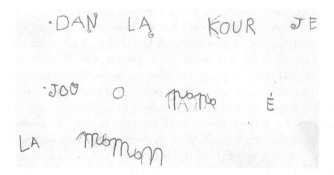

FIGURE 2.1 Tiphaine's writing.

FIGURE 2.2 Emy's writing.

FIGURE 2.3 Siméon's writing.

and he has a lot of trouble. Then she prompts him to continue, and he starts writing "*Pokémon*" by writing O for "*po*", which the teacher accepts, and then by proposing the letter C for "*ké*", which she also accepts (Figure 2.3). When she asks him what he hears at the end of the word "*Pokémon*", he says he can't hear anything more and she says, "Well, then if you don't hear anything more, if you don't know how it's spelled, if you're done, you put a little dot at the end to say it's over". He then exclaims vehemently that he is not finished, which he is right about, but the teacher firmly urges him to start drawing because the end of the session is drawing near, and he will have to move on.

The analysis of this session within the framework of "case-based reasoning" (Passeron & Revel, 2005) shows that when children with unequal resources are confronted with a *dispositif* of this type, the most advanced among them are valued, activate their knowledge, learn things and progress, whereas the less advanced are disqualified, produce lesser achievements, and fail to learn what they would precisely need to learn. Beyond mere literacy learning, such logics have been described in other research on preschools (Millet & Croizet, 2016).

Conclusion

Presupposing early childhood autonomy leads to valuing distal forms of socialization (in which the bodies of socializing agents and socialized children are distant) and regulations of activity that are not very explicit and produce vast differences. It perpetuates the reproduction of social inequalities in school. However, more equalizing socializing practices – because they do not presuppose the cognitive autonomy of young children – also exist, in the form of individual pedagogical experiences and arrangements with the norm that are not exceedingly objectified. They take place in a completely different socializing logic, one that is proximal and explicit: working with children, based on their real resources and not idealized ones, centring on their learning, anchored in the materiality of the instruments, the supports, and the objects of written culture.

The rewriting of the 2015 *curriculum* in June 2021 did not dispense with the recommendation of organizing writing trials and the notion of independent writing. However, it gave back importance to alphabetic techniques, which cognitive psychology has shown to be effective when children are ushered into the world of reading (Ecalle & Magnan, 2015). This is likely to promote the didactization of the *dispositif* in favour of word-encoding activities without speculation on the cognitive autonomy of children who do not yet master it. Such an evolution could be a sign of the demise of conceptions or practices assuming that children "invent" the alphabetical code from their own resources, but we cannot yet be sure. In particular, at the kindergarten level, we could witness a phenomenon similar to what has been uncovered when it comes to learning to read in first and second grade: the promotion of so-called "mixed" reading methods rather than entirely alphabetic-syllabic methods, the advantages of which for the children least acculturated to writing have been demonstrated by numerous scientific and empirical arguments (Deauvieau & Terrail, 2018; Garcia & Oller, 2015). In preschool and kindergarten, writing trials continue to be prescribed, leaving the field open to all sorts of local reinterpretations. If we retain the framework in practice in our field of inquiry, some of the prescribers of pedagogical standards who are in direct contact with teachers continue to adhere to the idea that children learn writing on their own as long as they are placed often in a situation inducing writing, while they cannot yet read or write independently. Their prescriptions are likely to maintain a situation of confusion that is hardly conducive to the development of explicit, proximal teaching practices.

Notes

1 This chapter, including the original French citations, was translated by Elisabeth Lamothe.
2 This applies to France's European mainland and excludes overseas territories.
3 Law n°2019-791 of July 26, 2019 for schools based upon trust, article 11.
4 Parents do have the option of not sending their child to school, but they have to make a reasoned request for authorization, and then they must homeschool their offspring on their own and submit to the tests conducted by the school institution.
5 It is defined as "a space within which the activities of members of professional groups concerned with the analysis and treatment of the same problem are organized" (Morel, 2010, p. 15).
6 In 40 years, no less than 6 programmatic texts have been elaborated: 1977, 1986, 1995, 2002, 2008, 2015; based on the same structure, this last programme was reshuffled in June 2021.
7 This refers to language and cognitive knowledge and skills made possible by the generalization of written culture: memorization, logical analysis, reorganization, reflexivity, abstraction and conceptualization, etc.
8 https://eduscol.education.fr/83/j-enseigne-au-cycle-1 (access date: September 26, 2022).
9 The chronotopic dimension of literacy, which is decisive in early learning, refers to the "link between space and time" and the ability to "move through space in an

orderly and controlled way, whether it is the space of the world or the space of the sheet of paper" (Laparra & Margolinas, 2016, p. 168).
10 Knowing the concepts of word, letter, written syllable, names, and the sounds of letters and some grapho-phonological relationships.
11 A public procedure that brings together experts and stakeholders concerned by an issue in order to compare opinions and identify consensus principles for action.
12 On this point, we refer the reader to our critical analysis of a widespread bias found in the French *école maternelle*, in the formal and real *curriculum*: in the name of a primacy of oral skills due to their age, young children should learn the segmentation of the written word (into syllables but also into phonemes) from activities carried out on sound material, possibly with the support of images. This bias puts children who are unfamiliar with written culture at a disadvantage, as they find it very difficult to take exclusively sound material as an object of study and to segment it into alphabetic categories (Montmasson-Michel, 2018, pp. 210–216).
13 Last year of the *école maternelle*, for children from 5 to 6.
14 A short text produced in a group of a few children with the help of a teacher about the pony activity, for example: "IR NOU SOM MONT DEBOU SUR LE PONEY" for "Yesterday, we stood on the pony".
15 Each child is expected to produce a sentence based on "writing production" instructions. Here are examples of instructions found in these two classes. In October: "Write a sentence about the activity we did at the stadium". In November: "Draw a moment from your fall vacation and write a sentence to caption your drawing. In January: "Draw your favourite gift" or "Write a greeting".
16 They are hierarchically above the teachers at the level of a territory (divided into districts by the National Education). Their mission is to implement educational policy at the school level and to assess the work of teachers and give them advice. Together with the pedagogical advisors who assist them (they are teachers who have been relieved of their duties), they are key players in the dissemination of pedagogical standards.
17 All names are pseudonyms to protect the privacy of the participants.
18 Emy: stay-at-home mother, high school degree with a focus in science [level 4], former sports instructor in the army; father army lieutenant, high school degree with a focus in science and then army entrance exam.
19 Siméon: mother is a nurse's aide in a medical-educational institution who is studying to become a social worker; she initially received a vocational diploma [level 3]; father is absent; maternal grandparents are retired nurses and very present.
20 Tiphaine: her mother is an insurance teleconsultant; her father is in charge of a workshop manufacturing automotive parts.

References

Bautier, E. (2010). Changements curriculaires: Des exigences contradictoires qui construisent des inégalités. In C. Ben Ayed (Ed.), *L'école démocratique: Vers un renoncement politique?* (pp. 83–93). Paris: Armand Colin.

Bautier, E. & ESCOL. (2008). *Apprendre à l'école. Apprendre l'école: Des risques de construction d'inégalités dès la maternelle.* Lyon: Chronique sociale.

Becker, H. S. (1952). Social-class variations in the teacher-pupil relationship. *The Journal of Educational Sociology*, 25(8), 451–465. https://doi.org/10.2307/2263957

Bernstein, B. (1975). *Class and pedagogies: Visible and invisible.* Washington: OECD. Centre for Educational Research and Innovation. Retrieved from https://files.eric.ed.gov/fulltext/ED124278.pdf (26.09.2022).

Besse, J.-M. (1990). L'enfant et la construction de la langue écrite. *Revue française de pédagogie*, *90*(1), 17–22. https://doi.org/10.3406/rfp.1990.1392

Besse, J.-M. (1993). De l'écriture productrice à la psychogenèse de la langue écrite. In G. Chauveau, M. Rémond, É. Rogovas-Chauveau, & Centre de recherche de l'éducation spécialisée et de l'adaptation scolaire (Eds.), *L'enfant apprenti lecteur: L'entrée dans le système écrit* (pp. 43–72). Paris: L'Harmattan INRP.

Besse, J.-M. (2001). L'accès au principe phonographique: Ce que montrent les écritures approchées. In G. Chauveau (Ed.), *Comprendre l'enfant apprenti lecteur* (pp. 130–158). Paris: Retz.

Besse, J.-M., Gaulmyn, M.-M., & Ginet, D. (1988). Introduction. In E. Ferreiro & M. Gomez Palacio (Eds.), *Lire-écrire à l'école: Comment s'y apprennent-ils? Analyse des perturbations dans les processus d'apprentissage de la lecture et de l'écriture*. Lyon: CRDP Lyon.

Bissex, G. L. (1980). *Gnys at wrk: A child learns to write and read*. Cambridge, MA: Harvard U.P.

Bissex, G. L. (1984). The child as a teacher. In H. Goelman, A. A. Oberg, F. Smith, & University of Victoria symposium on children's response to a literate environment: Literacy before schooling (Eds.), *Awakening to literacy: The University of Victoria symposium on children's response to a literate environment: Literacy before schooling* (pp. 154–173). Exeter, NH: Heinemann Educational Books.

Bourdieu, P. (1979). *La distinction: Critique sociale du jugement*. Paris: Editions de Minuit.

Bourdieu, P., & Passeron, J.-C. (1964). *Les héritiers: Les étudiants et la culture*. Paris: Editions de Minuit.

Brigaudiot, M. (1998). Pour une construction progressive des compétences en langage écrit. *Repères, recherches en didactique du français langue maternelle*, *18*(1), 7–27. https://doi.org/10.3406/reper.1998.2266

Brigaudiot, M. (2015). *Langage et école maternelle*. Paris: Hatier.

Calleja, B., Cloix, C., & Rilliard, J. (1998). Essayer d'écrire dès l'école maternelle: Un risque raisonné porteur d'apprentissage. *Repères, recherches en didactique du français langue maternelle*, *18*(1), 29–40. https://doi.org/10.3406/reper.1998.2267

Chamboredon, J.-C., & Prévot, J. (1973). Le "métier d'enfant". Définition sociale de la prime enfance et fonctions différentielles de l'école maternelle. *Revue française de sociologie*, *14*(3), 295–335. https://doi.org/10.2307/3320469

Chartier, A.-M. (2007). *L'école et la lecture obligatoire*. Paris: Retz.

Chartier, A.-M. (2011). Comment notre regard sur les jeunes enfants a changé: Les nouvelles psychologies du XXe siècle. *Actes des 5èmes Entretiens de la petite enfance*. Cinquièmes entretiens de la petite enfance 24 et 25 mars 2010, Cassis.

Chomsky, C. (1970). Reading, writing, and phonology. *Harvard Educational Review*, *40*(2), 287–309. https://doi.org/10.17763/haer.40.2.y7u0242x76w05624

Chomsky, C. (1971a). Invented spelling in the open classroom. *WORD*, *27*(1-3), 499–518. https://doi.org/10.1080/00437956.1971.11435643

Chomsky, C. (1971b). Write first, read later. *Childhood Education*, *47*(6), 296–299. https://doi.org/10.1080/00094056.1971.10727281

Clay, M. M. (1975). *What did I write?* London: Heinemann Educational.

Darmon, M. (2016). *La socialisation* (3e édition). Paris: Armand Colin.

David, J., & Fraquet, S. (2011). L'écriture en action et actions de l'écriture à l'école maternelle. *Le français aujourd'hui*, *174*(3), 39–56. https://doi.org/10.3917/lfa.174.0039

David, J., & Fraquet, S. (2012). *Ecritures approchées: Quels dispositifs didactiques au préscolaire?* https://www.forumlecture.ch/myUploadData/files/2012_2_David_Fraquet.pdf (26.09.2022)

David, J., & Morin, M.-F. (2013). Repères pour l'écriture au préscolaire. *Repères Recherches en didactique du français langue maternelle, 47*, 7–17.

Deauvieau, J., Reichstadt, J., & Terrail, J.-P. (2015). *Enseigner efficacement la lecture: Une enquête et ses implications.* Paris: Odile Jacob.

Deauvieau, J., & Terrail, J.-P. (2018). Le B-A-BA de la lecture. *La Vie des idées.* Retrieved from http://www.laviedesidees.fr/Le-B-A-BA-de-la-lecture.html (26.09.2022).

Durkin, D. (1966). *Children who read early: Two longitudinal studies.* New York: Teachers College Press.

Durler, H. (2015). *L'autonomie obligatoire: Sociologie du gouvernement de soi à l'école.* Rennes: Presses Universitaires de Rennes.

Ecalle, J., & Magnan, A. (2015). *L'apprentissage de la lecture et ses difficultés.* Paris: Dunod.

Fayol, M., & Jaffré, J.-P. (2014). Les orthographes inventées. In *L'orthographe* (pp. 32–54). Paris: Presses Universitaires de France.

Ferreiro, E. (1977). Vers une théorie génétique de l'apprentissage de la lecture. *Revue Suisse de Psychologie, 36*(2), 109–130.

Ferreiro, E. (1979). La découverte du système de l'écriture par l'enfant. In *Ministère de l'éducation. Direction des écoles, Apprentissage et pratique de la lecture à l'école: Actes du colloque de Paris des 13-14 juin 1979* (pp. 215–220). Paris: Centre national de documentation pédagogique.

Ferreiro, E. (1984). The underlying logic of literacy development. In H. Goelman, A. A. Oberg, F. Smith, & University of Victoria symposium on children's response to a literate environment: Literacy before schooling (Eds.), *Awakening to literacy: The University of Victoria symposium on children's response to a literate environment: Literacy before schooling* (pp. 154–173). Exeter, NH: Heinemann Educational Books.

Ferreiro, E. (1986). The interplay between information and assimilation in beginning literacy. In W. H. Teale & E. Sulzby, *Emergent literacy: Writing and reading* (pp. 15–49). Norwood, NJ: Ablex Pub. Corp.

Ferreiro, E. (1988). L'écriture avant la lettre. In H. Sinclair, *La production de notations chez le jeune enfant: Langage, nombres, rythmes et mélodies* (pp. 17–70). Paris: Presses Universitaires de France.

Ferreiro, E. (2000). *L'écriture avant la lettre.* Paris: Hachette.

Ferreiro, E. (2001). *Culture écrite et éducation.* Paris: Retz.

Ferreiro, E., & Gomez Palacio, M. (1988). *Lire-écrire à l'école: Comment s'y apprennent-ils?: Analyse des perturbations dans les processus d'apprentissage de la lecture et de l'écriture.* Lyon: CRDP Lyon.

Ferreiro, E., & Teberosky, A. (1979). *Los Sistemas de escritura en el desarollo del nino.* Mexico: Siglo XXI.

Ferreiro, E., & Teberosky, A. (1983). *Literacy before schooling.* London: Heinemann Educational.

Fijalkow, J., Cussac-Pomel, J., & Hannouz, D. (2009). L'écriture inventée: Empirisme, constructivisme, socioconstructivisme. *Éducation et didactique, 3*(3), 63–97. https://doi.org/10.4000/educationdidactique.576

Fijalkow, J., & Fijalkow, E. (1991). L'écriture inventée au cycle des apprentissages: Étude génétique. *Les Dossiers de l'Education, 18*, 125–167.

Fraquet, S., & David, J. (2013). Écrire en maternelle: Comment approcher le système écrit? *Repères. Recherches en didactique du français langue maternelle, 47*, 19–40. https://doi.org/10.4000/reperes.520

Garcia, S. (2013). *A l'école des dyslexiques: Naturaliser ou combattre l'échec scolaire?* Paris: La Découverte.

Garcia, S. (2018). *Le goût de l'effort. La construction familiale des dispositions scolaires.* Paris: Presses Universitaires de France.

Garcia, S. (2021). Différenciations adaptatives, palliatives et différenciations égalisatrices: L'exemple de l'apprentissage de la lecture. *Éducation et socialisation. Les Cahiers du CERFEE, 59*, Article 59. https://doi.org/10.4000/edso.13911

Garcia, S., & Oller, A.-C. (2015). *Réapprendre à lire: De la querelle des méthodes à l'action pédagogique.* Paris: Seuil.

Garcia, S., & Oller, A.-C. (2018). Mettre en place une pédagogie rationnelle: De la théorie sociologique aux obstacles sociaux. *Sociologies pratiques, 37*(2), 91–104. https://doi.org.ressources.univ-poitiers.fr/10.3917/sopr.037.0091

Garnier, P. (2009). Préscolarisation ou scolarisation? L'évolution institutionnelle et curriculaire de l'école maternelle. *Revue française de pédagogie. Recherches en éducation, 169*, 5–15. https://doi.org/10.4000/rfp.1278

Goodman, Y. (1986). Children's coming to know literacy. In W. H. Teale & E. Sulzby (Eds.), *Emergent literacy: Writing and reading* (pp. 1–14). Norwood, N.J: Ablex Pub. Corp.

INRP & Brigaudiot, M. (2004). *Apprentissages progressifs de l'écrit à l'école maternelle PROG.* Paris: Hachette éducation.

Isambert-Jamati, V. (1985). Quelques rappels de l'émergence de l'échec scolaire comme "problème social" dans les milieux pédagogiques français. In E. Plaisance, *L'échec scolaire. Nouveaux débats, nouvelles approches sociologiques. Actes du colloque franco-suisse 9–12 janvier 1984* (pp. 155–163). Paris: CNRS.

Jaffré, J.-P., Bousquet, S., & Massonet, J. (1999). Retour sur les orthographes inventées. *Les Dossiers des Sciences de l'Éducation, 1*(1), 39–52. https://doi.org/10.3406/dsedu.1999.878

Joigneaux, C. (2013). La littératie précoce. Ce que les enfants font avec l'écrit avant qu'il ne leur soit enseigné. Note de synthèse. *Revue française de pédagogie, 185*, 117–161. https://doi.org/10.4000/rfp.4345

Lahire, B. (2001a). La construction de l'"autonomie" à l'école primaire: Entre savoirs et pouvoirs. *Revue française de pédagogie, 135*(1), 151–161. https://doi.org/10.3406/rfp.2001.2812

Lahire, B. (2001b). *L'homme pluriel: Les ressorts de l'action.* Paris: Nathan.

Lahire, B. (2003). From the habitus to an individual heritage of dispositions. Towards a sociology at the level of the individual. *Poetics, 31*(5–6), 329–355. https://doi.org/10.1016/j.poetic.2003.08.002

Laparra, M., & Margolinas, C. (2016). *Les premiers apprentissages scolaires à la loupe: Des liens entre énumération, oralité et littératie.* Louvain-la-Neuve: De Boeck.

Leroy, G. (2020). *L'école maternelle de la performance enfantine.* Bruxelles: Peter Lang.

Millet, M., & Croizet, J.-C. (2016). *L'école des incapables? La maternelle, un apprentissage de la domination.* Paris: La Dispute.

Ministry of National Education. (2002). II - Ecole maternelle. In *Les programmes de l'école primaire.* (pp. 16–39). Arrêté du 25 janvier. Bulletin officiel de l'Education nationale, n°1 du 14 février Hors série.

Ministry of National Education. (2006). *Le langage à l'école maternelle*. Paris: CNDP.
Ministry of National Education. (2008). Programme de l'école maternelle: Petite section, moyenne section, grande section. In *Les programmes de l'école primaire* (pp. 12–30). Bulletin officiel de l'Education nationale n°3 du 19 juin 2008. Hors série.
Ministry of National Education. (2011). *Le langage à l'école maternelle*. Paris: Sceren CNDP CRDP.
Ministry of National Education. (2012). *Repères et références statistiques sur les enseignements la formation et la recherche*. Edition 2012. MEN, DEPP.
Ministry of National Education. (2015). *Programme d'enseignement de l'école maternelle*. B. O. spécial n°2 du 26 mars 2015.
Ministry of National Education, Youth and Sports. (2021). *Programme d'enseignement de l'école maternelle*. B. O. n°25 du 24 juin 2021.
Ministry of National Education and Culture. (1992). *La maîtrise de la langue à l'école*. Paris: CNDP: Savoir lire.
Montmasson-Michel, F. (2016). Une socialisation langagière paradoxale à l'école maternelle. *Langage et société*, *156*, 57–76. https://doi.org/10.3917/ls.156.0057
Montmasson-Michel, F. (2018). *Enfances du langage et langages de l'enfance. Socialisation plurielle et différenciation sociale de la petite enfance scolarisée*. [Thèse de Sociologie sous la direction de Mathias Millet et Gilles Moreau, Université de Poitiers]. https://hal.archives-ouvertes.fr/tel-02462031/ (26.09.2022).
Montmasson-Michel, F. (2020). Les toupies Beyblade et la Reine des Neiges à l'école du langage: Fabriques du genre et des rapports sociaux de classe à l'école maternelle. *L'orientation scolaire et professionnelle*, *1*(49), 313–337. https://doi.org/10.4000/osp.12141
Morel, S. (2010). *L'échec scolaire en France (1960-2010). Sociologie d'un champ d'intervention professionnelle* [Thèse de Sociologie, EHESS, Paris].
Ouellette, G., & Sénéchal, M. (2008). Pathways to literacy: A study of invented spelling and its role in learning to read. *Child Development*, *79*(4), 899–913. https://doi.org/10.1111/j.1467-8624.2008.01166.x
Pasa, L., Creuzet, V., & Fijalkow, J. (2006). Ecriture inventée: Pluralité des traitements et variabilité selon la structure syllabique. *Education et Francophonie*, *XXXIV*(2), 85–103. https://doi.org/10.7202/1079023ar
Passeron, J. C., & Revel, J. (2005). Penser par cas. Raisonner à partir de singularités. In J. C. Passeron & J. Revel (Eds.), *Penser par cas* (pp. 9–44). Paris: École des hautes études en sciences sociales.
Plaisance, E. (1986). *L'enfant, la maternelle, la société*. Paris: Presses Universitaires de France.
Read, C. (1971). Pre-school children's knowledge of English phonology. *Harvard Educational Review*, *41*(1), 1–34. https://doi.org/10.17763/haer.41.1.91367v0h80051573
Read, C. (1986). *Children's creative spelling*. London; Boston, MA: Routledge & Kegan Paul.
Renard, F. (2011). La construction des habitudes de lecture. *Savoir/Agir*, *17*(3), 75–79. https://doi.org/10.3917/sava.017.0075
Rosaz, J.-P. (2003). Constructeurs de mots en maternelle. Pour découvrir l'orthographe. *Les Dossiers des Sciences de l'Éducation*, *9*(1), 17–28. https://doi.org/10.3406/dsedu.2003.982
Sénéchal, M. (2006). Testing the home literacy model: Parent involvement in kindergarten is differentially related to grade 4 reading comprehension, fluency, spelling, and reading

for pleasure. *Scientific Studies of Reading*, *10*(1), 59–87. https://doi.org/10.1207/s1532799xssr1001_4

Sénéchal, M. (2018). *Comment les élèves appréhendent-ils l'écriture avant même tout enseignement? Conférence de consensus du Cnesco Ecrire et rédiger*. Lyon: Ifé; ENS Lyon. Retrieved from https://www.cnesco.fr/wp-content/uploads/2018/04/CCEcrits_note_Senechal.pdf (26.09.2022)

Sénéchal, M., & LeFevre, J.-A. (2002). Parental involvement in the development of children's reading skill: A five-year longitudinal study. *Child Development*, *73*(2), 445–460.

3

THE "PEDAGOGY OF AUTONOMY"

Similar educational tools for a variety of teaching practices

Julien Netter and Christophe Joigneaux

Introduction

One of the key features of the most recent "assessment" of educational practice is the increased emphasis on autonomy and self-reflection required of students from an increasingly early age (Lahire, 2001, 2005, 2008). Whether in France (Joigneaux, 2014) or Switzerland (Durler, 2015, 2016), the ideal preschool student is now expected to engage in activities on their own initiative by drawing on pedagogical resources (aids and materials) specifically designed for that purpose. While the pedagogy of autonomy and its associated resources ("game corners", "independent workshops", "sheets", "work plans", "responsibility boards", etc.) have grown in popularity in recent years, the uses to which they are put have evolved over time (Joigneaux, 2014, pp. 68–70; 2019, pp. 65–66).

In this chapter, rather than examining these uses from a diachronic perspective (over the course of several decades), we propose to take a synchronic approach focused on a particular preschool class (specifically, the second and third years of an *école maternelle* located in the French department of Seine-Saint-Denis consisting of children aged 4–5 years).[1] As part of a study of the RESEIDA network,[2] the practices of two classroom teachers (Camille and Stéphanie[3]), both of whom worked part-time with the same pupils, were observed over the course of several mornings (60 hours, almost all of which were filmed) during the academic year 2018–2019. The methodology used allowed us to dissociate the effects of the physical context (availability of certain pedagogical tools, spatial constraints, etc.) from the effects associated with the teachers' dispositions observed as part of the implementation of a pedagogy (or pedagogies) of autonomy. More specifically, the focus was on the different uses of tools pertaining to the pedagogy of autonomy as ideal-typified by Lahire (2001, 2005).

Given the range of uses associated with the kinds of tools implemented by Camille and Stéphanie, we may question the extent to which this ideal type constitutes a coherent whole. Indeed, the different practices employed by the two participating teachers point to the need for a subtler and more nuanced view than the distinction made by Lahire (2005) between cognitive and political autonomy. Lahire defines the cognitive form of autonomy as the "appropriation of knowledge", while the political form is defined as the appropriation of the "rules of social life" and discipline (p. 333). Other criteria for analysing and categorizing autonomy are needed to characterize different types of pedagogy. Observations suggest that a distinction can be made between at least two types of pedagogy for autonomy, distinguished according to the degree of systematicity with which student autonomy is developed or the temporal horizon of autonomy that each individual is seeking to develop. In the first case, "short-term" autonomy leads to the development of gestures that are of immediate use but provide little emancipation from the situation and therefore soon require teacher support and intervention. In the second case, "long-term" autonomy focuses on the deep and gradual incorporation of dispositions, which, though initially less effective as responses to dependency situations, are geared towards the attainment over time of a more complete form of autonomy. In what follows, our aim will be to assess the validity of this hypothesis. Insofar as they seemed to be especially typical of both the pedagogy of autonomy and the differences in practice that the approach allows for, we chose to focus the analysis on the following five points: the differentiated uses of the same pedagogical tool (a numerical strip), the different ways of using and dealing with student errors, the maintenance of classroom order, the management of student activities, and finally the use of metacognitive discourse.

The different uses of the numerical strip

Among the most characteristic tools and processes associated with the pedagogy of autonomy, Lahire emphasizes what he calls "*publicization*", according to which pupils are able to "*refer to visible elements (skills and knowledge, common rules, exercise instructions)*" (Lahire, 2005, p. 331; our translation) and thus "*have access to information (...) hitherto 'conveyed' by teachers alone*" (ibid., p. 330; our translation) but now formalized in tools such as files, books, dictionaries, worksheets, posters, and boards (ibid., p. 341). In characterizing this pedagogical ideal type, Lahire's focus is on the different uses that pupils make of the resources made available to them, highlighting the fact that pupils are not equally equipped to use them in the expected way (ibid., p. 341–347). The uses made of them by teachers have received less attention in the literature. Beyond any methodological considerations arising from the necessarily idealized nature of the proposed modelling, Lahire only highlights the (more or less) formalized and objectified nature of the learning environments created by teachers, reflected in practice by unequally developed publicization processes from one class to the next (ibid., pp. 333–334). Our corpus sheds further light on the more qualitative dimensions of the different ways in which this pedagogical model is put into practice. Again, our focus is not on the nature or number of pedagogical tools characterizing these practices (given that the two teachers observed in this study shared the same class) so much as on the way in which they used the same physical setting and resources, as well as the same pedagogical tools.

Among these tools, different uses of the numerical strip were observed.[4] Strips, which are now used in almost all classes of the French *école maternelle*, are often located below the (central) board, at the centre of what is known (in French) as the "gathering corner", a space used every day during periods of group work. Strips are often used by teachers and even pupils at the beginning of the day during the "roll call" and "date" rituals.[5] Their use in class implies an assumption among teachers that students can use them to find number words or other symbolic representations of the first integers, especially when displayed at child height. To find the word for a given number, pupils can tick the first boxes of the strip one after the other (so the box containing the number 1, followed by the box containing 2, and so on and so forth) by synchronizing their ticking with the reciting of a counting rhyme, consisting of the first integers, from lowest to highest (one, two, etc.). In other words, the approach to numerical strips suggests that teachers who have made this choice assume that their pupils have the ability to be, or to become, independent in performing this type of intellectual operation.

Since the two teachers shared the same class, it is conceivable that this disposition was imposed on one of them. However, an analysis of their respective practices shows that they shared this view, with both teachers requiring their pupils to use the numerical strip. There are other similarities. For example, both teachers explicitly set out their uses of the strip on a daily basis during learning rituals, clearly operating on the assumption that pupils should be explicitly taught how to use the tool. In addition, their explanations initially seemed relatively similar, with both taking full control of the box-ticking process, as well as the pace and the requirement to stop at the box containing the targeted number. In other words, pupils were simply left with having to recite the counting rhyme in synchrony with the successive counts. In short, both teachers sought to teach their pupils to use an aid conducive to developing their autonomy by drawing more specifically on the "reduction in degrees of freedom",[6] one of the support (or "supervision") functions identified by Bruner (1983; our translation).

However, on closer inspection, differences in practice are apparent, pointing to different conceptions of autonomy and, accordingly, different goals. What we find are contrasting practices around, and relationships to, language, with potentially significant implications for socio-educational inequalities. First,

Camille differed from Stéphanie in using reflexive discourse serving to articulate pupils' experience and present or future learning. For example, she would often remind pupils of the purpose of the numerical strip and the different strategies associated with its use. The final section of the chapter focuses more specifically on the role of metalinguistic and metacognitive practices, but we can already highlight one of the key characteristics of these practices. To make relatively decontextualized verbalizations of (abstract and therefore theoretically not visible) strategies more accessible, Camille typically accompanied them with dramatizations and non-verbal demonstrations. During moments of explicitation, she would often turn to the resources being used, whether the numerical strip or the other displays associated with it. Unlike Stéphanie, this enabled her to count more systematically and, therefore, to show the sequence that pupils should follow in focusing their attention on specific points. Her demonstrations were accompanied in some cases by the addition of written traces, as when she drew a cross above the number 13 on the strip to highlight the importance of remembering the number being searched for, with the cross marking the end of the count on the strip. In doing so, she explicitly drew attention to the strategies used in the development of, and bridge-building between, a range of information disseminated across vast graphic spaces (consisting, in this case, of all the displays referred to by Camille), as well as the value of retaining written traces of the information thus obtained to make it easier to use in future. What this highlights is the importance of seemingly minor gestures (Lahire, 2000) or "hypodidactic" methods (Johsua, 2003, pp. 139–142) and their link to cognitive autonomy and the reproduction of socio-educational inequalities, including at the preschool level (Joigneaux, 2009).

Different conceptions of student errors

The practices illustrated by Camille and Stéphanie were also found to differ when observing their responses to gaps between what schoolchildren did and what they were expected to do (Netter, 2018). These gaps may be referred to as errors. In Stéphanie's case, the slightest gap was immediately highlighted as an error and corrected. For example, after having counted the 22 pupils present in class, a pupil in the second year of the *école maternelle* was asked to locate the number 22 ("a 2 and a 2", as the teacher reminded her) on the strip but selected the number "11". Stéphanie then asked her classmate Enzo to invalidate the answer, noted that the number that she had picked out was the number 11, and said to the whole class, "Let's count, come on, let's go", supporting and accompanying the pupil in her counting until she reached the number 22. She then said to the student "22, 2 and 2" and showed her the label, which the pupil then handed over to her. This simple example highlights key features of her pedagogical practice. The first is that the focus of the entire episode was in compliance with a norm specific to the class (at least when

Stéphanie was the teacher) that may be summarized as follows: "You must give the teacher the correct label". The high degree of formality is clearly seen in the final gesture when the teacher showed the "right" label and asked the pupil to get it for her. There is a strong emphasis on adherence to school roles, with the role assigned to the pupil being to give (in this case physically) the correct answer to the teacher, whose role is to validate it immediately. Moreover, Stéphanie was observed questioning a pupil known to have a good grasp of numbers to validate the answer "11", without any other explanation being provided. In other words, the answer was presented (and perhaps conceived) as either right or wrong, with any wrong answers having to be immediately rejected. The role assigned to Enzo implies that a "good pupil" is assumed to be someone who has the right answer. Finally, the fact that the rationale behind the error was neither examined nor pointed out (for example, the proximity between "11" and "22", the fact that "1" rather than "2" is repeated) suggests that what Stéphanie values above all is simply demonstrating the different types of norms that must be established in class. The regulatory principle underlying the implied pedagogical ethos can be defined as follows: to present the correct answer to ensure that pupils are enlightened and appropriate the answer. Because pupils' autonomy is more assumed than constructed, the norms underlying their errors can be merely suggested without being exposed. In this normative context, learning can be ideal-typically defined as the systematic learning of a series of pre-defined correct answers to be given at the appropriate time.

Similar episodes were sometimes observed in the case of Camille, especially when it came to doing things quickly. However, more often than not, while errors were pointed out, they were also challenged. For example, having been asked to read out the number "13" on the board, one student said "30". The teacher then proceeded to ask the rest of the class for their views. Several pupils expressed their disagreement, prompting the teacher to ask, "Why do you disagree?" One pupil explained the difference between "13" and "30", at which point Camille interjected, "So what might have led her to believe that it was 30 and not 13?" The importance of this simple interjection, the effect of which is to shape and direct the entire conversation, should not be underestimated. What it does is encourage pupils to consider the underlying rationale of the error, resulting in a series of exchanges on positional notation. The practice even serves to challenge the different registers of norms in place in class, quite apart from, and prior to, any considerations around errors arising from their transgression. The point is invariably to highlight them indirectly by turning them into objects of reflection. This implies distinguishing stable norms related to others' knowledge, which may be viewed as more local and therefore seemingly less justified. For example, why write the date in the top left-hand corner of the board rather than in the right-hand corner? In this view, learning consists not in knowing a series of correct answers or correct ways of doing things so much as understanding the logic underlying their production. The pupil who made a mistake was not viewed by her classmates as ignorant but as a rational child who developed a thought, the logic of which departed from one of the norms that the teacher wanted to establish in class. In other words, Camille's goal was not simply to ensure adherence to a particular normative order but to help pupils acquire the intellectual tools needed to understand the underlying logic of that order. In that sense, we might say that Camille's aim was to ensure that pupils were able to access a form of autonomy differing from the kind of autonomy fostered in Stéphanie's practice. Camille's was found to be both more separate from the immediate context and broader in the sense that it was associated with dispositions making it accessible in a greater number of instances without the need for teacher support.

Ways of maintaining school order

Similarly, pupils' behaviour may be conceived as aligning to a greater or lesser extent with the behavioural norms required by the teacher. In Stéphanie's case, there was a significant emphasis on adherence to established norms combined with a lack of explanation around the underlying rationale. For example, while the pupils were counting, Stéphanie turned to a pupil who was chatting in the group corner and said in a somewhat brusque and angry tone, "Isia! Isia! That's no good at all! I'm watching you and it's not Johra disrupting you! That won't do at all! Please calm down straight away". She then concluded her interjection in a distinctly imperative tone amid a silence as total as it was temporary with, "Agreed, right?" Both the form and the content of the discourse signify the existence of a behavioural norm together with the fact that it has been transgressed and must be adhered to. The mention of the discrepancy is reinforced by the significant imbalance observed in the teacher-pupil interaction, of which Stéphanie makes full use. However, no effort was made to describe the norm from which Isia departed or to explain its rationale, or indeed to explain how to appropriate and apply the norm. A pupil such as Isia, who missed many days in her final year of the *école maternelle* without the reasons for her absence being known, was likely to misinterpret Stéphanie's words. For example, it was unclear whether she identified what was wrong about her behaviour. She may have assumed that a misunderstanding had occurred and that the teacher thought that she was bickering. While she understood that she should not talk, it is possible that she misunderstood the reason for silence in group work and the fact that she had to remain focused on the activity of one of her classmates to check her work and spot any errors. Finally, even assuming that she understood all of these things, there is nothing to say that she would have been able to regulate her behaviour, understood as a long-term objective, according to Vygotsky (2014), of human development. By contrast, it seems clear that, in the teacher's discourse, responsibility for non-adherence to the behavioural norm lies squarely with the pupil since there is no question of invoking an excuse. In other words, Isia was expected to comply with a norm whose meaning she may not have understood and that she may not know how to grasp, failing which she would be deemed guilty.

Camille's practice often contrasted with Stéphanie's in all these respects. Camille was also observed regularly calling the pupils to order. However, when she did so, it was invariably by explicitly verbalizing the behavioural rules that students were infringing. She also often drew attention to situations in which pupils adhered to behavioural norms. In this case, norms are thus "denaturalized" since they are not overlooked or passed over, meaning that they are not deemed so "normal" that there is no need to point them out, instead acquiring the status of learning objectives, the attainment of which is worth highlighting. As Camille said on one occasion as the pupils had just moved over to the group corner, "Well done for going to your usual places". She also spent much of her time explaining the purpose of behavioural norms. For example, when a pupil called Salimata appeared to be struggling to concentrate, looking around the class and sliding to the end of the bench where she was seated, Camille whispered to her, "Turn around and listen carefully", before adding, "Do you need a chair?" She then proceeded to quietly place a chair next to her. This seemingly innocuous interjection suggests that there is an important reason for behaving well and remaining properly seated. The assumption is that such behaviour is necessary to listen to what a classmate is saying. Here, the norm is not an end in itself but is instead directed towards a goal that is separate from it. Finally, Camille indicates that there are means or external stimuli that adults use (Vygotsky, 2014) to control pupil behaviour. The explicit presence of these stimuli is sometimes necessary, meaning that it may be legitimate in some circumstances, especially for children, to misbehave when such stimuli are lacking. The teacher thus operates as a "resource" person with the capacity to help pupils develop these abilities. In the example given here, the chair represented both a signal of the need to concentrate on what the classmate was saying and a physical support for the pupil's body.

For both teachers, maintaining the requirement for appropriate "school behaviour" was found to be a continuous and exhausting process in a class deemed "difficult". Indeed, from an autonomy point of view, both were unsuccessful in their attempts to ensure that pupils control their own behaviour. Two observations are necessary before concluding on this point. On the one hand, the classroom atmosphere was found to differ according to which teacher was leading the class. Pupils were calmer with Camille and required more frequent and more antagonistic interventions when led by Stéphanie. On the other hand, a distinction can be made between pupils' autonomy at a given point in time and the greater or lesser capacity of schoolchildren to become autonomous more rapidly. In other words, we may distinguish between a focus on autonomy in the short term associated with more immediate adherence to behavioural norms and an approach geared towards the longer term, the effects of which are less immediately visible but that translate over time into a greater ability for behavioural self-control.

Activity regulation

The differences between the two teachers are even more pronounced when considering pupils' cognitive activities, as already suggested by our examination of the uses of the numerical strip and the management of pupil errors. This is even more apparent when looking at both periods of group activity (see the earlier discussion) and periods during which pupils are scattered throughout the class during workshops, as was standard practice in French *école maternelle* for 30 from the early 1980s (Joigneaux, 2014) to the rise of Montessori education in recent years. Workshops involve groupings of tables spread throughout the class (or simply big tables), enabling schoolchildren to be placed "in groups" and to work on specific activities (with each workshop being assigned different activities).

This strategy is one of the most distinctive features of the pedagogy (or pedagogies) of autonomy, the effect of which is to loosen the constraints associated with the simultaneous teaching approach characterized by simultaneous learning tasks proposed to the same group (Chartier, Compère, & Julia, 1976). Workshops involve pupils performing different activities and different learning tasks over a limited period, making it more difficult for teachers to monitor and guide them simultaneously and in "real time", especially when pupils are scattered around the classroom. For workshops to become the pedagogical norm at preschool, it was necessary to assume that pupils could work on a regular basis in a relatively independent way within groups conceived as "autonomous" or "semi-autonomous workshops", with other groups being more teacher-led. The activities carried out in autonomous workshops can only be monitored and regulated by teachers from a distance, both spatially and temporally (Joigneaux, 2014).

Close observations and comparisons of Camille's and Stéphanie's practices during workshop periods showed that the kinds of pedagogical constraints described here were sometimes handled differently by the two teachers. For example, during a given period, Stéphanie tended to design all workshops as "autonomous workshops" by spending time correcting other work while the pupils worked independently in their workshops. Pupils were nonetheless permitted to come over to her to ask for help or to have their work assessed if they deemed it necessary. Camille took an altogether different approach, seeking instead to limit the moments during which pupils worked (completely) independently during workshops. To do so, she kept both the total number of workshops (there are generally only three) and the number of "autonomous" workshops (generally only one, or sometimes none when another adult is present) to a minimum. This was made possible by a range of spatial and organizational arrangements. The workshops consisted of a greater number of pupils (numbering seven or eight, as opposed to four or five generally). During a given period of workshop activity, Camille led two workshops (as opposed to one, as is generally the case). In spatial terms, the tables delimiting the workshops were positioned close to each other. Finally, Camille set the same activity in both workshops (as opposed to a different activity, which is standard practice). These seemingly inconsequential arrangements meant that she was able to shorten the (spatial and temporal) distance associated with the regulation of most pupils' activities, providing her with a more consistent view of the behaviour of a larger number of students. In addition, the reduced number of activities proposed during a given period also meant that her group explanations were more "public" since she was able to address a larger number of pupils. It seems likely that this also made it easier for her to monitor each pupil's work.

All of this may seem inconsequential in the sense that the two types of practices described here may ultimately seem relatively similar, differing only in terms of the uses made of the same teaching and learning framework associated with the pedagogy of autonomy. However, if we consider the impacts of these differences in activity regulation in terms of supposed or constructed autonomy, the gaps between the two practices are found to be far wider.

Different uses of "meta"

As we have already seen, the two teachers differ in their greater or lesser use of "meta" discourse – in the sense of a discourse which, through a process of *mise en abyme*, takes as its object class situations, i.e., objects through which openings are created to deploy discourse. These "meta" moments are rare in class, especially at preschool, where pupils require constant input from teachers and where there is never enough time. Making allowances for such moments presupposes making room for pauses during the "class flow" to allow for group reflection time, the effect of which is to delay the start of classroom activities and the performance of tasks, creating a risk that these will not be completed. In other words, maintaining a "meta" discourse requires significant effort on the part of teachers, while the associated benefits are not always clear to them.

Based on our observations, this type of discourse was found to be rare in Stéphanie's practice, which was heavily focused on significant devolution and practical physical matters (such as handing out materials) in the performance of schoolwork. By contrast, meta-discourse was found to be much more common in the case of Camille's practice. For example, while introducing a letter-cutting activity to several pupils, including Hamza, who seemed to want to get himself noticed, sometimes loudly so, Camille asked Lise, a relatively quiet pupil, to choose a letter to cut up. Lise selected the letter "o", which was then immediately followed by a loud "no!" from Hamza, who was keen to impose his choice. Camille turned to him calmly and said, "But it's what *she* wants, you'll be doing all this on your sheet *afterwards*", before adding in a light tone, "This is just an example. Right, I'm cutting up the letter". Camille's passing comment, "This is just an example", implies a major shift in discourse. In other words, she was no longer *in* the situation, cutting up letters and regulating the pupils' activity, but instead removed herself from the situation and, in doing so, also removed the pupils in question, chief among them Hamza, to talk *about* the situation. To use the term proposed by Russel (1908) in addressing paradoxes, Camille switched to a different "logical type". The effect of this was to provide her with a means of defining what the situation actually was, i.e., "an example", the implication being that there was little at stake and that there was no need to fight to get one's preferred letter cut up. As a result, Hamza immediately calmed down, joining the group of attentive pupils.

One of the major problems of school lies in the multitude of interpretations of situations made by pupils (Edwards & Mercer, 2013), which teachers struggle to reduce. The difficulty is that pupils' interpretations align to a greater or lesser extent with the interpretation theoretically expected by the teacher, translating, for pupils in the same class and in the same situation, into activities of widely differing educational value, which, through the accumulation of situations, eventually turn into learning inequalities (Bautier & Rochex, 2004). In terms of autonomy, the first requirement for pupils is to reach an interpretation that is consistent with the situation. However, this is not enough insofar as intellectual tools and materials are also needed to deal with the problems arising. These tools are often made available to pupils in class.

The question that arises is around their use, as was shown with the case of the numerical strip, but also the question of their interpretation – in other words, the definition of their role in the situation. In using the numerical strip, Camille seemed to be aware of this double constraint when articulating some of the gestures and cognitive or language operations that enable expected uses of the numerical strip tool ("uttering a number word while at the same time pointing to a single number", "remembering the number stopped at", etc.), the purpose of such uses ("looking for... finding the numbers written in numerals"...), and the errors to which they can give rise ("you start counting and then you forget the number you're looking for", etc.). More generally, it is both the situation and the objects that children encounter within that situation that are regularly defined by their use and their purpose. This enables pupils who are not familiar with the latter to understand the reasons why they encounter them. Such explicitation is found to be invaluable given the extent to which misinterpretations prevent any possibility of educationally "high-yield" autonomy, implying instead a context in which autonomy is exercised with difficulty and in which children find themselves isolated in dealing with the demands of school (Netter, 2012). Furthermore, "meta" verbalizations serve to emphasize a relation to highly reflexive language practices and uses. Many studies (particularly those that draw on intuitions first articulated by Vygotsky; see, for example, Vygotsky, 1997, p. 350) agree on the importance of the "meta" dimension to enable, encourage awareness of, and foster the ability to effect transfers of what is learned in a given situation to an increasingly broad range of situations. Autonomy thus constructed is, therefore, wider than the kind of autonomy constructed by Stéphanie since it is founded on more pronounced situations involving "reflexiveness". The aim is no longer simply to appropriate highly situated gestures since it is also a matter of developing ways of talking and thinking about what is done and why what is done is done – in other words, a relation to the world and to practice, with the latter's high educational "yield" having thus been reinstated (Lahire, 1993).

Conclusion

The practices compared in this study could both be described as "pedagogies of autonomy" given the tools and approaches involved, which are viewed as resources made available to pupils to enable them to perform their activities of their own initiative and thereby develop their autonomy. However, on closer analysis, the practices illustrated by the two teachers observed in this study serve to construct significantly different forms of autonomy. In the case of Stéphanie, we may speak of a focus on short-term autonomy, enabling students to meet her demands rapidly, at the risk of limiting the potential to broaden their range of skills and competencies in the longer term. Her behaviour is geared primarily towards the reproduction and understanding of expected activities or gestures, adherence to the rules of collective living (of which pupils are constantly being reminded), and the immediate utterance of the "right answer". Rather than being aimed at immediately satisfying her demands, Camille's practice appears to be geared towards allowing, over the longer term, for the transfer of skills and competencies developed in a given situation. Our analysis showed that Camille gives more importance to metacognitive reflections aimed at enabling schoolchildren to understand the implications of what they are doing, reformulating them within the terms of generic learning rather than the mere purpose of assessing the degree of "correctness" of their answers or behaviour. For her, the point is not simply to refer to or show what should be done or said in a given situation in the hope that pupils will subsequently go on to reproduce the "right answers". Rather, the aim is to transmit the ability to analyse how to understand and how to meet school demands that are not specific to the situation at hand, which thus come to be seen as an object of reflection.

Fundamentally, in Stéphanie's case, the type of autonomy assumed is a demanding form of autonomy since pupils must be sufficiently independent to realize that they need help or have their work validated. By contrast, Camille's preferred mode of supervision and regulation assumes a lesser degree of autonomy since she is more likely to intervene "in real time" (i.e., in close alignment with the temporality of pupils' activities) to validate or explain the work in which they are engaged. Our observations show that the broadest possible form of autonomy paradoxically requires providing pupils with significant guidance during activities geared towards supporting the appropriation of adapted dispositions rather than an expectation of immediate success. This is all the more true since the form of autonomy targeted by Camille requires greater cognitive and language skills on the part of pupils in the sense that it requires more language exchanges to characterize and justify the practices and strategies thus challenged, which presupposes equipping pupils accordingly. Access to the kind of "long-term" autonomy promoted by Camille appears to be the result of a "gamble", highlighting a high degree of initial trust placed in the children and in the future: in other words, they are assumed to be capable of gradually appropriating the dispositions that they are being encouraged to develop, and the future is conceived as the temporal horizon required for such learning, which may be longer or shorter depending on the pupil, with time being conceived in this approach as an ally rather than an enemy.

Since implementing this strategy is time-consuming, it can, in a given situation, prove detrimental to both classroom behaviour and task performance. However, the observations carried out as part of this study over the course of an academic year allowed for a comparison of students' progress with both teachers and showed that while pupils remained dependent on the highly contextualized support provided by Stéphanie, with Camille, they gradually built on learning possibilities that eventually became accessible to them. In doing so, they developed far more significant forms of "cognitive" and "political" autonomy, to use the distinction made by Lahire, which they were then able to partly transfer to situations encountered with Stéphanie.

These findings shed new light on the link established in the literature between "pedagogies of autonomy" taken as a whole and socio-educational inequalities. It seems important to qualify the link by distinguishing between different forms of these pedagogies, which can have different effects in terms of the development of autonomy in each student taken as an individual and inequalities within the classroom. However, it is also important to emphasize the cost associated with the pedagogical approach employed by Camille, meaning both a personal cost in terms of daily investment, energy, and permanent attention and cost over time in terms of training (generally self-training, which requires long-term commitment and determination). In other words, while some pedagogies of autonomy are not necessarily synonymous with increased inequalities, their use is likely to be at the cost of personal efforts and very specific predispositions. This would explain why such approaches are not more widespread given that little is done within the education system to reduce the costs associated with their implementation by individual practitioners.

Notes

1 Detailed explanations concerning the French *école maternelle* can be found in the chapters by Richard-Bossez and Montmasson-Michel in this volume.
2 The RESEIDA network is a collective of researchers from French-speaking universities specializing in the study of the construction of educational inequalities (RESEIDA stands, in French, for *Recherches sur la Socialisation, l'Enseignement, les Inégalités et les Différenciations dans les Apprentissages*, or Research on Socialization, Teaching, Inequalities and Differentiation in Learning).
3 Both names have been changed to protect the teachers' anonymity.
4 Numerical strips generally take the form of a strip consisting of boxes containing whole numbers written as numerals. They generally range from 1 (first box on the far left of the strip) to 10 (in *Petite Section*, i.e., the first year of the *école maternelle*) or 30 and above (in years 2 and 3).
5 In the French *école maternelle*, a typical day begins with welcoming students (sometimes accompanied by their parent(s)) in class, followed by "rituals", i.e., activities performed almost every day according to relatively consistent scenarios and interaction formats. The most common rituals include the "roll call" and "date" rituals. The roll call involves "calling out" the names of pupils in attendance and identifying those not present, which is often done by tallying both categories of pupils. In the case of the date ritual, the date is formalized both orally and in writing, which often gives rise to work on numbers when identifying the day of the month.
6 By "reduction in degrees of freedom", Bruner means "a simplification of the task by reducing the number of constituent actions required to reach the solution" (Bruner, 1983, p. 277; our translation).

References

Bautier, É., & Rochex, J.-Y. (2004). Activité conjointe ne signifie pas significations partagées. In C. Moro & R. Rickenmann (Eds.), *Situation éducative et significations* (pp. 197–220). Bruxelles: De Boeck.

Bruner, J. S. (1983). *Le développement de l'enfant: Savoir faire, savoir dire*. Paris: Presses Universitaires de France.

Chartier, R., Compère, M.-M., & Julia, D. (1976). *L'éducation en France du XVIe au XVIIIe siècle*. Paris: SEDES-CDU.

Durler, H. (2015). *L'autonomie obligatoire. Sociologie du gouvernement de soi à l'école*. Rennes: Presses universitaires de Rennes.

Durler, H. (2016). L'autonomie de l'élève et ses supports pédagogiques. *Recherches en éducation, 25*, 57–67. https://doi.org/10.4000/ree.5654

Edwards, D., & Mercer, N. (2013). *Common Knowledge: The Development of Understanding in the Classroom*. Oxon: Routledge.

Johsua, S. (2003). Entretien avec R. Amigues et M. Kherroubi. *Recherche et formation, 44*, 137–147.

Joigneaux, C. (2009). La construction de l'inégalité scolaire dès l'école maternelle. *Revue française de pédagogie, 169*, 17–28. https://doi.org/10.4000/rfp.1301

Joigneaux, C. (2014). L'autonomie à l'école maternelle: Un nouvel idéal pédagogique? *Recherches en éducation, 20*, 66–75. https://doi.org/10.4000/ree.8103

Joigneaux, C. (2019). À quoi jouent les élèves de maternelle? Des conceptions pédagogiques aux pratiques de classe. *Émulations, 29*, 59–71.

Lahire, B. (1993). *Culture écrite et inégalités scolaires: Sociologie de l' "échec scolaire" à l'école primaire*. Lyon: Presses universitaires de Lyon.

Lahire, B. (2000). Savoirs et techniques intellectuelles à l'école primaire. In A. Van Zanten (Ed.), *L'école, l'état des savoirs* (pp. 170–178). Paris: La Découverte.

Lahire, B. (2001). La construction de l' "autonomie" à l'école primaire: Entre savoirs et pouvoirs. *Revue française de pédagogie, 134,* 151–161. https://doi.org/10.3406/rfp.2001.2812

Lahire, B. (2005). Fabriquer un type d'homme "autonome": Analyse des dispositifs scolaires. In B. Lahire (Ed.), *L'esprit sociologique* (pp. 322–347). Paris: La Découverte.

Lahire, B. (2008). La forme scolaire dans tous ses états. *Swiss Journal of Educational Research, 30*(2), 229–258. https://doi.org/10.24452/sjer.30.2.4790

Netter, J. (2012). Circulation réelle du travail entre classe et hors classe. In P. Loségo (Ed.), *Actes du colloque "Sociologie et didactiques: Vers une transgression des frontières"* (pp. 426–438). Lausanne: Haute école pédagogique de Vaud. http://www.hepl.ch/sociodidac (accessed 29.02.2022).

Netter, J. (2018). *Culture et inégalités à l'école. Esquisse d'un curriculum invisible.* Rennes: Presses universitaires de Rennes.

Russell, B. (1908). Mathematical logic as based on the theory of types. *American Journal of Mathematics, 30*(3), 222–262. https://doi.org/10.2307/2369948

Vygotsky, L. (1997/1934). *Pensée et langage.* Translated by F. Sève. Paris: La Dispute.

Vygotsky, L. (2014). *Histoire du développement des fonctions psychiques supérieures.* Translated by F. Sève. Paris: La Dispute.

4

THE DIDACTICS OF AUTONOMY IN MULTIGRADE CLASSROOMS

Laura Weidmann and Ursula Fiechter

Introduction: From teacher- to learner-centred classroom settings

The shift "from teaching to learning" has become a major trend in education around the globe (Biesta 2013). It focuses on the needs of the individual learner and calls for the adaptation of teaching in classrooms to these individual needs. Instead of instructors standing in front of their classes, teachers are now considered teacher-coaches: their primary requirements focus on diagnosing and supporting their pupils' individual learning (e.g., Reusser 2019). Student autonomy becomes a central concern within individualized teaching settings: the focus on each learner as a unique individual requires adapting teaching to individual needs and fostering pupils' autonomy. Pupils shall become autonomous learners who are to be supported in becoming able to adapt to new challenges and to solve problems. Furthermore, autonomous learners become an important condition in individualized settings, as teachers face the challenge of coping between the individual needs of their pupils and their own limited (time) resources (Breidenstein 2014).

The focus on individual learning is accompanied by the appreciation of individual differences. The new leading ideal is no longer that of treating classes as homogeneous entities, but to focus instead on the heterogeneity of pupils. As a consequence, heterogeneous class organizations are on the rise in the Canton of Bern in Switzerland. More than 50 percent of primary school classes are organized as multigrade classes (e.g., Fiechter et al. 2021b, p. 11). Multigrade classes offer a unique insight into the strategies by which teachers deal with the expectations of adapting to the individual needs of pupils. In our ethnographic research project on multigrade teaching and learning processes (Fiechter et al. 2021a),[1] we placed the spotlight towards the strategies involved in creating differentiated learning events for multigrade classes. Comparing two cases from our study, this chapter focuses on the question of how teachers differentiate in multigrade classrooms. How do these differentiating measures address pupils and how is autonomy part of the teaching concept?

To begin with, we shall contextualize our research question with a discussion of didactical differentiation in multigrade classes and then analyse the inherent conceptions of autonomy before we discuss our case study. In its conclusion, the chapter sheds light on the two opposing patterns of two teachers' pedagogical practice and manners of reasoning on the question of individualization or differentiation in classrooms, and how concepts of pupil autonomy may influence a teacher's didactic strategies.

Didactical differentiation in multigrade classes

Multigrade classes have increased in the German-speaking part of the Canton of Bern over the past 20 years. This is partly due to the high number of rural communities that have been spreading across vast areas of the canton. In order to offer schools in the vicinity of those rural communities, the canton has also maintained the tradition of multigrade classes at a time when it was considered outdated. However, multigrade classes have also recently become popular in urban regions, where the discussions rather rest on ideas of progressive education (*Reformpädagogik*), to stimulate social learning and to facilitate the "child's self-activity" (Laging 2010, p. 6).[2]

Multigrade classes vary in the form and degree in which the different grades engage in the same tasks or topics, or simply share the same classroom (Veenman 1995, p. 319). Regardless of how teaching in multigrade classes is organized, didactical differentiation is essential. Teachers of multigrade classes must contend with the fact that the diversity of learning goals and preconditions among their pupils is more explicit and urgent. They are to choose and arrange teaching and learning content in a way that accommodates various dispositions. To this end, teachers are compelled to abandon conservative concepts of teaching, which address pupils as a homogeneous group that shares the same knowledge and skills. As Laging (2010, p. 6) observes it, multigrade classes are often introduced to foster a constructivist and individualized understanding of learning and differentiated concepts of classroom settings and teaching. Understanding learning processes in a constructivist way means addressing the preconditions of pupils so they can have access to the learning arrangements and learning goals. In order to achieve this aim, teaching didactics shall offer open and differentiating learning opportunities (e.g., Reusser, Stebler, Mandel, & Eckstein 2013, pp. 21–22). "Differentiation" is hence recommended as a key didactic concept to address any class, be it a mono- or multigrade class setting (ibid., p. 57). The concept refers to various didactic measures that "open up different approaches [...] for the learners in the same teaching situation" (ibid.). Although didactic frameworks avoid calling for complete individualization in an explicit manner, they do suggest that practitioners should aspire to "a good fit between instructional offerings and individual usage options" (ibid.). Consequently, learner autonomy becomes an important factor within various approaches to didactical differentiation. It helps teachers in managing the differentiated classroom settings and addressing the needs of their pupils by supporting them as individuals or as groups. This constructivist understanding of learning has taken to the Swiss-German didactical discourse, and consequently to the competence-oriented curriculum *Lehrplan 21* in German-speaking cantons in Switzerland (cf. D-EDK 2014).

Autonomy concepts in differentiated classroom settings

The importance of pupil autonomy is reflected in the curriculum (D-EDK 2014), where various aspects of autonomy are outlined and formulated as major learning goals. Thereby, the curriculum makes teachers responsible for fostering autonomy-related skills in their pupils (Erziehungsdirektion des Kantons Bern 2016, p. 9). Autonomy-related learning goals are formulated as a part of the "general competences" (*Überfachliche Kompetenzen*), which are prominently positioned in the opening of the curriculum: under the sub-category of "self-competences", items such as "Solving tasks / problems; Acquiring learning strategies, planning, implementing, and reflecting on learning and work processes" are listed (ibid., p. 15). Additionally, "methodical competences" should empower pupils to achieve academic goals, by equipping them with behavioural skills that are required to succeed in school and beyond. Taken together, the "general competences" are designed to enable pupils to become individuals who are capable of "pursuing and reflecting on prescribed and self-defined goals and values" (ibid., p. 4).

In the discussion about individualized teaching and autonomy of pupils, Ricken (2016, p. 10) describes autonomy as a social concept that leads to a specific form of subjectivation, which oscillates between "independence" and "self-legislation". In the pedagogical context, this self-legislation translates into the appropriation of the school's social order by the pupils. This process aims at producing school subjects who are conditioned to fulfil educational expectations and achievements. These conditions apply strongly to pupils in multigrade classes.

In order to provide customized learning opportunities for individuals, teachers of multigrade classes have to address every pupil according to his or her abilities. Thereby, to render the diversity manageable, multigrade teachers often make up groups along different categories (Fiechter et al. 2021a; also, Reh 2011, p. 47), which are addressed as comparable entities and must be able to work autonomously, without the teacher's help and supervision for some time. In this process of clustering or differentiating, a teacher practices difference through explicit, implicit, legitimate, or illegitimate categories (ibid.). Hence, this practice exemplifies how the seemingly objective and neutral term "heterogeneity" implies, in fact, a deeply personal choice and interpretation of certain features by the teacher (Eckermann 2017, pp. 27–28).

As a consequence, autonomy becomes a normative expectation in today's schooling, in multigrade teaching especially, and a dominant factor among the goals of education more generally. More specifically, competences, which are linked to autonomy and methodical skills and subjugation, become part of educational assessment and achievement (Reh & Rabenstein 2012).

Thus, normalized expectations of self-regulation and autonomy lead to new or different forms of acknowledgement of what is a "normal" or "high-performance" pupil (Reh & Rabenstein 2012). Autonomy thereby becomes a precondition for being a "good achiever" (ibid.). Pupils are (pre-)classified along their ability to self-direct their activities and to manage and make use of the teaching and learning materials (e.g., books, worksheets) and to complete them within a defined amount of time. It becomes a central task for pupils in their classroom routine to "not only learn[ing] to learn, but also to organise an operating process" (Reh 2011, p. 48) since these "second-order activities" (ibid.) are benchmarks for their subjectivation and categorization and differentiation in the eyes of the teacher.

These tendencies are further accentuated in multigrade classes, where the request for teachers to differentiate and for pupils to organize their learning processes themselves is even more dominant. Following a poststructuralist perspective on subjectivation, our interest in the case studies lies in identifying the implicit or explicit concepts of autonomy teachers have and how these are applied through the differentiated treatment of pupils according to their subjectivation as autonomous or non-autonomous learners.

Two case studies: Different concepts and expectations of autonomy lead to different ways of teaching

The main topic of our previous research project was the (re-)construction of common learning tasks in multigrade classes within cycle 2 (ranging from grade 3 to 6, ages 9 to 13, respectively) in different school subjects (Mathematics, German, French, English as well and Nature, Humans, Society (NMG)) (Fiechter et al. 2021a).

Data were collected through classroom observation sessions, interviews with teachers, and learning/teaching materials. The data were analysed according to the sequence-analytical method. Especially in the interviews, teachers emphasized the importance of routines and the goal for pupils to become self-directed in one form or another. Although autonomy has neither figured as a predefined keyword in the presentation of the project nor in the framing of our interview questions, it repeatedly surfaced as an important issue in the teachers' narratives. Hence, in the following section, we shall survey these explicit and implicit references to investigate the concepts of autonomy as they emerged in the statements and behaviour of teachers. Based on descriptions of classroom situations and interviews with the teachers, we shall analyse the criteria and categories by which the teachers differentiate the pupils in their class. In this way, we can reconstruct how pupils are addressed and what subjectivation processes they undergo.

We chose to select and compare two cases from our research project and reflect on the (different) ways in which pupil autonomy is discussed by teachers and appears in their teaching and assessment practices. Both study sites are located in remote rural areas; one classroom comprises 17 pupils ranging between grades 4 and 6 of the primary level, and the other is composed of 16 pupils between grades 3 and 6 (Fiechter et al. 2021a). Both cases are based on observations we made in classes dealing with "Nature, Humans, Society" (*NMG*). This school subject is considered particularly suitable for multigrade classes because its didactical concepts are seen as most developed according to the requirements for differentiated and individualized teaching (Adamina 2014; 2019; Adamina & Hild 2019; Weidmann & Adamina 2021).

Both chosen cases show how three or four grades engage in a learning process on the same topic but at different levels. Thus, teachers are required to offer different approaches to the topic, so learners find a way of accessing it. We describe how the teachers differentiate and meet the individual preconditions of their learners, how they distinguish and address different levels of the learning subject, and what understandings of autonomy resonate in these practices.

"They don't have to bring anything along, but they get many opportunities to train and experience self-efficiency"

The first case study is set in a primary school that introduced multigrade settings many years ago. The class contains grades 4 to 6. After sixth grade, pupils attend a secondary school located in the nearby district capital.

The teacher whom we observed in this case works closely together with her co-teacher. They often design common teaching projects across different school subjects. These projects are differentiated along grade levels, as the teacher explains in the interview: the fourth graders encounter the main topic for the first time, whereas fifth graders have already heard about it the year before and are required to deal with the topic in more depth. The sixth graders, who are coming into contact with the subject for the third time, need to learn about it systematically and need to be able to share their knowledge with the younger pupils.

In the lessons we observed, the project topic was "Features of Life". From this overview, the focus shifted to fauna, then was narrowed down to vertebrates. The pupils were to gain insight into the main characteristics of all vertebrates, get an overview of different vertebrate species (fish, amphibians, mammals, reptiles, birds), and learn the characteristics and the classification of selected mammals, and transfer the classification to other species. In order to evaluate their learning progress at the end of the project, the pupils were to answer questions in one-on-one interviews with the teacher. The interview questions varied according to the grade levels; this is important, especially for the assessment of the 6th graders, who must meet specific learning goals in order to justify their selection into the differentiated levels of the secondary school.

By means of our protocols, we investigated how differentiation procedures were implemented by the teacher during class time. The following sequence is taken out of a class conversation on the "Features of Life", which marks the opening of a whole project. The fifth and sixth graders watched a documentary on the topic beforehand, which is referred to in the following example. After the lunch break, the teacher initiated the discussion by showing a set of objects – a bouquet of flowers and a burning candle among other things – and asking whether they were alive and why, or why not. After a short discussion in coincidentally collated pairs, the teacher drew the conversation onto the classroom level, whereby she inquired what the pupils had discussed.

T: Then, you have talked about the candle. What do you think about it? Heidi, what have you been discussing?
H: It cannot procreate. It cannot pass on genetic information. [...]
T: You are right, no genetic information is passed on. The fifth- and sixth-grade pupils have heard that in the film: What does this mean, to pass on genetic information? Florian?
F: Um...if two creatures pass on their genes to their children.
T: Can you give a simple example? What have you inherited from your parents? Is there anything that you keep on hearing? The same eyes or height...?[3]

In this quotation (translated by us), the teacher refers to a documentary that had been shown only to the fifth and sixth graders, and she requires them to summarize one aspect for the fourth graders. Hereby, the more advanced pupils are addressed as more knowledgeable regarding a specific topic. At the same time, they are requested to pass this knowledge on to the fourth graders, under the teacher's guidance.

This example illustrates three elements of the teacher's involvement in subjectivation and of her conception of autonomy, respectively. First, the differentiation between the more and the less advanced is focused on a scholarly subject and merely of temporary value since each fourth grader is sure to become eventually a fifth and a sixth grader. Thereby, addressing the younger pupils as dependent and in need of instruction is only temporary and restricted to the specific scholarly knowledge at hand. By asking the pupils in higher grades to pass on information to less advanced ones, the teacher dilutes their more advanced status in the classroom by instigating the transfer of specialized knowledge. In this situation, autonomy is understood as relational and in development. Second, this form of differentiation demands some effort on the part of the older ones as well, and they are therefore not merely the teacher's help or deputies but further supported and required to advance their own competences by summarizing the documentary. And third, pupils in higher grades are not completely left to their own devices, but by means of a resource-intensive class conversation, their reproduction or summary of acquired knowledge is controlled by the teacher. This strategy helps to minimize the passing on of wrong concepts to the younger pupils, and their consolidation in the older pupils' minds. Thereby, she assumes responsibility for the improvement of their knowledge by understanding her role as someone who offers learning opportunities and involves the more advanced pupils in this process. She controls the correctness of the information passed on by the more advanced pupils. At the same time, she is very attentive to social cohesion within the class. As she states in the interview, she very much thinks about the composition of the groups who work together in class. In all the lessons we observed in her class, the pupils either worked together in teams or were involved in a class conversation with the teacher. It is therefore a recurrent characteristic in her teaching that the topic and learning task are almost constantly public, with group discussions and classroom conversations being dominant forms. These forms of teaching emphasize her idea that a classroom community is a training ground for understanding and practicing one's role, motivations, and autonomy. This is supported by the differentiation she makes: fourth and fifth graders are slowly acquainted with the topics and led into the roles of the ones who are familiar with and increasingly becoming experts in the given topics.

Although autonomy has not figured as a predefined keyword for the interviews, all interviewed teachers mentioned it – in one form or another – as an important issue. The teacher in the previous example tells us that in her classroom organization, pupils have many opportunities to practice autonomy. In this way, she adheres to her remark that autonomy is not a prerequisite for her pupils, but rather something that is trained in class:

I: What are the requirements for learners in a multigrade class?
T: They just have to get the opportunity to exercise autonomy. They get the opportunity to be in a group with visible differences and find their own strengths and weaknesses. They don't have to bring anything along in that sense. [A]nd…there are certainly children who are closer to it, who can do it faster […] they get an overview very quickly. […]

And I mean, when someone looks at my class, I've heard that a few times now, from [teaching interns]: "Wow, they are so autonomous!" […] But I think here they also have a training ground to be[come] autonomous. [I] mean, the children arrive here with a basis already. […] Right? They get here, after having already practiced things: being autonomous, being self-effective, and have felt, hey.… Yes!

This statement carries a specific – and particularly broad – concept of autonomy. The teacher views it as a realization of self-efficacy, in the sense of "[having an] overview" and understanding one's own effects on the surroundings. To this end, the pupils should develop an understanding of their own resources and learn how to use them.

In this case study, the teacher also understands autonomy as something that is not to be found in equal proportion in every pupil upon their arrival in class and that needs to be practiced in everyday situations – within and beyond school. Along this line of understanding, she sees multigrade classes as a particularly good opportunity to practice but emphasizes that it would be out of place to set "self-competences" (Erziehungsdirektion des Kantons Bern 2016, p. 15) as a precondition to succeed in this setting. The pupils ought to prove their achievements in the sixth year. Yet it clearly transpires throughout the observations that some pupils' preconditions suit autonomy more than others. They have the possibility to contribute. In the interview, she explains, "If I set up groups, I think about who from 6th grade could take the lead, because she or he is more advanced. Sometimes I put a 5th grader next to her or him, who also knows a lot about the subject. Thus, they can support each other in coaching the younger pupils in the group. This doesn't always work, but I try". Autonomy is, in the teacher's eyes, a line of development. Assumedly, she sees it as a precondition for the pupils' understanding of where and how they can make an impact as a person.

In many ways, this case study presents an exception among what we saw during the field research: much more often, we witnessed relatively rigid subjectivations of individual pupils by teachers, which were hard to overcome over the years that the pupil spent in the classroom with the same teacher. One such case is illustrated in the next part.

"One cannot assume to be able to work with everybody in a similar way..."

The class involved in the second case study is made up of 16 learners from grade 3 to grade 6. The school is located in a very small community, much like the first one. The school consists of two classes, one for cycle 1 and one for cycle 2, resulting in a combination of four grades within each class. This is due to the regulation of the cantonal educational authority, which requires a minimum of children entering cycle 1 to keep a school open. Hence, although multigrade classes have a longer tradition in this community, the multigrade setting in this case is also a consequence of the decreasing population in the area.

The teacher is experienced in teaching multigrade classes. Like her counterpart in case 1, she teaches the class in a team of two, with both teachers being in charge of certain school subjects. The following example is also drawn from the classes in "Nature, Humans, Society". The teacher makes a four-year schedule during which the topics will not be repeated. Hence, each pupil tackles each topic only once.

The lesson which we shall discuss came at the end of a two-week project phase, during which the pupils did research on an animal of their choice. The learners were encouraged to choose an animal that they were not yet well acquainted with. The scale of the assessment of the student production was, like in the first case, differentiated along grade levels: the third and fourth graders were to produce posters, whereas the fifth and sixth graders were to give a PowerPoint presentation in front of the class. The criteria for the assessment process accordingly differ as well. The fifth and sixth graders are to be able to research the internet for information about their animals, identify similarities and differences with other species, and recognize the common structure of the skeleton of animals. The third and fourth graders are expected to demonstrate the ability to recognize relevant information in texts about their animals, summarize, structure it to be presentable on a poster, and complete it with pictures they collected from the internet. Accordingly, the teacher divides the class into two subgroups (third/fourth year and fifth/sixth year). This way she saves time, as she states in the interview: "I'm just less strict with the 5th than with the 6th. It seems to me that if I always prepared everything fourfold, at some point my time is also limited". The difference between third and fourth graders, as well as between fifth and sixth graders is made by the extent to which the teacher provides content support, depending on her individual assessment of each pupil's needs. It is thus a more informal and adaptive line of differentiation.

The (self-directed) task process is supported by a manual that each pupil received initially: it is designed differently for the two groups (third/fourth graders and fifth/sixth graders) and describes step by step what to do and contains the evaluation criteria, so pupils know what they need to pay attention to. Classroom observation shows that the teacher's assistance is mainly focused on formal aspects and technical skills like printing pictures downloaded from the internet.

Beyond the grade levels, this teacher – like many others in our sample – regularly differentiates between "weaker" and "stronger" pupils within each grade. These subjectivations seem almost unavoidable to minimize complexity in multigrade classes, and they correspond to the desire for differentiating beyond the grade level. Yet, they are sensitive from the point of view of equal opportunity, as they offer room for subjective and opaque bias on the part of the teacher.

Another excerpt from the interview with this teacher shows how she applies these categories in the process guide she had handed to the pupils to monitor and "self-direct" their projects:

I: How did the process manual seem to work out in your opinion?
T: So, I certainly helped them in the process. They also kept asking me, "Where am I now [in the process of tasks]?", "What do I need to do

next?" But I do have the feeling that it helped them. Because otherwise I would have had some [pupils] who would have just been cutting things out, and then cutting them again at school... um.... I have simply experienced that afterwards [without a process guideline] they lose focus on the content, especially the weaker ones.

In her description, the "weaker" pupils are likely to lose focus of the underlying – or main – objective of the task at hand. Often, the full characterization of what makes a pupil "weak" or "strong" remains vague, relative, and derived from a comparison with fellow pupils. Generally, however, this ascription includes autonomy as a central component. It is understood as the ability to remain on track and to work along the pre-scripted procedures. In the present case, these aspired methodical skills and autonomy are illustrated by the process manual, which is meant to offer support for those who (self-)identify as "weaker". With regard to her expectations of pupil autonomy, another statement by the teacher suggests her pragmatism:

I: How have your teaching practices changed since you operate in a multigrade setting?
T: Now, I certainly benefit from my experience. Or also from knowing the subjects and the teaching materials [Lehrmittel]. I know certain things, certain processes („...) That helps me. And from having acquired certain things in this way. Or also the pupils. They know how things work with me. They also know exactly where to find things. All of that has now become very structured, and I think that helps a lot, when operating in a multigrade classroom.

This explanation shows how classroom routines, or second-order activities (Reh 2011, p. 48; see chapter 3), are highly valued and afforded considerable preparation by this teacher. This seems necessary to keep up her resources for what she perceives as the core of her teaching efforts, namely, to help pupils systematically prepare for their presentations.

The following case is exceptional in this class in that it presents the individual, and externally – pathologically – legitimated, subjectification of a pupil as one with a learning disability. However, it presents the ambivalence of individualized subjectivations in the form of reduced learning – and autonomy – expectations.

In the last lesson of the project phase, each pupil gives a presentation about the animal he/she has done research on for the past two weeks. The presentation of one pupil in the sixth grade, Rolf, especially stood out. He has a diagnosis justifying reduced learning goals and therefore is receiving a lot of support for autonomous tasks. He finishes his presentation about the ibex with a very interesting anecdote about the ibex's disappearance from the Swiss territory and how smugglers reintroduced them across the border from Italy.

The didactics of autonomy in multigrade classrooms   **85**

R: "That was my presentation. Are there any questions?"
Some hands
are raised: "How were the ibexes stolen from the Italians?"
R: "I'm not sure, but I believe they were caught and transported across the Alps".

The class applauds, Rolf returns to his seat. The teacher casually adds that although she is not an ibex expert either, she doubts that they were stolen, but thinks they were rather probably reintroduced by a consensual contract with the Italians.

After the lesson, we asked the teacher to elaborate on her impression of Rolfs' performance in the lesson that had just ended.

T: I find now, for example, Rolf, [… h]e is really, really tremendously weak. And that's for him, what he showed today, for me, that's amazing. Really. That he was able to stand up like that, he was able to say the sentences fluently– so really, that's a [grade] six for him as a RiLZ* pupil, for me.
I: Also compared to what, or how he presented last time? So really on an individual scale?
T: Yeah. He'd never done a presentation at all. Like that. And that's for me now so, yeah, that's for me the biggest success. She has also just now said that – […] the IF teacher.** She has also helped him a little bit.
* *RiLZ:* Reduced individual learning goals ** Remedial teacher

This excerpt shows how this teacher evaluates a pupil according to an individualized scale, as she reflects on his performance. Her statement furthermore discloses that the teacher neither has any expectation concerning his autonomy in the preparation nor regarding the performance or the content of the presentation.

Despite receiving the highest grade on his own scale, the teacher does not compare him with his undiagnosed and/or uninhibited classmates. This may be regarded as a truly individualized accompaniment of a pupil's progress. Furthermore, the fact that he has received help from a remedial teacher (*Heilpädagogin*), *a priori* dismisses him from competing with the rest of the class who have received only as much support as is standard for their respective grade. Within this individualized setting, the pupil in question has a benchmark on his own due to his classification as a pupil with special needs. His medical diagnosis is transformed into such a staunch pedagogical subjectification that he is unlikely to get rid of it. This classification prevents him from opportunities of showing what he would be capable of achieving and being an expert in something autonomously and therefore to move beyond the teacher's expectations tied to his classification. He will remain a pupil who is unable to learn anything without the teacher's help.

In this example, a teacher categorizes a pupil's autonomy *a priori*. After the task is completed, it is again used as a vital element to the teachers' evaluation of a pupil's scholarly performance. This double usage of autonomy as an essentializing criterion of differentiation and evaluation can lead to a hopeless spiral of marginalization, as this case illustrates.

Rolf has shown a lot of personal interest and effort to do research and present his findings on the ibex. However, the teacher's concluding comment in class negates, or at least puts into question, what Rolf has researched on his own, while at the same time dismissing it as unimportant. By this act, she neglects and denigrates his intellectual autonomy and his capability of being an autonomous learner.

This shows that the teacher prioritizes the methodical skills and class-routine aspects of autonomy over creative engagement with the subject matter. The acquisition and mastery of second-order activities (organizing a working process along required routines, procedures, rituals, and rules) are clearly prioritized over first-order activities, such as the substantial engagement with the learning task itself (Reh, Rabenstein & Idel 2011; see also: Reh 2013, p. 48).

Contrasting the case studies

Autonomy becomes a precondition for being a "good achiever" (Reh & Rabenstein, 2012). Facets of autonomy constitute the general competences formulated in the curricula, and they play a decisive role in the selection of different performance groups at the end of primary school. Our analysis provides insight into two distinct forms and degrees in which the autonomy of pupils is tolerated, promoted, or even assumed as a prerequisite in multigrade class settings, and the kind of subjectivation resulting from a teacher's perspective.

The teacher in case 1 sees her teaching and the multigrade setting as a practice ground to develop autonomy by cooperating and conversing with classmates who are older or more autonomous and in this sense act as role models. She invests considerable time in classroom conversations that include all learners across the three grades. Thereby, the whole class is involved in the production of shared knowledge, and the subject matter remains the central focus of discussion. Since the topics are repeated year after year, pupils have the opportunity to deepen their knowledge of the topic and consciously observe their own improvement over the three years. Her concept of autonomy implies personal commitment to class content, thus, first-order activities (Reh 2013, p. 48). Conversely, teacher 2 prepares a lot of support material, so that pupils can work towards two different target levels on their own. The work process and teacher support vary by grade and additionally by the expected degree of autonomy. As she explains, "weaker" pupils get lost if they are not intensely supported. Since she plans her programme over four years, pupils encounter each topic only once and cannot revisit and observe their own knowledge development regarding this precise matter. This case exposes the scope of resources that is demanded of a teacher in designing, accompanying, and assessing the individual learning process of each pupil. The teacher reacts to this challenge by clearly prioritizing method over content: she is therefore not able to absorb and appreciate the content quality of the product – not only in the case of the pupil with reduced learning goals. Instead, the final product, consisting of the presentation of the completed work, gets recognition solely for its methodical achievements, not leaving much room for the subject matter to be commented upon. There is also no classroom discussion on commonalities or connections between the individual pieces of work, or among different topics worked on together as a class. In this case, autonomy refers to second-order activities.

In the first case, the teacher creates opportunities for pupils to experience and practice autonomy by encountering the topic repeatedly, to become aware of their own progress. They are asked to add new knowledge to their existing ideas and to make them all converge in a playful way, while the teacher shows interest in both the factual and fantastic elements of their creations. The pupils work in teams a great deal and assessments are conducted in a private manner so that the differences between them are not so obvious, except for the grade levels, e.g., the expectation for sixth graders to act as role models. The older pupils are expected to have the upper hand when it comes to knowledge and are therefore required to support the younger pupils by sharing information. In the examined sequence, this peer-to-peer teaching format is closely accompanied and controlled by the teacher so as not to deputize real teaching responsibility. This subjectification as older or younger pupil is temporary since all pupils move through each grade level over the course of the three school years.

The teacher of the second case study instead enacts predefined subjectivations through her teaching and classroom activities. In this case, categories of "weaker" and "stronger" pupil within a grade level and/or a pathological diagnosis are constantly resorted to as scale reference for her interactions with individual pupils. Thereby, autonomy acts among the parameters for their expected performance, it defines the form and extent of teacher support and, consequently, the highest achievable mark. This concept of autonomy weighs heavily on methodical competences as guiding principles. It seems in line with the idea that pupils learn methods to follow individualized goals and interests. As we have observed, however, the individualizing part of the topical content remains in a very restricted and predefined range and is only marginally taken into account in the assessment of competences. It is also quite likely that the teacher in example two understands her efforts as a gradual build-up of pupils' autonomy, in which pupils must first prove themselves as autonomous in the form of adapting to school norms and techniques. Only at a further stage – and only if the teacher has distinctive resources to allow and appreciate it – may they indulge in a kind of autonomy that includes the pursuit of own authentic ideas, goals, and values.

Conclusion: The didactics of autonomy

Autonomy is understood – in parts – as something that needs to be expanded and practiced in school. Yet it also serves as the basic element of differentiation among learners and therefore becomes a prerequisite, especially in multigrade classes. Multigrade classes emphasize the fact that a "narrowly guided class lesson" (Reusser 2019, p. 159) is no longer a teaching option, and pupil autonomy becomes a central condition for successful teaching and learning (Ricken, Casale & Thompson 2016). This requires teachers to be highly flexible, agile, and well-prepared in order to adapt learning tasks and classroom settings to a diverse set of learning subjects (Reusser 2019, p. 159). In response, many teachers differentiate along group and/or individual categories through both formal and informal – subjective – markers of distinction. The case studies make it clear that the practice of differentiation by the teachers is based to a considerable degree on their informal, implicit, and highly variable concepts and expectations of pupil autonomy. In the first example, the teacher implies autonomy as something attainable, and she sees herself as responsible for fostering it in the classroom. She addresses and subjectivizes the pupils as young people who are gaining knowledge and autonomy through common interaction. Meanwhile, the second case shows how expectations of autonomy are mainly based on working methods (research and presentation). Subjectivation occurs through her estimations of individual learning preconditions, in reference to a grade or diagnosis.

To name this implicit differentiation practice, both teachers address groups of pupils as "stronger" or "weaker" or more or less advanced. The use of these categorizations varies in strict implementation and relevance between the two teachers. In both cases, however, they gain importance when transition into secondary school is imminent. The case studies have shown that the prevalent need for clustering pupils together gives teachers' personal criteria considerable weight. The power that lies in a teacher's subjectivation ought therefore not to be underestimated, since these ascriptions are at times hard to shake off during a pupil's educational journey and "render each pupil more public in their singularity" (Reh 2011, p. 47). The conceptions of autonomy resorted to by teachers strongly shape how they support and evaluate individual pupils. From an equal opportunity perspective, therefore, it seems imperative to elaborate on the concept, its sub-concepts, and the specific responsibilities of a teacher in promoting the acquisition of the relevant competences, as well as the limits to this responsibility.

Generally, it can be assumed that it is more difficult to teach autonomy in the classroom if it is seen as a prerequisite and a matter of constant lagging-behind of some pupils. Conversely, when it is understood as an explicit mandate in the curriculum, teachers may be more likely to address it as a learning objective. More pragmatic and clearer distinctions among the autonomy facets in the curriculum could help make autonomy a more feasible school-based endeavour and turn it into a less secretive, subjective matter. This will require, among other things, to explicitly distinguish between first and second-order activities, and to work on how they are to be valued and assessed.

Notes

1 The project called "*Die Konstruktion des Unterrichtsgegenstands im jahrgangsübergreifenden Fachunterricht auf der Mittelstufe*" ("The construction of a learning subject in mixed-grade classrooms") (17 s 0001 01) was funded by the PHBern and carried out from August 1, 2018, until July 31, 2020.
2 Quotations from the literature, fieldnotes, and interviews are translated by the authors.
3 All names are pseudonyms.

References

Adamina, M. (2014). Sachunterricht in der deutschsprachigen Schweiz – aktuelle Entwicklungsarbeiten zu Lehrplan und kompetenzorientieren Lernsituationen. In H.-J. Fischer, H. Giest & Markus Peschel (Eds.), *Lernsituationen und Aufgabenkultur im Sachunterricht* (pp. 25–38). Bad Heilbrunn: Verlag Julius Klinkhardt.

Adamina, M. (2019). Lernen unterstützen – adaptiv-konstruktiv lehren. In P. Labudde & S. Metzger (Eds.), *Fachdidaktik Naturwissenschaft. 1.-9. Schuljahr. 3.,* extended and updated edition (pp. 183–196). Bern: Haupt Verlag.

Adamina, M., & Hild, P. (2019). Mit Lernaufgaben Kompetenzen fördern. In P. Labudde & S. Metzger (Eds.), *Fachdidaktik Naturwissenschaft. 1.-9. Schuljahr. 3.,* extended and updated edition (pp. 119–134). Bern: Haupt Verlag.

Biesta, G. (2013). Interrupting the Politics of Learning. *Power and Education* 5(1), 4–15. https://doi.org/10.2304/power.2013.5.1.4

Breidenstein, G. (2014). Die Individualisierung des Lernens unter den Bedingungen der Institution Schule. In B. Kopp et al. (Eds.), *Individuelle Förderung und Lernen in der Gemeinschaft. Jahrbuch Grundschulforschung 17* (pp. 35–50). Wiesbaden: Springer Fachmedien. https://doi.org/10.1007/978-3-658-04479-4_3

Eckermann, T. (2017). *Kinder und ihre Peers beim kooperativen Lernen. Differenz bearbeiten - Unterschiede herstellen.* Wiesbaden: Springer Fachmedien. https://doi.org/10.1007/978-3-658-15752-4

Erziehungsdirektion des Kantons Bern (2016). *Lehrplan 21. Grundlagen.* Retrieved from https://be.lehrplan.ch/container/BE_Grundlagen.pdf (checked on 2/10/2022).

Fiechter, U., Adamina, M., Ganguillet, S., Misini, T., Reck, B., Schwab, S., Wälti, B., & Weidmann, L. (2021a). *Jahrgangsübergreifendes Lehren und Lernen im 2. Zyklus. Exemplarische Unterrichtsanalysen und fachdidaktische Herausforderungen. Beiträge für die Praxis.* Bern: hep Verlag AG.

Fiechter, U., Ganguillet, S., Misini, T., Schwab, S., & Weidmann, L. (2021b). Einleitung: Jahrgangsübergreifendes Lehren und Lernen im Zyklus 2. In U. Fiechter, S. Ganguillet, T. Misini, S. Schwab, & L. Weidmann (Eds.), *Jahrgangsübergreifendes Lehren und Lernen im 2. Zyklus. Exemplarische Unterrichtsanalysen und fachdidaktische Herausforderungen* (pp. 7–20). Bern: hep Verlag AG.

D-EDK, Deutschschweizer Erziehungsdirektoren-Konferenz (Ed.) (2014). *Lehrplan 21. Kanton Bern*. Retrieved from https://be.lehrplan.ch/index.php (checked on 12/27/2021).

Laging, R. (2010). Altersmischung - eine pädagogische Chance zur Reform der Schule. In Ralf Laging (Ed.), *Altersgemischtes Lernen in der Schule. Grundlagen, Schulmodelle, Unterrichtspraxis* (4th ed., pp. 6–29). Baltmannsweiler: Schneider-Verl. Hohengehren.

Reh, S. (2011). Individualisierung und Öffentlichkeit. Lern-Räume und Subjektivationsprozesse im geöffneten Grundschulunterricht. In S. Amos, W. Meseth & M. Proske (Eds.), *Öffentliche Erziehung revisited. Erziehung, Politik und Gesellschaft im Diskurs* (pp. 33–52). Wiesbaden: VS Verlag für Sozialwissenschaften.

Reh, S. (2013). Die Produktion von (Un-) Selbständigkeit in individualisierten Lernformen. Zur Analyse von schulischen Subjektivierungspraktiken. In A. Gelhard, T. Alkemeyer & N. Ricken (Eds.), *Techniken der Subjektivierung* (pp. 189–200). Paderborn: Fink.

Reh, S., & Rabenstein, K. (2012). Normen der Anerkennbarkeit in pädagogischen Ordnungen. In N. Ricken & N. Balzer (Eds.), *Judith Butler. Pädagogische Lektüren* (pp. 225–246). Wiesbaden: Springer VS.

Reh, S., Rabenstein, K., & Idel, T. S. (2011). Unterricht als pädagogische Ordnung. Eine praxistheoretische Perspektive. In W. Meseth, M. Proske & F. O. Radtke (Eds.), *Unterrichtstheorien in Forschung und Lehre* (pp. 209–222). Bad Heilbrunn: Verlag Julius Klinkhardt.

Reusser, K. (2019). Unterricht als Kulturwerkstatt in bildungswissenschaftlich-psychologischer Sicht. In U. Steffens & R. Messner (Eds.), *Unterrichtsqualität, Konzepte und Bilanzen gelingenden Lehrens und Lernens. Grundlagen der Qualität von Schule 3* (pp. 129–166). Münster: Waxmann Verlag.

Reusser, K., Stebler, R., Mandel, D., & Eckstein, B. (2013). *Erfolgreicher Unterricht in heterogenen Lerngruppen auf der Volksschulstufe des Kantons Zürich*. wissenschaftlicher Bericht. Universität Zürich, Institut für Erziehungswissenschaft.

Ricken, N. (2016). Die Sozialität der Individualisierung. Einleitende Bemerkungen. In N. Ricken, R. Casale, & C. Thompson (Eds.), *Die Sozialität der Individualisierung* (pp. 7–17). Paderborn: Ferdinand Schöningh.

Ricken, N., Casale, R., & Thompson, C. (Eds.) (2016). *Die Sozialität der Individualisierung*. Paderborn: Ferdinand Schöningh.

Veenman, S. (1995). Cognitive and noncognitive effects of multigrade and multi-age classes: A best-evidence synthesis. *Review of Educational Research* 65(4), 319–381. https://doi.org/10.3102/00346543065004319

Weidmann, L., & Adamina, M. (2021). Fach Natur, Mensch, Gesellschaft: Tiere und Stoffe als Beispiele für Lerngegenstände. In U. Fiechter, M. Adamina, S. Ganguillet, T. Misini, B. Reck, S. Schwab, B. Wälti & L. Weidmann (Eds.), *Jahrgangsübergreifendes Lehren und Lernen im 2. Zyklus. Exemplarische Unterrichtsanalysen und fachdidaktische Herausforderungen* (pp. 39–56). Bern: hep Verlag AG.

5
"NOTICE HOW YOU FEEL" AND "TRAIN YOUR BRAIN"

Mindfulness meditation as a technology of the self in education

Jeanne Rey

Introduction

Imagine yourself at the entrance to a magical garden. As you open the door, you see bright flowers of every colour, tall trees gently swaying in the breeze, and a clear endless sky above. It's a special place where you can feel calm and relaxed. Now imagine that this garden lies at the foot of a majestic mountain. Visualize its grandeur, with towering peaks that touch the sky. Feel the solid ground beneath your feet, connecting you to the mountain's strength and stability. Take time to observe the mountain's surroundings. Observe the lush greenery, the waterfalls, and the serene sounds of nature. This is your sanctuary of peace, a place of tranquility and inner calm. As you contemplate the mountain, you feel a sense of awe and inspiration. Now imagine yourself beginning to climb the mountain. Step by step, you rise. Notice the cool breeze against your skin and the caressing warmth of the sun on your face. Each step brings you closer to a greater sense of serenity. As you ascend, notice the breathtaking views before you. Take time to appreciate the beauty that surrounds you – the immensity of the landscape, the luxurious valleys, and the endless sky. When you reach the summit, find a comfortable place to rest and admire the panorama. Close your eyes and let the calm and serenity of the mountain wash over you. Breathe deeply and allow yourself to be overcome by a sense of peace. Imagine a warm, golden light beginning to shine in your chest. This golden light represents gratitude and love. Feel it spreading from your chest, flowing to all parts of your body and filling you with a sense of happiness and love. Now, you are one with the mountain: rooted and resilient...

DOI: 10.4324/9781003379676-7
This chapter has been made available under a CC-BY license.

It is a bright Monday morning in the primary school section of an international school located in an urban region of Switzerland. Eight-year-old children sit or lie on benches, carpets, or on the floor of the colourfully decorated classroom. Most of them have shut their eyes, some move slightly, and the general feeling emanating from the scene is one of a peaceful moment of relaxation. A female voice speaking in slow monotone conjures up images and sensations related to mountain scenery while eventually drawing parallels between the mountain and one's body parts. Mary, the teacher, has the students listen to a YouTube programme offering guided meditations for children.[1] The soundscape is made of nature sounds (water, birdsong) and bells, as well as slow keyboard sounds, creating an atmosphere one is more likely to find in one of the Swiss wellness industry's numerous spas and thermal centres than in a school. During the 10-minute sequence, the children remain almost immobile and seem to be immersed in the scene described. The voice evokes a harmonious garden decorated with colourful plants and animals before inviting the audience to climb a majestic mountain. It insists on sensory feelings, images, and smells, both in the depicted imagined scene and within the children's bodies. It also invites the audience to cultivate positive feelings such as love, joy, and gratitude.

I witnessed the scene in Mary's classroom in May 2018 after ten months of field research in the International School.[2] One element that caught my attention during my fieldwork on the Swiss international school landscape[3] – which I had started three years earlier – is the tendency to quickly embrace pedagogical innovations and to proudly feature them while advertising their school on the private school market. Such innovations also tend to spread quickly, and other schools adopt them as well so that they soon become a standard among international schools. The origin of these innovations may vary. They may either be of technological nature or be promoted by international organizations or research-based policies or stem from the latest educational trends. While some of these innovations are adopted by the whole school (e.g., a new centralized teaching organization using iPads), others might just be implemented by some teachers on a voluntary basis (e.g., the latest method in foreign-language learning). Mindfulness meditation represents one of these pedagogical innovations, practiced by some voluntary teachers with their pupils, yet offered in one form or another in nearly all the international schools I visited in Switzerland.

At the International School, mindfulness is one of many activities offered to teachers and pupils. Mindfulness is promoted as a schoolwide pedagogical concept. It is one of the after-school activities offered to children. Training programmes were also offered to teachers at the school, and a partnership was established with external researchers to assess its benefits. The research found that the training programme led to more mindfulness, more self-compassion, more openness to other people, as well as improved quality in relationships. A silence room was created in the school that provides a space for those who want to meditate. Some teachers can also take part in continuing education programmes abroad. All are offered on a voluntary basis, and some teachers went so far as to practice mindfulness meditation with their pupils on a daily basis. That was Mary's case.

"Showing self-agency" (which translates in French as "*être autonome*") is one of the seven key competences mentioned in one of the school curricula whose general goal is to help children become "successful", "happy", and "productive".[4] According to school concepts, autonomy as a competence is related to the capacity to analyse the demands of one's environment and consequently apply resources for adequate action. In this chapter, I will discuss how far the practice of mindfulness is referred to as a resource aiming at helping children to achieve agency in their learning and social lives. I will discuss how the specific focus put on sensory, emotional, and cognitive processes during and after mindfulness practice may be instrumental in this. I will argue that this practice can be heuristically conceptualized by referring to the concept of "technology of the self" developed by Foucault and discuss the limits thereof. I will further analyse the pedagogical uses of mindfulness practice: in what context and how is mindfulness practiced at school? What are the teacher's pedagogical intentions? To what conceptions of autonomy does it relate to?

In order to address these questions, I will rely on data collected in the context of a research project (EDUtrans) on international schools in Switzerland and in transnational arenas (Rey, Bolay, & Schubiger, 2019; Rey, Bolay, & Gez, 2020, 2021). The ethnographic research was conducted between 2015 and 2018 in 21 international schools located in Switzerland, as well as in other international schools in North America (Toronto and Chicago) and East Africa (Nairobi). It involved either short visits or long-term immersion stays, including at the International School; teachers and expert interviews; and observations at job fairs (for prospective teachers) and school fairs (for prospective parents), where international schools marketed themselves to attract teachers and pupils. The practice of mindfulness meditation became an emergent aspect of the ethnographic research process and caught my attention as one of the pedagogical innovations featured by many international schools, partly because it sharply contrasted with Swiss public schools where mindfulness meditation had had little visibility until then or was deemed controversial. This chapter will focus on observations I made in the International School's primary school section, and in particular in Mary's classroom, as well as on interviews with teachers and instructors (including for mindfulness meditation) and on the analyses of official documents and school communication material. For a broader contextualization of my observations in Mary's classroom, I will also rely on data gathered during the broader ethnographic research project conducted in other schools. Firstly, I will describe a routine sequence of mindfulness meditation in Mary's classroom and how this practice coexists with other "techniques of government" in daily school life. Secondly, I will situate the practice of mindfulness meditation in schools as the result of the historical, institutional, and scientific translation of a Buddhist contemplative practice into a pedagogical practice. I will then address controversies that have emerged with the spread of mindfulness meditation and suggest that these controversies may be better understood when conceptualizing mindfulness meditation as a technology of the self. Thus, I will address the teacher's pedagogical intentions for practicing mindfulness meditation and to what extent autonomy is an issue here, as well as the importance of contextual factors. To conclude, I will argue that the neoliberal critique of mindfulness meditation is relevant yet limited in grasping the variety of contexts and pedagogical intentions at stake.

Discipline and technology of the self at an international school

Building on the work of Foucault (1988, 2015), discipline and the technologies of the self may be approached as two different "modes of government" that rely on different dynamics. Both technologies of the self and discipline produce specific outcomes, yet their main focus and mode of operation are different. Discipline creates order and one of its main focussing points is the body. Discipline has long been associated with institutions such as prisons, factories, the army, hospitals, and schools, where order is central in the arrangement of space, objects, and bodies. By contrast, technologies of the self create subjects, and their main focus is the work that one accomplishes on oneself. Discipline is externally imposed and associated with (positive or negative) sanctions when one does (not) comply. Technologies of the self need to be adopted and their efficacy at least partly relies on their appropriation by the subject. The ethnographic description that follows will set the ground for discussing how both disciplinary practices and technologies of the self may coexist in a school and how far mindfulness meditation may be understood as a technology of the self, as well as the limits of this conceptualization.

As the day starts in the primary section of the International School, pupils aged 6–13 walk towards the schoolyard with their nanny, mom, or dad. One mother wears a sports outfit, another a blazer indicating she is on her way to work. One father wears a suit with a tie, while another is dressed in casual jeans and a T-shirt. In the schoolyard, children line up in a specific location depending on their age group, which is in turn divided into class groups. When they are allowed to enter the main building, one class after the other, children are asked to walk and remain silent. At times, a teacher asks an undisciplined pupil to return to the main door and walk again to the classroom in a more disciplined manner. Once the children reach their classroom corridor, the line starts to dissolve, and the children resume their noisy chats.

Mary's classroom comprises 24 seven- and eight-year-old second graders with heterogeneous backgrounds in terms of previous school experiences, nationalities, and languages spoken at home. Most of the international school parents work in multinational corporations based in the region, among which there are large corporations in the food industry, pharmaceutical companies, banks, and corporations active in the trade of raw materials or the extractive industry. International organizations constitute the second sector of occupation, with the World Health Organization, the United Nations, and the United Nations Refugee Agency, among others, attracting expatriates to the region. Another substantial share of the parents work for non-governmental organizations, missions, and diplomatic corps, as well as foundations. This international microcosm is reflected in the staff and student bodies with up to 140 different nationalities to be found in the largest international schools in the region, and more than 80 different mother tongues spoken at home, among which English prevails.

Loud pop music sometimes welcomes the children as they enter the classroom and continue the task they were previously working on. They might get the help of Laura, the assistant teacher, who directs them, corrects their papers, prepares the learning material, and tidies up the classroom. By contrast with Mary, the main teacher, Laura never addresses the whole class but rather remains alert to the issues that might arise at any moment. "It's not visible, but my radar is always 'on'", she said to me. A child's voice speaks loudly to the whole school out of the loudspeakers: "Today in the library, we are gonna read a story in Croatian". A parent reads a story in the library every morning in a different language. Mary asks her students, "Do you recognize that voice?" It is the voice of the brother of one of the children. After some working time, the children reach Mary's "morning ritual", as she calls it. Mary's morning ritual mostly starts with a sequence in a circle, when she introduces a topic and discusses an issue while referring to the children's choices, individual behaviours, experiences, or tastes. That day, Mary talks about the pumpkin, basil, and coriander that the children planted. Meanwhile, a girl is chatting and not listening. Mary interrupts and asks the girl, "How do you feel when someone doesn't listen to you? I didn't choose the rules of this class. Who did it?" A child replies, "We did". Another child objects that she was not present when they made up the rules. Mary answers, "Even if you were not in this class, it would be fair if you listened to others". Then she addresses the whole class in the circle, "If you have a message, bring it to me, otherwise get ready for dancing". She asks which dance the children would like to choose. Three popular songs are put forward by the children and the class ends up voting for the 'Freeze' dance. A video of the dance from the YouTube platform is then projected onto a large screen, with loud bass. The loud voice says "We are going to sing a song about dancing and freezing. So when I say dance, you are going to dance, and when I say freeze you are going to freeze". Children dance and freeze, and then dance and sing another song.

Then, Mary transitions to the mindfulness part of the morning routine. "You can find yourself a breathing spot while the song is ending", she says. As the children are used to the transition, they immediately lie on the ground, on a carpet, or on a bench. At this moment, an issue develops between two pupils. As she usually does, Mary reacts to interpersonal issues between children by asking them questions and referring to their developing sense of responsibility, "Is it your problem or is it Lizzy's problem?" When the issue is solved, Mary asks what type of breathing the children wish to do now. One day, a child answered, "We all invented our own breathing," to which Mary assented, "Yes this is true, we all invented our own breathing". The children suggest several options, including "Five mountains", "Happy forest", "Tooth fairy breathing". Mary lets the children vote and notes that there is a draw. "A lot of people are not voting though", she says. Meanwhile, several children started to whisper again. "I want you to realize by yourself when you're being distracted". "Train your brain".

Children lie on the ground while a slow even-pitched recorded female voice conjures up images and sensations related to mountain scenery, while eventually drawing parallels between the mountain and one's body parts. During the sequence, Mary sometimes intervenes in order to insist on specific aspects: "If you close your eyes, it will be easier for you to imagine and feel". "If not, chose one spot". She also corrects the position of some children. "Try to feel that you're the mountain and feel as strong as the mountain". "Try to notice when your brain is thinking to something else". "Good job for focusing on yourself". "Check in with yourself. Notice how you feel". Meanwhile, Laura and a special education teacher prepare some material for future learning activities that the children will do alone or in small groups across several workshops. The sequence ends when the recorded voice saying, "Thank yourself for the good work".

From a Buddhist practice to the classroom: A historical translation mediated by science

In order to understand how Mary came to practice mindfulness meditation in her classroom, it is helpful to address the conditions surrounding the growing interest in mindfulness meditation in science, care, business, and education in the West. Supported by a growing field of clinical studies, mindfulness practice – which was until then mostly associated with the counterculture (Kucinskas, 2018) – was introduced into care institutions in the context of stress reduction and mental health programmes in the 1970s. According to Kabat-Zinn (2003, p. 145), mindfulness is related to "particular qualities of attention and awareness that can be cultivated and developed through meditation", which can be defined as "the awareness that emerges through paying attention on purpose, in the present moment, and nonjudgmentally, to the unfolding of experience moment by moment". In order to understand the growing, yet uneven, popularity of mindfulness in schools, I will provide an outline of the complex translation process that prepared the ground for the spreading of mindfulness practices in the care sector and, more recently, in education. This process relies on the translation of a contemplative practice, which in Western epistemology is categorized as "religious"[5], into a scientific discourse through the development of neurosciences. This translation from a repertoire of religious practice into a scientific object of investigation is central in the process of how mindfulness became a secular practice and thereby was able to move into secular institutions such as health care and schools.

Key actors of this translation include Prof. Jon Kabat-Zinn, an American scientist and Buddhist practitioner, who launched and tested the "Mindfulness-Based Stress Reduction Programme". This eight-week programme launched in the 1970s gained some recognition in medical and scientific circles as it was proved to be efficient in preventing specific mental troubles. While commenting on mindfulness-based interventions, Kabat-Zinn (2003) acknowledges the Buddhist origin of mindfulness meditation, yet he argues that mindfulness is not inherently Buddhist, but rather is about attention, which is a universal process. He refers to the approach of the historical Buddha as an inquiry into the nature of the mind, rather than as a founder of a religious tradition. Over the last decades, contemplative practice became objectified as a legitimate scientific object of inquiry in the growing field of neurosciences (Tang, Hölzel & Posner, 2015). The objectification of meditation through neuroscientific imagery helped shift its status from religious to secular. Mindfulness became perceived as an evidence-based practice, which was confirmed both through semi-experimental designs that validated its efficacy in preventing mental troubles and a growing field of neurosciences that created an epistemic status for meditation as a "real" phenomenon. This new status came along with a decontextualization of contemplative practice from its social, philosophical-religious contexts and epistemologies and a recontextualization into new social, philosophical, and religious contexts and epistemologies. Mindfulness became increasingly popular in the business sector, in the wellness industry, in therapy, and more recently in education. There, research also played a role in framing mindfulness as an educational practice. While there was hardly any scientific publication on mindfulness in education around 2000, the field has significantly increased since then (Schonert-Reichl & Roeser, 2016), and over the last years, research programmes on mindfulness in schools have been launched in several prestigious universities. Expected benefits of mindfulness include the enhancement of children's capacity to self-regulate their attention and their emotions (Meiklejohn et al., 2012; Maynard et al., 2017).

Yet, the Buddhist origin of mindfulness meditation complicates its adoption as a secular practice in educational contexts, and mindfulness is also referred to as a practice at the intersection of religion, science, and healing (Ergas, 2014). This tension is increased by the blurred boundaries between research and practice, as many key actors of research on mindfulness also happen to be engaged in contemplative practice. This tends to make its reception in educational contexts where religious issues tend to be sensitive and more difficult, while popular references to mindfulness meditation navigate between various neuro-scientific, spiritual, and medical discursive regimes, as we shall see from the Swiss context of our research. In several Swiss cantons, authorities restricted the practice of mindfulness in public schools. As I conducted this ethnographic research, one Swiss canton banned the "Mindfulness-Based Stress Reduction Programme" as a non-recognized project for public schools due to the lack of scientific evidence and questioned its alleged non-denominational nature. Another Swiss canton also decided to reject a mindfulness programme that was initially slated to be offered in schools on a larger scale. This reluctance may partly be attributed to the ambivalent connotation of a meditation practice framed as secular, yet with explicit Buddhist roots.[6] On the other hand, some teachers in Swiss public schools practice mindfulness with their students. Associations and training sessions for schools and teachers developed, including recently among institutions of teacher education. Books with teacher experiences or guidelines get published in Switzerland and some students in education conduct their thesis on the subject. While caution is observed on the part of educational authorities, mindfulness practice is also gaining popularity among some teachers in Swiss public schools.

From depoliticization to self-entrepreneurs: Mindfulness as a technology of the self

Teachers adopting mindfulness meditation primarily acknowledge its potential benefits. Yet, this practice also raised its share of controversies. The development of mindfulness meditation in a wide array of domains, from therapy to schools and the business world, also led to growing defiance. Critical scholarship highlighted that while mindfulness may enhance resilience, it also tends to enhance political resignation and passivity. In the business world and in education, meditating may help professionals and students alike to cope with the pressure of an ever-growing competition and the expectations of ever-higher productivity. The development of mindfulness in the business sector, notably among the Big Tech companies like Google, is largely based on the belief that improving employees' well-being would eventually enhance the company's productivity. In these circles, mindfulness has been promoted by professional, educational, or economic elites that were unaware of their own privileged position with regard to the effects of mindfulness (Kucinskas, 2018). Regarding causal attributions, failure tends to be perceived as an individual rather than a systemic problem, and thus mindfulness meditation fails to address the cause of collective suffering and systemic changes that need to be addressed (Purser, 2019). Eventually, with some exceptions in the context of social activism, mindfulness meditation deals with how to comply with the context rather than transforming it. Thus, the practice would then lead to a depoliticization of the stance of individuals – although that might be contrary to some of its pioneers' expectations.

As has been shown by Foucault, the "medical gaze" (like other scientific discourses) produces subjects that are inherently situated in relation to the norms produced by medical discourse (Foucault, 1997). Barker (2014) thus argues that mindfulness meditation contributes to an extended medicalization of life. According to her, its practice expands the definition of disease to include emotional ups and downs, as well as the need for therapeutic intervention. Paradoxically, while mindfulness meditation supposedly opposes the rationalization of life, it turns out to be a strong disciplinary practice, as it extends the magnitude of "therapeutic surveillance" (p. 172) to every breath and moment. Building on Barker's argument, Reveley (2016) analyses how this technique may be instrumental in constructing an educational subject that is in line with neoliberal ideology. This process consists in placing a greater part of moral responsibility on the children with regard to their well-being, self-protection, and self-surveillance. Reveley thus argues that mindfulness meditation either may be a beneficial meditative technique or may be turned into a neoliberal self-technology institutionalized as a form of "therapeutic education".

Yet in a certain manner, this discussion is too narrow to capture the contextual variations of the practise of mindfulness meditation in schools. First, the use of mindfulness in a classroom is not limited to therapeutic purposes. It is thus important to take the intentions of the teachers practicing mindfulness at school into consideration, as it is likely that these intentions are of a pedagogical rather than therapeutic nature – an idea I shall develop in the next section. Second, the supposedly innovative character of mindfulness meditation must be put into perspective as one among many techniques of government in schools. These techniques have developed along a continuum framing norms as either external or internal to the subjects. On one end, disciplinary practices aim at creating order by situating norms as external to the subject, targeting primarily bodies and behaviours. Examples include the "classical" forms of punishment or the more recent trend of "positive discipline". On the other end of the continuum, technologies of the self situate the locus of agency as internal to the subject and derive effectiveness by framing the way subjects get to relate to themselves (and their environment), possibly aiming to develop self-awareness, self-reflection, self-regulation or any form of self-development. Examples include moral education (see as an illustration of Foucault's discussion of Loyola's exercises) or the practice of mindfulness meditation. Mindfulness meditation is not exceptional in that sense and shows continuities with other techniques of government that have long been developed in schools.

From the ethnographic vignette presented earlier, we can analyse how both disciplinary practices and technologies of the self are set in the daily routine of the children at International School. Discipline manifests itself in the lining up of the students in the schoolyard, and the walking in silence in the hall creates a specific order that both pragmatically allows for managing the flux of the pupils' circulation in the common school space and asserts that there are rules to be followed. This practice targets the pupils' bodies via specific practices (standing in line, silence) and sanction follows transgression of the rule (by starting the whole process again). Discipline is a collective concern for teachers in the school (for instance, with regard to the behaviour of their charges in the shared space outside the classrooms), and it is also an issue for many teachers with their pupils, notably with regard to classroom management. One example is the popularity of continuing education on positive discipline in international schools, which aims at developing disciplinary practices that favour positive sanctions and encouragements over negative sanctions and punishment (Bolay & Rey, 2019). By contrast, Mary makes little use of disciplinary practices involving rules and (positive or negative) sanctions. Her interventions mostly rely on maieutics, asking children to reflect on their attitudes and behaviour, and appealing to a collectively defined agreement rather than an externally imposed rule. Of particular interest is Mary's stance towards the children during and after the practice of mindfulness. She constantly refers to their own judgements or how they should raise their awareness about their feelings, their conduct, and their reflections on the best thing for them to do in specific situations. By repeatedly calling upon their sense of responsibility, she invites and enables them to perceive themselves as autonomous in their choice and behaviour, as self-governing learning subjects. She also grounds her expectations in their awareness of their own cognitive behaviour ("Train your brain"), state of mind and cognitive processes ("I want you to notice by yourself when you're being distracted".), and sensory feelings ("Check in with yourself. Notice how you feel").

Pedagogical intentions and the concept of autonomy in an uncertain world

Foucault argued that techniques of government also rely on self-government, which implies the work that a subject operates on themselves. What the practice of mindfulness also reveals in the case we studied is how this *dispositif* aims at raising the children's awareness of their sensations, emotions, and thoughts in order to become autonomous and self-confident learners. Mary reported to me that she developed mindfulness in her class as a response to the pedagogical difficulties she experienced due to the complex and heterogeneous profiles of the children. Among 24 pupils, 13 had special needs of some kind, mostly related to a specific language, or cognitive or psychological needs. She told me that since she implemented her morning routine including mindfulness meditation, the atmosphere of the class had changed: she experiences more serenity among the children and insists that they have never complained about going to school again. She attends a yearly training programme in the USA on learning and neurosciences which inspired her implementation of mindfulness meditation, and she said that it radically changed the way she teaches, as mindfulness meditation has now become fundamental to her work. While she thinks that her class may sometimes look chaotic to external visitors – partly because she uses few disciplinary techniques, she perceives it as a normal dimension of learning processes and activities in her classroom.

Taking a step back and turning to sociological theories, mindfulness practice may also offer a space of "functional deceleration" in a context of general social acceleration, following Rosa's thesis (2013), which is also characteristic of the international school environment. While the international corporate, financial, or diplomatic microcosm to which the pupils' families belong are engaged in professional contexts where technological acceleration prevails, children also experience the accelerating pace of their educational lives (Bolay & Rey, 2019). International schools train students to become autonomous and cope with the expectations of flexibility and mobility that characterize the multinational corporation model. In this context, the temporal dimensions of teaching practices and technologies in international schools are in line with the temporality associated with the social position of pupils: they are fast and shift rapidly. With the help of the teaching assistant, the children engage in activities that follow each other at a rather quick pace, transitions are smooth, both aiming at avoiding boredom while maximizing the children's enjoyment of the activities and rationalizing their capacity to concentrate through targeted physical or intellectual practices. Every moment of the children's day is filled and planned, from school to breaks to after-school activities organized by the school, and there is rarely a moment of "lost time" in the busy schedule of the ten-hour day most children spend at any international school. Meditation, like other body-mind practices, may well offer this moment of functional deceleration in a context of general acceleration of the pace of life in this international microcosm.

Mary, like many teachers in her school, mentions the challenges of children's lives in this specific milieu: rather privileged on the economic level yet going through multiple transitions and mobilities due to their parents' career paths, spending long hours at school, even more time with their nanny, or confronted by parental anxieties. She refers to mindfulness with at least three different pedagogical intentions. First, it offers an answer to her classroom management issues, providing clues on how to cope with a highly heterogeneous classroom and with the diverse learning and educational needs of the students. Second, it sustains the capacity of the children for socio-affective regulation and well-being, and fosters their autonomy as social actors and members of the classroom community. In the third place, it aims at developing cognitive self-regulation among learners by becoming aware of their cognitive processes (by observing their own thoughts and attention capacities), as well as reflecting on their own cognitive strategies. Overall, Mary intends to help the children regulate their emotions, be aware of the necessary conditions for learning, and reflect on their behaviour as learners, in other words, to foster autonomy in a complex and uncertain world.

Conclusion

McNay (2009, p. 63) pointed out that under neoliberalism, "individual autonomy is not an obstacle or limit to social control but one of its central technologies". Discourses on mindfulness promote indeed the concept of a responsible, autonomous individual dedicated to self-improvement (Arthington, 2016). Yet injunctions to autonomy in educational contexts are inherently paradoxical and rely on the "wilful" internalization of educational expectations by pupils (Durler, 2015). The analysis of the techniques and *dispositifs* which mediate this process is therefore of central importance in order to understand how autonomy is enacted daily in school practices. We have discussed how, in the mind of the promoters of mindfulness meditation in educational settings, this practice is expected to develop specific qualities and sustain learning processes, like socio-emotional competences and socio-emotional learning. By observing this mindfulness meditation contextualized in Mary's classroom, we could also point to pedagogical intentions related to the development of metacognition and reflexivity: mindfulness is about developing awareness in order for the children to become reflective in their own behaviour as social actors and learners. Thus, it positions the children as endowed with agency in their learning process. This reflective way to frame autonomy echoes the specific microcosm to which the school belongs, namely an "educational cosmopolitan enclave" where the children of diplomats and CEOs mingle with local elites before moving on to other cosmopolitan enclaves across the globe (Bolay & Rey, 2021; Rey, Bolay, & Gez, 2021). There, flexibility and adaptability are central attitudes for coping with mobility and changing economic or work environments, and these attitudes are also cultivated in international schools. In response to this context, school actors also express the need to create a sense of belonging among the so-called "third culture kids". Body-mind techniques like mindfulness meditation are also instrumental in this, as they ritualize the daily routine and represent a space of shared experience and practice, a moment of functional deceleration beyond performance and competition.

By conceptualizing mindfulness meditation as a technology of the self, we highlighted the processes by which this practice implies the government of the individual subjects – namely, by framing the relation that subjects develop to their thoughts, sensations, emotions, and more largely to themselves and their environment. Yet the exclusive framing of mindfulness meditation as a neoliberal technology may also be limitative as it underplays the importance of the context, the differentiated and socially stratified dimensions of how such *dispositifs* unfold in a given context, and the pedagogical intentions of the teachers.

Notes

1 For copyright reasons, the author could not include quotations from this program in the introductory paragraph but instead created a simulation of a YouTube mindfulness programme for children inspired by a Chat GPT text on the same topic.

2   For anonymity reasons, the name of the school, teachers, and children are fictive, and minor contextual information are changed.
3   This chapter is based on data collected in the context of the research project EDUtrans on the "Transnationalisation of Swiss Private Education", which was funded by the Swiss National Science Foundation (project number 161231).
4   The other competences are to become lifelong learners; knowing how to interact with others, with the world, and with diverse tools and resources; transdisciplinarity; and multiliterate thinking.
5   For a critique or problematization on the category of religion, its Western epistemology, and normative assumptions, see Asad (1993) or Gez, Droz, Rey, and Soares (2021).
6   It should be noted that while mindfulness meditation can be practiced without any reference to Buddhist symbols and rituals, as the description of Mary's classroom practice shows, some teachers choose instead to include symbols from Buddhist or other oriental spiritualities, which does raise questions about the alleged strictly secular status of mindfulness mediation.

References

Arthington, P. (2016). Mindfulness: A critical perspective. *Community Psychology in Global Perspective, 2*(1), 87–104. https://doi.org/10.1285/i24212113v2i1p87

Asad, T. (1993). The construction of religion as an anthropological category. *Genealogies of Religion: Discipline and Reasons of Power in Christianity and Islam, 2*, 27–54.

Barker, K. (2014). Mindfulness meditation: Do-it-yourself medicalization of every moment. *Social Science & Medicine, 106*, 168–176. https://doi.org/10.1016/j.socscimed.2014.01.024

Bolay, M., & Rey, J. (2019). Les temporalités de l'éducation internationale: Pratiques et technologies de l'accélération sociale. *Anthropologica, 61*(1), 137–149. https://folia.unifr.ch/global/documents/312670

Bolay, M., & Rey, J. (2021). Frontiers of cosmopolitism: Educational enclaves and the extractive roots of international schools. *Critique of Anthropology, 41*(4), 421–437. https://doi.org/10.1177%2F0308275X211059655

Durler, H. (2015). *L'autonomie obligatoire. Sociologie du gouvernement de soi à l'école.* Rennes: Presses universitaires de Rennes.

Ergas, O. (2014). Mindfulness in education at the intersection of science, religion, and healing. *Critical Studies in Education, 55*(1), 58–72. doi:10.1080/17508487.2014.858643

Foucault, M. (1988). Technologies of the self. In L. H. Martin, H. Gutman, & P. H. Hutton (Eds.), *Technologies of the self. A seminar with Michel Foucault* (pp. 16–49) London: Tavistock Publications.

Foucault, M. (1997/1963). *Naissance de la clinique* (5th éd.). Paris: Presses Universitaires de France.

Foucault, M. (2015/1975). *Surveiller et punir. Naissances de la prison.* In M. Foucault (Ed.), *Oeuvres II* (pp. 261–613). Paris: Gallimard.

Gez, Y. N., Droz, Y., Rey, J., & Soares, E. (2021). *Butinage: The art of religious mobility.* Toronto: University of Toronto Press.

Kabat-Zinn, J. (2003). Mindfulness-based interventions in context: Past, present, and future. *Clinical Psychology: Science and Practice, 10*(2), 144–156. doi:10.1093/clipsy.bpg016

Kucinskas, J. (2018). *The mindful elite: Mobilizing from the inside out*. New York: Oxford University Press.

Maynard, B., Solis, M., Miller, V., & Brendel, K. (2017). Mindfulness-based interventions for improving cognition, academic achievement, behavior, and socioemotional functioning of primary and secondary school students. *Campbell Systematic Reviews*, *13*(1), 1–144. https://doi.org/10.4073/CSR.2017.5

McNay, L. (2009). Self as enterprise: Dilemmas of control and resistance in Foucault's The birth of biopolitics. *Theory, Culture & Society*, *26*(6), 55–77. https://doi.org/10.1177/0263276409347697

Meiklejohn, J., Phillips, C., Freedman, M. L., Griffin, M. L., Biegel, G., Roach, A., & Saltzman, A. (2012). Integrating mindfulness training into K-12 education: Fostering the resilience of teachers and students. *Mindfulness*, *3*(4), 291–307. https://doi.org/10.1007/s12671-012-0094-5

Purser, R. (2019). *McMindfulness: How mindfulness became the new capitalist spirituality*. London: Repeater.

Reveley, J. (2016). Neoliberal meditations: How mindfulness training medicalizes education and responsibilizes young people. *Policy Futures in Education*, *14*(4), 497–511. https://doi.org/10.1177/1478210316637972

Rey, J., Bolay, M., & Gez, Y. N. (2020). Precarious privilege: Personal debt, lifestyle aspirations and mobility among international school teachers. *Globalisation, Societies and Education*, *18*(4), 361–373. https://doi.org/10.1080/14767724.2020.1732193

Rey, J., Bolay, M., & Gez, Y. (Eds.) (2021). Cosmopolitan enclaves: Spatial and cultural (under)privilege in education, expatriation and globalization. *Critique of Anthropology*, *41*(4), 158.

Rey, J., Bolay, M., & Schubiger, E. (2019). Généalogie de l'élève cosmopolite et marchandisation de l'international dans des établissements privés en Suisse, In A. Sieber Egger, G. Unterweger, M. Jäger, M. Kuhn, & J. Hangartner (Eds.), *Kindheit(en) in formalen, nonformalen und informellen Bildungskontexten. Ethnografische Beiträge aus der Schweiz* (pp. 259–278). Wiesbaden: Springer.

Rosa, H. (2013). *Social acceleration. A new theory of modernity*. New York: Columbia University Press.

Schonert-Reichl, K., & Roeser, R. (Eds.) (2016). *Handbook of mindfulness in education. Integrating theory and research into practice*. New York: Springer.

Tang, Y., Hölzel, B., & Posner, M. (2015). The neuroscience of mindfulness meditation. *Nature Reviews Neuroscience*, *16*(4), 213–225. https://doi.org/10.1038/nrn3916

SECTION II
Teachers' guidance of pupil autonomy in secondary schools

6

(UN)SUPERVISED AUTONOMY

Getting pupils to "take responsibility" for their learning

Héloïse Durler and Crispin Girinshuti

Introduction

The category of autonomy has become increasingly important in the field of education in recent decades. Today, pupils are commonly expected to be active, to take responsibility for their learning activity through individualized school work formats (Durler, 2015; Lahire, 2005; Périer, 2014). An argument often put forward is that promoting autonomy would make it possible both to address the heterogeneity of pupils and to optimize individual learning, to help pupils with the greatest difficulties while supporting the "potential" and motivation of each one, in line with the new expectations of "inclusive education" (Cerna et al., 2021).

However, the forms of autonomy generated within these educational settings are opaque and their relation to school inequality rather ambiguous. While individualized arrangements are presented as a solution to adapt teaching to the specific needs of the individual learner, it is unclear whether and how these can contribute to enhancing equity and equal opportunities or, on the contrary, rather reinforce school inequalities. In particular, it remains to be seen what practices are put in place in the daily life of the classrooms to promote pupils' autonomy: How do teachers manage to get pupils to work autonomously? What obstacles do they encounter? What are the pupils' practices?

The present contribution relies on a research project that furthers previous work on classroom practices aimed at fostering pupil autonomy in primary schools (Durler, 2015) and in private Montessori schools (Leroy et al., 2021). We will analyse the observations made during a didactical project carried out with two classes at the end of compulsory secondary education in mathematics in a large rural school. Our field is part of a larger ethnographic research project on self-directed learning in lower secondary schools in Switzerland.[1] Here, we discuss insights from our study site located in Romandie (see Chapter 7 for an analysis of the "German-speaking" field site).

By bringing together classes from two different levels, the pedagogical project aims to improve the autonomy of pupils by changing the usual organization of teaching. These ambitions raise a series of questions: What practices have teachers put in place to foster pupil autonomy? How do pupils work in this context? In particular, how differently do the teachers support performing pupils and how do low-performing pupils deal with the demands of autonomy? Through the presentation of our observation data, we will show that what is central to the approach adopted by the teachers is the desire to make the pupils responsible for their own work. In order to break away from an authoritarian relationship of vertical transmission of knowledge and imposition of discipline, a certain amount of freedom is granted to them, at different levels (spatial, temporal, in work methods, etc.). This led us to examine in the first part the extent to which didactic prescriptions promoting approaches that develop pupil autonomy are linked to the issue of school inequalities. In the second part, we present the practices of the teachers observed in our field research, in order to understand how and to what end pupil autonomy is promoted. In the third part, we tackle the constraints that hamper the initial ambitions of teachers. We conclude the chapter with a reflection on the risk of increasing inequalities linked to this desire to introduce practices aimed at pupil autonomy.

Autonomy-oriented learning arrangements as *dispositifs*

Autonomy in the school context is the subject of numerous studies in the educational sciences and didactics, which question the means to be used to promote pupil autonomy, often with a prescriptive aim. From this perspective, it may concern for example the question of learning materials that promote autonomy, in particular the impact of the use of new technologies (Amadieu & Tricot, 2014), didactic choices, and the organization of pupils' work (Liquète & Maury, 2007) or the effects of collaboration among pupils (Connac, 2016). The reasons why this prescription is so important lie at the crossroads of various influences. On the one hand, pupil autonomy is closely linked to a vision of the individual that emphasizes freedom of choice, self-government, and even personal fulfilment, a legacy of certain principles advocated by the *new education movement (le mouvement d'"éducation nouvelle")*. It is also part of a context of reduced public spending, a search for greater efficiency and lower-cost "solutions", and a transformation of what is expected from pupils that is more or less linked to the world of employment (Leroy, 2022). On the didactic level, the promotion of autonomy often goes hand in hand with the promotion of socio-constructivist approaches based on a critique of transmissive teaching (Garcia, 2013), which views teachers as the authority and pupils as passive receivers. Instead, these approaches emphasize project-based teaching and the active child. They now constitute the ordinary practices of public schools, whether in primary school or in secondary school (Barrère, 2013) or in the choice of learning materials (textbooks, children's literature, for example) (Bonnéry, 2015). According to this socio-constructivist perspective, each pupil should necessarily discover by themselves, thanks to the mediation of the group and the teacher, the steps leading to the elaboration of knowledge that is not transmitted by the teacher. These pedagogies are supposed to give "meaning to learning" (Kerroubi & Rochex, 2004) and have often been favoured with regard to low-performing pupils. At the same time, the individualization of the treatment of pupils' difficulties is on the increase, with the demand to differentiate, to set up personalized programmes, etc., contributing to the spread of the idea that pupils have a personal responsibility (Garcia, 2021) in relation to their academic performance.

From a sociological perspective, there have been warnings that this autonomy-oriented pedagogy increases educational inequalities (Anyon, 1997/1980; Bernstein, 2007/1975; Bonnéry, 2011; Dannepond, 1979; Demailly, 1990; Isambert-Jamati et Grospiron, 2007/1984; Joigneaux, 2009; Lahire, 2005; Perrenoud, 1984; Plaisance, 1986). The criticism is that the transfer of autonomy to the pupils in particular is not appropriate for pupils with learning difficulties. Authors argue that these pedagogical developments would tend to raise the overall level of requirements, without transmitting to the pupils the prerequisites enabling them to acquire school knowledge in the situations that arise. In this regard, Basil Bernstein (2007) makes a useful distinction between "visible" and "invisible" pedagogies: "visible pedagogy" corresponds to the traditional conception of teaching, in which the learning content is defined in advance, broken down, and sequenced, and the assessments are explicit. In the "invisible" model, on the other hand, the tasks are global, the sequencing is loose, and the pupil is barely aware of the aims of the tasks. Insofar as autonomy pedagogies tend to approach the invisible model, they contain the risk of increasing the difficulties of pupils from working-class backgrounds due to the emergence of socio-cognitive misunderstandings (Bautier & Rayou, 2009) for pupils who are less familiar with school expectations.

In order to understand the issues, particularly in terms of educational inequalities, linked to pedagogies that promote pupil autonomy, we adopt a perspective that is attentive to the processes of socialization (Darmon, 2006; Lahire, 1998, 2005), of the "social fabrication of individuals" (Lahire, 2013), and we endeavour to describe the "social frameworks" in which autonomy is constructed and exercised (Geay, 2011). In particular, this perspective makes it possible to reflect on the subjects that are produced within a context that emphasizes increased leeway granted to pupils (freedom of choice, empowerment, the right to express one's opinion, etc.).

To understand the – sometimes contradictory – relationships between pedagogical intentions and the conditions making it possible for pupils to appropriate these aims and to mobilize or construct the resources necessary for their appropriation, we use the French theoretical concept of *"dispositif"* (Bonnéry, 2009, 2011; Durler, 2015; Foucault, 1975; Lahire, 2005). Talking about *"dispositif"* allows one to understand how the principles favoured in the use of techniques, objects, and practices aimed at making pupils gain knowledge, outline the features of the ideal pupil and define the qualities that they must demonstrate, the relationship to knowledge that they must adopt, and the power relations in which they must be involved (Lahire, 2005).

Investigating autonomy in lower secondary school

To understand how pupil autonomy can be concretely put forward in pedagogical practices, we focus on an autonomy-based project to teach mathematics to two 11th-grade classes, with pupils aged around 15. The teaching project gathered pupils with different levels in mathematics from these two classes for joint lessons in the same room over a three-month period. Our observations started a few months before the implementation of the "pedagogical experiment". First, we made observations of the different classes, talked with the two teachers involved, Fabrice and Muriel,[2] and participated in a field trip where the two classes were brought together and mixed so that the teachers, as they told us, could better observe the behaviour of the pupils, understand the affinities between them and prepare the constitution of the groups for the next teaching sequence. Second, we closely followed the project, observing the activities in the classroom during a total of 38 hours. Usually, we both stayed in the classroom, shadowing (McDonald, 2005) the work of the two teachers and focusing on the interactions of a few pupils. In addition to these classroom observations, we also held informal discussions with teachers and pupils before and after the observed periods and shared more festive moments (outings, Christmas activities, meals with teachers in restaurants). We also administered a questionnaire and held focus groups with pupils in each class.

In this secondary school, pupils are separated into two groups by level ("standard" and "strong") in mathematics, French, German, English, and natural sciences, and they are therefore in separate classes for these subjects. Prior to the project, Fabrice was in charge of a "standard" math class of 18 pupils (11 girls and 7 boys), while Muriel was responsible for a "strong" level class of 16 pupils with an equal gender distribution. For the duration of the project, the two classes were held in a room larger than the usual classrooms, the school's conference room, and the teachers were both present during the teaching periods.

The educational project lasted from November 2019 to January 2020. The *dispositif* is characterized by three working methods, each lasting approximately four weeks. These phases of the pedagogical experiment were defined beforehand by the two teachers, who thus wished to set up distinct arrangements involving increasing autonomy of the pupils in their work. The first method (in November) consisted in having the pupils work in workshops and in working groups. The teachers formed fixed groups of five to six pupils, usually mixing the two performance levels. They were given instructions on how to work through a chapter of geometry using several sequences of theory and exercises to be completed together. Each group had to choose a sequence to start with (in no predetermined order) but had to complete all of them within four weeks. The second method (in December) was based on a "work plan", which pupils had to follow. They had to hand in the results of their work individually and regularly to the teachers in order to get feedback on their progress. At the same time, the teachers kept a record of the progress of the pupils' work, reproduced in a table projected on a screen that was constantly visible to all pupils and on a computer accessible to pupils. It is designed as a double-entry table, where each row corresponds to a pupil and each column to an exercise. In each cell, a number indicates how many corrections and feedbacks the teacher has sent to the pupil, with a system of colours for the cell to indicate whether the exercise has been completed correctly (green), whether there are minor corrections to be made (orange) or more important ones (red).

The last method (in January) used is the "flipped classroom": many resources are made available to pupils (mainly video instruction but also manuals, mobile phone applications, etc.) who must work according to "objectives" predefined by the teacher. Pupils are therefore given a list of objectives. They are then free to choose how to achieve them: they are free to choose the exercises to be carried out and the materials to be used, the manner of working (alone or in groups), and the time and location for working (in class or at home).

Each of the sequences corresponds to a subject in the 11th-grade mathematics programme: geometry, equations, functions. For each of them, the teachers were available to answer the pupils' questions, but did not give a "frontal lesson". The teachers offered "workshops" on request and after registration of the pupils to "lift the blocks" the pupils may have experienced at certain points. These three methods explicitly aimed at promoting the autonomy of the pupils, as explained here by the teachers:

> Convinced that each pupil should be able to progress at his or her own pace, the pupils will have the opportunity to discover working methods that empower and develop the autonomy of each one.
> *(Extract from the letter sent to the parents in August 2019)*[3]

More specifically, one main objective was made clear by the teachers: to make pupils responsible for their learning, giving them the freedom to take ownership of the learning content and letting them decide by themselves when to take the tests. We will now look at how these initial intentions translate into the daily practice of teachers and pupils.

The way of making pupils responsible for their learning

Giving pupils choices

Based on strong criticism of the negative effects of the traditional school system, the two teachers intended to enhance pupils' choices and room for manoeuvre in learning. At the beginning, in early November, teachers told pupils that they were free to use the space as they saw fit. They could sit in the corridors, in the conference room, work in the position of their choice, etc.

> A group asks to set up their table in the corridor. Muriel answers, "There is no problem". The pupils take a table and chairs and set up outside the classroom.
> *(November 8, 2019 – field notes HD)*

Choice even becomes imperative, as Fabrice says, "You don't have much choice, you're going to have to choose. You're going to have to get interested" (September 17, 2019 – field notes HD). In the teacher's words, a distinction is made between "mobilization", which would be compulsory, and "motivation": "We don't ask you to be motivated, it's not compulsory. But you have to mobilize yourself and maybe motivation will follow" (September 17, 2019 – field notes HD). The attitude required towards work is therefore that of voluntary "mobilization", which should lead to satisfaction for the pupils, potentially a source of motivation for learning. "Mobilization" here is therefore similar to "effort", but is never designated as such. It is primarily words that refer to freedom that are used (such as "choice", "will") as an impetus towards responsibility: "You are responsible for doing as you wish" (September 17, 2019 – field notes HD).

> Fabrice: "(…) you are totally free, you come here, you can start work straight away. (…) We will help you if you need it, we are here at your disposal, and everything is allowed. Really, everything is allowed, as long as you work, that's it. Don't ask us if you may go to the toilet, don't ask us if you may stand up".
> *(November 25, 2019 – field notes CG)*

This freedom given to pupils extends to the work itself. The pupils have to "manage" it themselves, according to the objectives given to them, as Fabrice announces, "It is you who will choose what you are going to do. We're not going to tell you anymore" (January 6, 2020 – field notes HD). In this perspective, pupils have the possibility to decide when to take the assessment test:

> Fabrice: "You decide when you take the written test over a three-week period. Do you agree? You can choose that. Great! Well, good job. Have fun".
> *(November 12, 2019 – field notes HD)*

The teacher's last remark ("Have fun") refers to an important aspect of the pedagogical approach: the pupils have to enjoy their work.

> Fabrice: "I hope you will have fun taking control of your learning and working as you like. In general, you often have a teacher who imposes a lot of things upon you and that doesn't necessarily suit you. So, my goodness, it may be destabilizing, but I seriously hope that you will have pleasure in doing a bit of that".
> *(January 6, 2020 – field notes HD)*

During our visits, indeed, a relaxed atmosphere prevailed, in which pupils chatted, joked, shared food, stood up, moved around. As the following exchange finally shows, the teachers intended to establish a general climate of trust, and the pupils had to feel that they had the teachers' trust on their side:

> While the pupils continue their test, Fabrice and Muriel talk. Muriel says that the problem with sitting so close is that they can cheat. Fabrice tells her that it's okay, "if they do it in a smart way". "It's important to show that we trust them, it's part of the process". Muriel says to me, laughing: "Fabrice is cool, isn't he?"
> *(December 6, 2019 – field notes HD)*

Trusting pupils and leaving the choice to them can be understood as techniques of "concernement" (Lahire, 2005) aiming at the fact that the pupils can no longer say that the tasks do not interest them since they have chosen them themselves. Having "willingly" chosen their activity, the pupils are strongly encouraged to pursue it to the end. The "pedagogical trap" (ibid., p. 330) then closes on them: they cannot fail to complete what they have "chosen" to do; they are deemed "responsible" for their choice, and they must therefore take responsibility for it.

In the teachers' vision, the goal of autonomous learning for pupils goes hand in hand with the conception that the teacher must take a back seat. In an email sent to us in April 2019, the teachers presented their project as follows:

> We wish to experiment with three sequences between the end of October and the end of January 2020 with the main objective of developing "autonomous learning" for our pupils. (…) In this process, the objective

is that the pupils acquire the ability to construct their own knowledge, with the teacher no longer considered as the holder of knowledge but the resource person who provides the framework and tools enabling the pupils to find their best potential.

(Email of April 5, 2019, sent by Fabrice)

Teachers are no longer the "holders of knowledge", but they become "resource persons". This appears through the idea that it is not the teacher who asks for a task to be done, but the pupils who have to respond to instructions, written by a "designer" who could be someone other than the teacher. Fabrice said, "To work well, you'll have to respect the instructions. If you are told to work alone, it's because the person who conceptualized the thing thinks it's right" (September 17, 2019 – field notes HD). Teachers regularly remind pupils that they have to manage their time and make time trade-offs in relation to learning objectives that they have to identify:

Fabrice: "The important thing is the acquisition of objectives (…) But don't count on us to give you homework. It's your responsibility, OK? But that doesn't mean there is no homework"

(November 5, 2019 – field notes HD)

Teachers emphasize the idea to their pupils that they have to fend for themselves, arguing that they will not be assisted by a teacher forever: "You won't always have a teacher around" (November 5, 2019 – field notes HD). The withdrawal of teachers can be perceived physically, with pupils being completely left alone at times (in the corridors or in the hall), causing one pupil to jokingly say, "Isn't there a teacher here?" (December 10, 2019 – field notes CG).

While freedom of choice is emphasized as a means of empowering pupils, it is inextricably linked to helping them work without teachers, as Fabrice explains it to us, "Giving them autonomy is one thing, but it's also about them having a range of possibilities to get into the work without us" (November 8, 2019 – field notes HD). In this spirit, pupils are regularly asked to seek support from each other, to help one another, as Muriel also tells them, "We ask you to learn to collaborate" (November 8, 2019 – field notes HD). The withdrawal of the teacher is thus accompanied by a clear encouragement to collaboration:

Fabrice: "To work, you really do as you like. You have Mrs Muriel and myself as a resource, but get used to being resources among yourselves".

(November 25, 2019 – field notes CG)

Pupils are encouraged to seek out teachers "wisely", i.e., not to be "assisted", but to get help in planning work. Pupils should therefore understand that they should not remain alone when they stall but should take the initiative to ask for support from others. Asking for support from others is understood as a way of making progress in their independent work. In fact, this "withdrawal" can be seen in interactions in which the teachers place the responsibility for the choice of the working method on the pupil:

> Chloé (Strong level[4]) asks Fabrice about the exercises: "Does that mean we have to do them all?" He replies by telling her what he would do, but that it is a method that suits him, not necessarily her. "If I were you, I would proceed in order until I feel confident. You can do anything, make it your own".
> *(January 7, 2020 –field notes HD)*

By positioning themselves as a "resource person", the teachers' objective is also to provide individualized support, offering more to those with greater needs. Fabrice points out that "you can say what you like about this type of teaching, but what is certain is that the teacher has time to devote to those who need it most" (November 4, 2019 – field notes CG). Later, pupils are reminded of this by Fabrice: "you have two teachers available who have nothing else to do but to help you. So really, we don't have anything else to do but to take an interest in you" (January 6, 2020 – field notes HD).

Confronting pupils

Our observations show that the *dispositif* requires a significant investment on the part of the teachers: through practices of close observation of their pupils, a significant amount of time spent preparing and correcting the pupils' work but also various forms of verbal interaction aimed at encouraging and motivating them. Indeed, autonomy conceived as shifting the responsibility for learning onto the pupil does not only have a didactical aim. Fabrice, in particular, states that he wants to participate in the transformation of the individual:

> That's typical, it's very confronting for the pupil, but in my opinion, in terms of learning, it is a game-changer. It doesn't change the fact that they have to learn maths, but it changes their attitude.
> *(December 3, 2019 – field notes HD)*

The expression "confrontation", understood as a moment that can be unpleasant, "destabilizing" for the pupil, but with a potential for transformation, is regularly used by Fabrice during our exchanges, but also during the interactions he has with the pupils. Sometimes, this "confrontation" is expressed in a terse tone, clearly indicating that the pupils are in charge, that they are no longer going to be "cocooned": "It's up to you to take notes that are necessary to know where you stand. That's your business, you're the ones who are going to have to be responsible for it" (September 17, 2019 – field notes

HD). The pupil's accountability can also be achieved through forms of "provocation" by the teacher:

Fabrice: "But you, what did you want to do? Ask yourself the right questions. You still haven't understood that. Don't forget that you're in a group. You have *to rely on it*".

Maeva (Standard level): "Nobody relies on the group. But we're not doing the same exercises".

Fabrice: "OK, carry on like that, ignoring what I've told you, it's your problem" (November 5, 2019 –field notes HD)

To "confront" pupils means to make them "aware" that they "are in charge". This is not only done through speeches but also through the use of teaching materials. For example, the tables summarizing the status of the pupils' work plan constitute a confrontation technique: the progress of the pupil's work, made public, is intended to raise awareness. Thus, the aim is to encourage pupils to seek help and not have learning constraints imposed upon them. In other words, making pupils autonomous does not mean abandoning them to their difficulties, it means encouraging them to take the initiative in the process of acquiring knowledge. It should be noted that this project was not intended to be implemented to the detriment of the most difficult pupils; on the contrary, the teachers regularly reaffirmed their concern to see these pupils make progress and showed a marked interest in them throughout the project, whether through close observation of these pupils or, more generally, through the adoption of close physical postures, the teacher being most of the time kneeling next to the pupil. However, if the teachers aim at individualizing teaching to the benefit of those most in difficulty, our observations indicate that the teachers devoted more time to the pupils who ask for it and that the "strong" pupils are those who make the most demands on the teachers (November 2019 – field notes CG). As a matter of fact, pupils tend to spend long periods of time raising their hands to call the teachers and complained about wasting time:

> Charles (Standard level) tells Loïc (Strong level): "You've been calling the teacher for five years. You don't know why you call her anymore".
> *(November 12, 2019 – field notes HD)*

Thus, while the didactical arrangement implemented aims to make pupils responsible for their learning, the teachers' stated ambition is, more generally, to have an influence on the pupils themselves, on their attitude, and their state of mind. If the pupil's freedom seems to be central, it is accompanied by techniques designed to ensure that the pupil is mobilized in the expected direction. The teacher's action consists either of "confronting" the pupils by close observation of the pupils' work, mobilizing speeches, or the use of teaching aids, making individual progress visible to all. In addition, the teachers mention the need to regulate the pupils when they are having difficulties in their learning or in their attitudes towards work. As Fabrice himself summarizes it, "There is the autonomy that they don't have and we have to help them. There are some who are confrontational there are some who need to be regulated, because they are totally deviating" (December 3, 2019 – field notes HD).

Thwarted autonomy

Despite all the efforts of the teachers to make pupils responsible, the latter adopted practices that deviated from the teachers' expectations. In response, the teachers started to resort to forms of constraint that were not included in the design of the project. Thus, although their aim was to grant free choice to the pupils, during the course of the project, we observed a rather immediate recourse to external constraints, particularly in response to what they consider to be "disturbing" behaviour:

> I move to the back of the room. In the meantime, the ambient noise has increased. In the classroom, there is laughter, someone knocks over a chair. (…) Fabrice speaks up, "Today, (…) I also see people who let themselves be taken in by the game in the wrong way. That means that there are some who really get caught up in … there are games, there are possibilities, there are openings, I can do what I want to some extent, but I'm not mature enough to assume that, and I do something else, and I start playing or doing something else. What bothers me the most is that it's detrimental to those who have become very mature in their work and that you don't provide an atmosphere that is conducive to becoming really better. That bothers me a lot".
>
> *(November 22, 2019 – field notes, CG)*

Indeed, we observed the teachers wavering between freedom or tolerance for even "inappropriate" use of the provided freedom on the one hand and forms of constraint or pressure to counter what might appear to be school deviance on the other hand, particularly when pupils do not hand in their work on time.

> Fabrice and Muriel decide to split up a group of boys, because they are making too much noise. Fabrice: "we have to give them a little less freedom. They are not mature enough for that kind of freedom".
>
> *(January 14, 2020 – field notes HD)*

This shift from freedom to constraint manifested itself in the use of space. In the beginning, teachers told pupils that they were free to use the space as they saw fit. They could sit in the corridors, in the conference room, work in the position of their choice, etc. But the constraint became tighter as the weeks went by, so much so that for the second half of the project, pupils were no longer allowed to leave the classroom.

The hardening of constraints was also obvious concerning temporal freedoms. The aim of letting pupils work at their own pace was revised by the teachers as the project progressed, as they felt compelled to follow the curriculum. Due to this time pressure, the teachers demanded from those pupils who had not finished their work on time to come to school at 7.30 am, before the start of classes. During these 45 minutes of restraint, the pupils had to complete the work requested in silence. Furthermore, even if there was officially no homework, teachers implicitly expected pupils to work at home to fulfil the time schedule. The system itself is designed in such a way that the pupils have all the materials (boards, video clips) online at their disposal to work at home.

On the part of the pupils, there were forms of resistance to the accountability process that was put in place. This resistance can manifest itself in the daily life of the pupils by an absence of work or lack of discipline. This resistance can also be expressed openly, as shown by the exchange between the teacher, Fabrice, and the pupils when he informs them of the teaching methods that will be used between November and January:

Fabrice: "How do you imagine this. Will it go well? I'm waiting to hear your opinion on how you're dealing with all this". (Silence from the audience for a few seconds)

Charles (Standard level): "I prefer when the work is given to me because it's hard to concentrate with my mates around".

Nell (Standard level): "I think it's more efficient to give us a list of exercises. Now we'll have to read the content of all the workshops, it'll take time". (…)

Eva (Standard level): "I'm already not very motivated by maths, I prefer having things imposed on me. I don't know, I feel a bit bad about it".

Fabrice: "I'm very sensitive to that. I'll be there to help you. However, you are to choose what's good for you. I'm not abandoning you, I'm not leaving".

Imany (Standard level): "I prefer it when someone imposes things on us. It requires much more responsibility than before".

Fabrice: "It's destabilizing". (…)

At 1:45 pm the bell rings, and the pupils go out into the corridor. We talk to Fabrice. He says he is happy that the pupils have expressed themselves, even if it is not positive (September 17, 2019 – field notes HD).

It is interesting to note that the freedom given to the pupils extends to being able to express that they do not like the working method. However, these discussions leave the observer with a paradoxical impression: it seems that if pupils are allowed to express themselves, they may also internalize the idea that expressing one's opinion does not serve much purpose since the working method is imposed upon them.

In sum, our observations of teachers' and pupils' practices show contradictions inherent to the implementation of a "compulsory autonomy" (Durler, 2015) in the school context. On the one hand, the teachers, even though they do not wish to position themselves in an authoritarian manner vis-à-vis the pupils, are forced to adopt constraining practices to make the pupils work, which runs counter to the project of empowering the pupils in which they should take the initiative in their work. The pupils, on the other hand, do not easily accept the accountability they are subjected to. Through resistance practices, they force teachers to place constraints on them and tell them what to do. In other words, they demand the possibility to not be autonomous, motivated, and responsible for their work. In this way, the pupils' empowerment project is thwarted insofar as the pupils adopt practices that deviated from the teachers' expectations, forcing them to resort to forms of constraint that were not included in the project.

Recourse to parents: An "imperative"

It is noteworthy that the observed pedagogical *dispositif* seems to include recourse to parents in the case of difficulties, as one of the teachers clearly expressed it in an email he sent us:

> This type of confronting method for the pupils allows us to create this kind of situation and precisely to allow certain pupils to progress and to become more independent and mature when working, but I admit that without the help of the parents the challenge often remains daunting.
> *(Extract from an email sent to us by Fabrice, January 12, 2020)*

Parents are perceived as a necessary resource, as Fabrice tells us: "in fact there is a lot [to do] outside the classroom" (January 14, 2020 – field notes HD) but also as a potential source of conflict, if they do not adhere to the project, if they question the practices or if they refuse to collaborate with the teachers. In this logic, there are therefore two types of parents who pose a problem: parents who are seen as "critical" (who challenge and monitor the teachers) and parents who are seen as "uninvested" (who insist that teachers should assume total responsibility for schoolwork, who feel that they should not do the work for them). In the following extract, Fabrice anticipates a possible refusal of the parents to support him, thus leaving him with a "problem", the impossibility of relying upon them.

> Fabrice: [...] And soon, I'm sure I'll get calls from parents, or I'll call the parents, and two or three of them will say, "deal with it", you know? We'll have this problem.
> *(December 3, 2019 –field notes HD)*

The pedagogical project aimed at encouraging the autonomy of pupils is thus accompanied by work with parents in order to get them to adhere to it and initiate coordination, as Muriel explains to us here:

> I communicate a lot with Sean's parents [Strong level] [...] as I felt he was not ready at all for the test, I wrote to the parents (conversation in appendix). They phoned me twice this week to coordinate on a common discussion with Sean who seems to have seriously started to work on his test preparation and shows us a clean and complete work. So, his parents seem to have finally sided with us and by working together with them, we are starting to see positive results.
> *(Extract from an email sent to us by Muriel, January 10, 2020)*

In all cases, a great deal of work was done to convince parents of the merits of the approach and encourage them to continue the work done in class at home, whether through individual discussions or at teacher-parent meetings. This trend is reflected in the orientation of parents' practices by teachers in order to make them "pedagogical auxiliaries" (Thin, 2009). Parents should therefore follow up on their children's homework and take up the discussion on motivation to work from the same perspective as teachers. Teachers thus express a conception according to which the school cannot be its own recourse in the event of pupils' difficulties. This assumed outsourcing of part of the pedagogical work produces inequalities among families who are differently equipped to enter into this collaboration (Delay, 2013; Périer, 2019) and take on this work but also has repercussions on the work of teachers since it implies a more or less informal form of education of parents by teachers (Conus & Nunez Moscoso, 2015; Deshayes et al., 2019; Durler, 2015; Scalambrin & Ogay, 2014; Van Zanten, 2012).

Conclusion

Through the presentation of empirical material from field observations, we have seen how teachers concretely go about leading pupils into autonomous work. We have highlighted the initial attentions, the socialization goals expressed, the preferred didactic paths: freedom of choice, mixing pupils with unequal levels of performance, ensuring the withdrawal of teachers and encouraging collaboration between pupils, the emphasis on individual responsibility and mobilization through forms of "confrontation". In particular, we found that far beyond learning mathematics, the *dispositif* aims to change individual learning behaviour by making pupils responsible for their work. In fact, the *dispositif* does not work as expected: not all pupils accept the compulsory autonomy; some enjoy the freedoms without mobilizing themselves, and the low-performing pupils in particular demand more authoritarian teacher guidance. The teachers also eventually thwart the proclaimed pupil autonomy in order to achieve the given learning goals after all.

We argue that if these contradictions appear, it is because this empowerment requires pupils to possess resources, linked to forms of relationships to time, to school work, etc., that are not directly constructed in the classroom. The path of "confrontation" favoured by the teachers we observed clearly shows that the autonomy expected of pupils relates to an injunction: in the event of a problem, the aim is for the pupil to "remobilize" (mobilize resources that are conceived as personal), rather than to reflect on the construction, in class, of these resources.

At the same time, there is an almost systematic appeal to parents in case of difficulties. These observations are in line with the tendency documented elsewhere (Durler, 2015, 2019) to shift more of the responsibility for educational work onto the pupil and his parents. Generally speaking, the propensity to shift part of the work to the "client" (consumer, user, beneficiary, patient, etc.) is a cross-cutting development in the organization of work (Dujarier, 2008; Tiffon, 2013), largely discussed in the commercial world and which has yet received little comment in the world of education (Losego & Durler, 2019).

In summary, seen as the result of individual mobilization, through forms of "confrontation" aimed at bringing pupils to "take responsibility" for their learning, this conception overlooks the resources (cognitive, behavioural, etc.) needed for autonomous learning during classes. One can assume that it could increase the risks of educational inequality since parents are endowed with more or fewer resources, cultural capital, educational knowledge, etc., to support their children and leads teachers to reluctantly adopt coercive practices when pupils do not possess them.

Notes

1 Project *Führung zur Selbstführung. Eine ethnographische Studie zu schulischen Settings des selbständigen Lernens* (2017–2022) (SNF-100019_173035/1), supported by the SNF and the Universities of Teacher Education Bern and Vaud. The project relies on participant observations and ethnographic interviews in five schools with different classroom organization in the French- and German-speaking parts of Switzerland.

2 Aliases
3 Oral and written quotations in French have been translated by the authors.
4 Strong level in mathematics.

References

Amadieu, F., & Tricot, A. (2014). *Apprendre avec le numérique. Mythes et réalités.* Paris: Retz.

Anyon, J. (1997/1980). L'origine sociale des élèves et le programme caché des activités scolaires. In J.-C. Forquin (Ed.), *Les sociologues de l'éducation américains et britanniques* (pp. 225–253) Paris/Bruxelles: De Boeck. (Translation of: Anyon, J. (1980). Social class and the hidden curriculum of work. *Journal of Education, 162*(1), 67–92.)

Barrère, A. (2013). La montée des dispositifs: Un nouvel âge de l'organisation scolaire. *Carrefours de l'éducation, 36*(2), 95–116. https://doi.org/10.3917/cdle.036.0095

Bautier, E., & Rayou, P. (2009). *Les inégalités d'apprentissage. Programmes, pratiques et malentendus scolaires.* Paris: Presses Universitaires de France.

Bernstein, B. (2007). Classe et pédagogies: Visibles et invisibles. In J. Deauvieau & J.-P. Terrail (Eds.), *Les sociologues, l'école et la transmission des savoirs* (pp. 85–112). Paris: La Dispute.

Bonnéry, S. (2009). Scénarisation des dispositifs pédagogiques et inégalités d'apprentissage, *Revue française de pédagogie, 167,* 13–23. https://doi.org/10.4000/rfp.1246

Bonnéry, S. (2011). Sociologie des dispositifs pédagogiques: Structuration matérielle et technique, conceptions sociales de l'élève et apprentissages inégaux. In J.-Y. Rochex & J. Crinon (Eds.), *La construction des inégalités scolaires. Au cœur des pratiques et des dispositifs d'enseignement* (pp. 133–146). Rennes: Presses Universitaires de Rennes.

Bonnéry, S. (Ed.). (2015). *Supports pédagogiques et inégalités scolaires. Études sociologiques.* Paris: La Dispute.

Cerna, L. et al. (2021). Promoting inclusive education for diverse societies: A conceptual framework. *OECD Education Working Papers, 260.* Paris: OECD Publishing. https://doi.org/10.1787/94ab68c6-en

Connac, S. (2016). Autonomie, responsabilité et coopération: Ce qu'en disent les élèves utilisant un plan de travail, *Éducation et socialisation* [Online], *41.* https://doi.org/10.4000/edso.1725

Conus, X., & Nunez Moscoso, J. (2015). Quand la culture scolaire tend à structurer la négociation des rôles d'enseignant et de parent d'élève. *La Recherche en Éducation, 14,* 8–22.

Dannepond, G. (1979). Pratique pédagogique et classes sociales. Etude comparée de 3 écoles maternelles. *Actes de la recherche en sciences sociales, 30,* 31–45. https://doi.org/10.3406/arss.1979.2657

Darmon, M. (2006). *La socialisation.* Paris: Colin.

Delay, C. (2013). L'impératif scolaire du partenariat et son appropriation partielle au sein de familles populaires: Un exemple genevois. *Éducation et sociétés, 32,* 139–153. https://doi.org/10.3917/es.032.0139

Demailly, L. (1990). *Le collège. Crises, mythes et métiers.* Lille: Presses Universitaires de Lille.

Deshayes, F., Payet, J.-P., Pelhate, J., & Rufin, D. (2019). "C'est déjà les parents qu'il faudrait éduquer!" Intentions, opportunités et tactiques d'une pratique enseignante inconfortable. *Sociétés et jeunesses en difficulté, 22.* http://journals.openedition.org/sejed/9569 (accessed: 02.09.2022).

Dujarier, M.-A. (2008) *Le travail du consommateur, de Mac Do à E-bay, comment nous coproduisons ce que nous achetons*. Paris: La découverte.
Durler, H. (2015) *L'autonomie obligatoire. Sociologie du gouvernement de soi à l'école*. Rennes: PUR.
Durler, H. (2019). Orienter les pratiques parentales. Une externalisation du travail enseignant. In H. Durler & P. Losego (Eds.), *Travailler dans une école. Sociologie du travail dans les établissements scolaires en Suisse romande* (pp. 123–145). Neuchâtel: Alphil.
Foucault, M. (1975). *Surveiller et punir*. Paris: Gallimard.
Garcia, S. (2013). *A l'école des dyslexiques. Naturaliser ou combattre l'échec scolaire?* Paris: La découverte.
Garcia, S. (2021). Différenciations adaptatives, palliatives et différenciations égalisatrices: L'exemple de l'apprentissage de la lecture. *Education et socialisation 59*. https://doi.org/10.4000/edso.13911
Geay, B. (2011). L'impératif d'autonomie… et ses conditions sociales de production. In M. Jouan & S. Laugier (Eds.), *Comment penser l'autonomie? Entre compétence et dépendances* (pp. 151–168). Paris: Presses Universitaires de France.
Isambert-Jamati, V., & Grospiron, M.-F. (2007/1984). L'exemple du "travail autonome" au deuxième cycle long, études de linguistique appliquée. In J. Deauvieau & J.-P. Terrail (Eds.), *Les sociologues, l'école et la transmission des savoirs* (pp. 189–225). Paris: La Dispute.
Joigneaux, C. (2009). La construction de l'inégalité scolaire dès l'école maternelle. *Revue française de pédagogie, 169*, 17–28. https://doi.org/10.4000/rfp.1301
Kerroubi, M., & Rochex, J-Y. (2004). La recherche en éducation et les ZEP en France. 2. Apprentissage et exercice professionnel en ZEP: résultats, analyses, interprétations. *Revue française de pédagogie, 146*, 115–190. https://doi.org/10.3406/rfp.2004.3101
Lahire, B. (1998). *L'homme pluriel. Les ressorts de l'action*. Paris: Armand Colin.
Lahire, B. (2005). Fabriquer un type d'homme "autonome": Analyse des dispositifs scolaires. In *L'esprit sociologique* (pp. 322–347). Paris: La découverte.
Lahire, B. (2013). *Dans les plis singulier du social: Individus, institutions, socialisation*, Paris: La découverte.
Leroy, G. (2022). *Sociologie des pédagogies alternatives*. Paris: La Découverte (coll. Repères).
Leroy, G., Dubois, E., et Durler, H. (2021). Quelle liberté de l'enfant dans les classes Montessori? Sociologie de la socialisation montessorienne en école privée. Dans F. Darbellay, Z. Moody et M. Louviot (Eds.), *L'école autrement? Les pédagogies alternatives en débat* (pp. 229–247). Neuchâtel, Suisse: Alphil. http://hdl.handle.net/20.500.12162/5116
Liquète, V., & Maury, Y. (2007). *Le travail autonome. Comment aider les élèves à l'acquisition de l'autonomie*. Paris: Armand Colin.
Losego, P., & Durler, H. (2019). Introduction. Pour une sociologie du travail pédagogique. In H. Durler & P. Losego (Eds.), *Travailler dans une école. Sociologie du travail dans les établissements scolaires en Suisse romande* (pp. 7–33). Neuchâtel: Alphil.
McDonald, S. (2005). Studying actions in context: A qualitative shadowing method for organizational research. *Qualitative Research, 5*(4), 455–473.
Périer, P. (Ed.) (2014). L'autonomie de l'élève: Émancipation ou normalisation? *Recherches en éducation, 20*. https://doi.org/10.4000/ree.7675
Périer, P. (2019) *Des parents invisibles. L'école face à la précarité familiale*. Paris: Presses Universitaires de France.
Perrenoud, P. (1984). *La fabrication de l'excellence scolaire*. Genève: Droz.

Plaisance, E. (1986). *L'enfant, la maternelle, la société*. Paris: Presses Universitaires de France.
Scalambrin, L., & Ogay, T. (2014) "Votre enfant dans ma classe". Quel partenariat parents-enseignante à l'issue du premier entretien? *Éducation et sociétés*, *34*(2), 23–38. https://doi.org/10.3917/es.034.0023
Thin, D. (2009). Un travail parental sous tension: Les pratiques des familles populaires à l'épreuve des logiques scolaires. *Informations sociales*, *154*, 70–76. https://doi.org/10.3917/inso.154.0070
Tiffon, G. (2013). *La mise au travail des clients*. Paris: Economica.
Van Zanten, A. (2012). *L'école de la périphérie. Scolarité et ségrégation en banlieue*. Paris: Presses Universitaires de France.

7
DOING REFLEXIVITY IN A SELF-DIRECTED LEARNING SETTING

Regula Fankhauser, Judith Hangartner and Ditjola Naço

Self-reflection has gained central importance in the educational reform discourse in many countries. The recently introduced curriculum for compulsory education in the German-speaking Swiss cantons, for example, prominently emphasizes self-reflection as a competence. Being capable of "self-reflection" and "reflection on one's own learning process" are identified and operationalized by the curricula as basic interdisciplinary competences. In accordance with the policy trend, reform-oriented schools that prioritize new curricular objectives, such as individualized teaching and autonomous learning, highlight the importance of self-reflection on their home pages, school programmes, and mission statements. Autonomy-oriented school settings promise to successfully support self-reflection with specific tools such as learning logs or individual coaching sessions. Finally, self-reflection appears as a comprising strategy in teacher education and training. The guiding pedagogical framework of our own University of Teacher Education defines self-reflection as an instrument that should enable pupils and lecturers to "reflect on and successfully practice their daily work" (PHBern, 2012).

Given the popularity of the topic, it is surprising that self-reflection is far less prominent in educational research. Didactical and practice-oriented approaches identify self-reflection as indispensable for the optimization of the learning process and operationalize it for teaching practice (Gläser-Zikuda & Hascher, 2007; Helmke, 2003, 2009; Hilbe & Herzog, 2011). Furthermore, psychological approaches conceptualize self-reflection as a facet of metacognition in models of self-regulated learning. Beyond these strands of scholarly concern, self-reflection is conspicuously absent in educational research in general and in empirical classroom research in particular. Overall, the questions about how self-reflection takes place in pedagogical settings and to what extent these practices can be understood as self-reflection at all, therefore, remain largely unanswered. We think that this discrepancy between the omnipresence of the programmatic discourse and the scarcity of empirical research hints at the "taken-for-granted nature of reflection" (Fejes & Dahlstedt, 2013, p. 24).

To problematize the ostensible self-evidence of reflection as an instrument for improving learning outcomes, it seems necessary to cast the critical gaze in two directions. On the one hand, it calls for zooming out and for asking how the increased popularity of the concept is located in a broader socio-political context. On the other hand, it requires zooming into the concrete pedagogical practices of reflection and examining these efforts with regard to their programmatic framework as well as their inherent difficulties. The current chapter falls into four parts. First, we reconstruct the socio-political framework within which self-reflection is to be situated and we conceptually analyse the theoretical construct. Second, we recapitulate the rather scarce empirical research that focuses on reflective practices in classroom settings. Third, we will present our own empirical material, and, finally, we will draw a conclusion attempting to shed light on some of the fundamental problems associated with reflection within the educational context.

Self-reflection as a central imperative in reflexive modernity

The prominence that reflection has gained within the educational discourse since the end of the 20th century is related to the socio-political development in the second or late modernity, known as "reflexive modernity" (Beck, Giddens, & Lash, 1994; Beck & Holzer, 2004). This development is characterized by a growing degree of complexity, opacity, and a decrease in reliable means of orientation. In this increasingly contingent and unstable environment, the individual is challenged to make decisions in a situation of uncertainty, without a reliable basis for decision-making at their disposal. Thus, the "ultimate responsibility of decision-making" (Beck, 2007, p. 347) is placed upon the shoulders of the individual. Within reflexive modernity, the individual is required to make rational decisions through reflective practices such as questioning and examining, planning, assessing, and calculating (Wiesenthal, 2009). In this context, the critical self-reflection of one's own preferences and wishes is a central aspect of autonomy (Dworkin, 2015). The demanded reflexivity serves as a compass for the always momentary decision-making processes under conditions of uncertainty.

Transferred to the social sciences, the central aspects from the philosophical understanding of reflexivity – the thinking of thinking, recognition of recognition (Forster, 2014) – are maintained, while the frame of reference is expanded. While the classical philosophical concept is concerned with the subject and limited to it, a social science perspective may widen reflexivity to a whole social system, a historical epoch, or a specific scientific practice (cf. exemplarily for a "reflexive educational theory", Rieger-Ladich, Friebertshäuser, & Wigger, 2009). Thereby, a clear-cut, systematic distinction between reflection and reflexivity can hardly be made (ibid.). While in the case of a subject it may be helpful to distinguish between reflection as a practice and reflexivity as an attitude, this distinction is barely possible in the case of social (sub-)systems. Leaving this distinction, it can be concluded that the "reflexive turn" refers to a new mode that affects the individual level, social systems, or scientific practices, which uses reflexive distance to critically assess the premises and consequences of decision-making under increased uncertainty.

The discourse on "lifelong learning" seamlessly follows the theory of reflexive modernity. In the context of contingent conditions of decision-making, the outcome of learning processes is fundamentally open. Learning then becomes a form of permanent and never-ending reorientation and adaptation to economic and social changes. Thereby, the focus is no longer on the accumulation of knowledge and qualifications but on a reflexive understanding of learning. Reflexivity instead of reflex is the motto of the demanded adaptation to transformation and uncertainty (Edwards, Ranson, & Strain, 2010). The theory of lifelong learning initially was developed in adult education, especially in professionalization theories. Schön's (1983) early concept of the "reflective practitioner" served as an inspiration and marks a discourse that has prevailingly concentrated on teacher professionalization since the end of the 20th century (Altrichter, 2000; Chak, 2006; van Manen, 1995). The concept of the "reflective practitioner" also works within this discourse on teacher professionalization as a response to crises and difficulties that are identified as belonging to "reflexive modernity": confronted with new and unpredictable problems, trained routines fail and need to be adapted and readjusted. Here, reflection is supposed to function as a kind of transmitter that translates the observations of previous actions into an improvement strategy. While "reflection-in-action" takes place implicitly and during the action itself, "reflection-on-action" steps out of this flow. The latter mode distances itself during the act of explicating and tries to become aware of the action's inherent logic.

Reflective practice has been understood as the ideal of professional teaching practice and a "central guiding principle in teacher education" for several decades (Neuweg, 2010, p. 44). It is assumed that gaining awareness of one's own action-guiding beliefs, norms, and emotions inevitably leads to improved practice (critically Fejes & Dahlstedt, 2013). Thus, reflexivity and autonomy have become "magic words" in teacher education and training (Wrana, 2006). They are implemented within autonomy-oriented learning settings in the form of portfolios, learning journals, feedback loops, and coaching sessions. This didactic of reflexivity has also managed to reach classrooms at the school level – at least in German-speaking countries. An autonomy-oriented practice controlled by reflexivity is considered superior to rehearsed routines. This dichotomous view creates an opposition between the rational, self-governing subject on the one hand and conventions, traditions, and ritualization on the other. Successful "uncertainty management" (Wiesenthal, 2009, p. 38) is connected to a reflexive actor, who increasingly reflects not only on his own actions but also on her own self for the purpose of optimization. And while one analytically may distinguish between an epistemological form of reflection that focuses on one's actions and an ontological one that centres on the self (Rolfe & Gardner, 2006), the systematic distinction is often difficult to make in practice: the optimization of action and of the self overlap; thus, the demand of optimization reaches the self.

Actor-centred theoretical approaches assume that the autonomous reflexive actor is able to examine their own practice from the outside, in order to reflect on and intentionally change it. Thereby, the distinction between reflection and practice is not only a categorical but also an essentialist one. Sociological theories of practice, on the other hand, understand reflection itself as a practice. "Doing reflection", the performance of reflecting, is a cultural practice, which, like other practices, draws on culturally shaped patterns and codes and produces specific subject positions (Reckwitz, 2009). Rather than programmatically propagating reflection as a strategy for coping with crises and optimizing one's own practices, a practice-theoretical perspective focuses on the doings of reflection itself. It is then a matter of analysing the cultural conditions in which reflexivity is embedded and of scrutinizing the social effects it generates.

Ethnographic perspectives on pupil self-reflection

A few authors in the field of German-speaking educational ethnography address the phenomenon of "doing reflection" in individualized, autonomy-oriented classrooms. Rabenstein and Reh (2007) analyse various forms of pupils' learning process documentation and related teacher-pupil conversations. The authors conclude that the pupils' documents are primarily a monitoring tool in the hands of teachers, while pupils perform as self-reflecting and improving learners during the conversations with their teachers. Menzel and Rademacher (2012) scrutinize the structural logic of questionnaires used for pupil self-assessment in a Montessori school. They show that the questionnaire is formulated in such a way that it requires pupils to relate themselves to their social environment in a self-problematizing way. This demand, the authors conclude, does not foster self-assessment competences but obliges pupils to position themselves in relation to the school demands (ibid., p. 91). Under the disguise of autonomy and reflexivity, the identification with and the internalization of the school norms is pursued. Therewith, the instrument subjugates the pupils while obfuscating its governmental technology of power at the same time.

Finally, Martens (2018) focuses on teaching sequences in which pupils are encouraged to openly reflect on their own learning behaviour in front of the class. He also concludes that the point of reference for these reflective practices is not the pupil's own self and preferences but the teacher's expectations (ibid., p. 100). Ultimately, it is a matter of fulfilling the school norms and integrating them into the system of performance evaluation. In sum, the studies show how self-reflection is reduced to self-evaluation as part of a school-based assessment process, which ultimately fosters the reproduction of school norms and expectations.

These briefly summarized ethnographic studies suggest that reflective practices are uniformly enacted in the classroom. Moreover, the constricted gaze on the observed micro-practices prevents them from including the structural dimensions of the field in their analysis. In contrast, our discussion pays attention to the possible varieties of these practices and considers the structuring effects of the field.

Practices of self-reflection in a self-directed learning setting in Switzerland

The following analysis is based on an ethnographic research project on autonomy-oriented classroom settings at the lower secondary level.[1] The project encompasses five case studies in the French and German-speaking parts of Switzerland.[2] The project analyses from a practice-theoretical perspective the sociality of classrooms that distinguish themselves by a focus on pupils' self-directed learning. With a practice-theoretical perspective (Reckwitz, 2002) and following Foucault's (2000) notion of governmentality, the project is particularly interested in the practices of guidance and self-guidance that the *dispositif* of autonomous learning produces in the classroom, and beyond, in the school as an organization. Fieldwork included participant observation in a variety of classroom settings, as well as in coaching interactions, team meetings, and school conferences. These observations of teachers' and pupils' practices were, when possible, supported by audio recordings and supplemented by ethnographic interviews with teachers, pupils, and headteachers.

The following discussion is concerned with pupil self-reflection, which was in all five case studies an important issue. The analysis monitors the extraordinary efforts made to stimulate pupil self-reflection in one of the case studies. The research in this school comprised 90 visits or a total of 200 hours spent in classrooms and team meetings between October 2017 and February 2020.[3]

The school is located in an urban neighbourhood where residential and industrial zones merge together. It accommodates around 600 pupils from age 12 to 15 from diverse socio-cultural backgrounds. The school was built only a few years ago: therefore, the construction of a new school building was developed in line with the new pedagogical concept. Instead of conventional classrooms, larger pedagogical units with heterogeneous student composition form the backbone of the school. These units materialize the transformation of the classic disciplinary classroom towards an autonomy-oriented setting with individualized support of pupils. The centrepiece of the pedagogical unit is the learning studio, complemented by two smaller rooms: one for subject class instruction and one for group work. Architecturally similar to an open office, the learning studio offers working space for 60 pupils and several teachers. The learning studio is where the pupils spend about one third of their time, sitting at their personalized tables and working individually on their given tasks (Hangartner, Fankhauser, Budde, Forkby, & Alstam, 2022). The rest of the time, the 60 pupils of the unit are organized into sub-groups for class teaching. These groups vary depending on the subject and usually transcend either grades or performance levels. As a result, pupils meet in a wide variety of learning constellations during a school week. The pedagogical unit is supervised by a small team of five to seven teachers. They are responsible for subject teaching, as well as for individual coaching during the three years that the pupils spend in the learning studio. The pedagogical units thus create small, social habitats within the school at large.

Accompanying self-directed learning in the learning studio, self-reflection is an explicit cornerstone of the school's pedagogical concept. The importance of self-reflection as part of the autonomy *dispositif* is made obvious by the devices created for this purpose: at least once per quarter year, each pupil meets with her or his coach for a session in which the pupil's learning progress and behaviour are evaluated and goals for the following weeks are defined (Hangartner, Kaspar, & Fankhauser, 2019). One lesson per week is reserved for heterogenous learning groups in which the pupils are supposed to reflect on their learning. According to the school's pedagogical vision, the exchanges taking place in these groups should assist the pupils towards improving their social and self-competencies. In addition to these interactive opportunities for self-reflection, teachers use written tools to guide the pupils' reflection: a learning journal is to be used for planning and reflection. Furthermore, various standardized forms for reflection and the self-assessment of learning sustain the preparation of coaching sessions or parent-teacher meetings. The mid-term school report includes such a self-evaluation form, with which the pupils, in addition to the teachers, are to assess their performance and behaviour. In addition to the regular coaching appointment, the weekly learning group meetings and the self-evaluation forms, the pupils are also asked to engage in self-reflection situationally, for example, to reflect on extracurricular projects.

While the multitude of tools reflects the proclaimed importance of reflection for autonomous learning, the experiences that we witnessed during fieldwork came across as ambivalent. At a school conference a few months after the beginning of fieldwork, the principal reported on the results of an internal evaluation that included not only teachers but also pupils and their parents. Among the critical evaluation results, reflection tools were identified as a challenge, right after the prominent issue of excessive teacher workload. The principal summed up the feedback by saying that "something doesn't work out" concerning the learning groups, that the teachers were uncertain about the success of the coaching sessions, and pupils assessed that the learning journals were totally unnecessary.[4] The principal concluded that in the long term, the instruments for reflection were challenged and that new ideas would have to be sought. However, the teams should not stress out and could continue to work as they did before or as they saw fit.

The criticism of the reflection tools revealed by the evaluation was also evident in the two pedagogical units in which we did our research. Already at the beginning of fieldwork, the "learning journal" was presented to us with the comment that the pupils were reluctant to use it properly. Instead of using it for planning and reflection, they used it merely as a daily planner. In the learning group lessons observed in the first months of fieldwork, the expected reflection did not take place. For example, pupils were asked to reflect on communication strategies, give feedback on each other's presentations, or help each other with the "learning jobs". The majority of the pupils were reserved towards the prescribed exchange in the groups that were heterogenous in age and performance level. The pupils tended to complete the demand of group work as quickly as possible and without any content-related discussion so that they could return to working on their individual learning tasks as soon as possible. Based on the pupil feedback that the learning groups amounted to "wasted time", the teacher teams discussed adaptations of the tasks and goals of the learning groups in both pedagogical units. Finally, the learning groups were spared the imperative of reflection; instead, pupils were allowed to work on specific tasks (e.g., planning for the winter camp) in groups selected by the pupils or to devote more time to individual work on the learning tasks.

In one of the pedagogical units, a new reflection tool, the so-called green booklet, was introduced to encourage individual reflection on the learning process (see the following section). In the interview with the ethnographer, the teachers disclosed ambiguous stances towards the standardized reflection tools. While some teachers valued the forms as a means of preparation for the coaching interview, others criticized the instrument as useless since the pupils would only mechanically fill them out.

All in all, the school used a variety of devices to encourage the pupils' reflection on their learning. By evaluating the experiences with the reflection tools, the school as an organization itself demonstrated a reflexive self-understanding. In the realm of pedagogical practice, however, dissonances were revealed between the teachers' sincere efforts to implement the conceptual objectives and the critical reactions of the pupils, accompanied by doubts from some teachers as well. Due to the ever-so-ambivalent experiences, the teachers opted for a pragmatic approach by trying out new reflection instruments and putting the old ones aside.

In the following part, we shall discuss the differences between the logic of the reflection instruments and their – varied – processing by the pupils, using the example of two reflection tools. The first instrument is the "green booklet" mentioned earlier; the second example analysis is a reflection prompt in the context of a weeklong project on climate change. Both examples are written reflection tasks that we explore as materialized manifestations of reflective practices. Given the limited insights into how teachers dealt with these particular reflection exercises, we analyse their written traces to identify the cultural codes they activate and the subject positions they produce.

Doing reflexivity: The "green booklet"

The "green booklet" consists of a notebook in which pupils should write down their reflections. The notebook is accompanied by a reflection questionnaire, from which the teacher chooses a question on which the pupils are to reflect. The questionnaire began by instructing the pupils to briefly review the past school week and to take five minutes to write notes down in the green booklet. The instrument thus serves the intention to evaluate previous experiences and to derive helpful insights for the upcoming week. The five sections dividing up the questionnaire ("Subject-related", "Work behaviour", "Personal level", "Emotions", "Self-reflection") contain three to six questions each. The thematic differences between the blocks are blurry, leaving the last section filled with all the leftover questions. Beyond the thematic division, the questionnaire roughly contains two categories of questions. The first category calls for expressing the perception of one's own experiences, interests, meaningfulness, feelings, and motivation in relation to school subjects or learning. It asks for example: "What is important to me in relation to the content learned in subject XY?" These questions ask pupils to connect their selves to learning as a process and its content. Through such subjectifying introspection, learning becomes something that belongs to one's own and that is not dictated from the outside.

The questions belonging to the second category intend to evaluate and improve learning. Here, time management and efficient planning, the choice of learning partners, and learning achievements are put to the test. The focus is not to attain subject-specific goals but to optimize learning as a technology and process. The integration of these two different sorts of questions imparts the questionnaire with cultural codes of both self-development and self-optimization (Reckwitz, 2009, p. 174). Due to this dual approach, pupils are addressed as autonomous, self-responsible subjects actively acting on themselves through self-reflection (Edwards, 2008). The formulation of the questions using the "I"-form implies that introspection does not come across as externally imposed, but rather as a skill that the pupils internalize while simultaneously acquiring the technique of self-interrogation. So, what does the application of the tool look like in practice?

Reflection through the use of the green booklet was scheduled for Monday mornings at the beginning of class when pupils gathered in the learning studio. After its introduction at the beginning of the year, the green booklet was used regularly for five months and a total of nine times. The booklets were still lying around on desks some weeks after the next school year had started, but they had not been put to use again. The majority of the selected questions belong to the second category of self-optimization, with the exception of the question "What makes me satisfied/dissatisfied when learning?" and the question about connections between the topics of different subjects. The following insights are based on an analysis of the booklet entries of five pupils (from different grades and performance levels), as well as on interviews with the pupils.

The first striking impression when looking through the entries in the booklets are their brief length and their formality. Furthermore, the pupils' entries conspicuously reveal a prevalence of self-accusations and moral intentions of improvement. The pupils' use of identical, general formulations however suggests that pupils repeated corresponding appeals. The repetitive completion of self-assessment forms which the pupils are accustomed to seems to contribute to the transformation of reflection prompts into routines of processing (Matter & Brosziewski, 2014). In contrast to these dominant patterns, two questions – asking about the connection between the different subject contents and about one's own contribution to a productive learning environment – were answered in such a diverse way that these do not seem to belong to the usual repertoire of self-reflection questions.

In the following, we take a closer look at the variety of the pupils' answering behaviour. The question chosen belongs to the subject-related section and asks about typical mistakes pupils make and how to avoid them. The answers repeat the dominant patterns but nevertheless disclose distinctions among the pupils.

The first and very obvious observation that can be made when looking at the answers (depicted in Table 7.1) is their lack of connection to subject-related learning. Nonetheless, the entries nuance the trend of generalized self-diagnosis and moral intentions of improvement. Pupil M.'s entry reveals the internalization of school expectations when it comes to evaluating her learning strategies and their improvement. The diagnosis of her mistakes shows both a conscientious effort to meet school requirements and self-criticism for putting herself under too much pressure. In contrast, the self-reproaches of E., N., and S. as well as the resolutions (also of M.) are formulated in such a way that they

TABLE 7.1 Answers (translated) to the question about typical mistakes and how to avoid them from the "subject-related" block

	Where do I make the same mistake again and again?	*How can I avoid it in the future?*
E., boy, first grade	That I talk too much during class.	? idk (I don't know).
M., girl, second grade	I always put myself under pressure when I have a test, for example, or a lot of tasks that I still have to do.	Just by starting and going step by step.
N., girl, third grade	I usually keep learning the wrong way for a test.	I should take more time for the English tasks because I always do that at the last minute.
S., girl, third grade	I start working too late. The same goes for the learning tasks.	Keep at it. Try harder.
T., boy, first grade	I forget that the others might not be so good at a given subject, and I say it's easy.	I could just keep it to myself.

refer to routine norms of school communication. These answers raise the hypothesis that the standardized citation of school norms involves an aspect of silent resistance on the part of the pupils: by routinely performing standardized self-critique and promising improvement, pupils may protect themselves from the requirements of self-inspection. Nevertheless, the demands of self-inspection, as well as their formula-like confessions, might impact the pupils and shape their subjectification. In contrast to his four classmates, T.'s self-thematization, which is exceptional both in terms of the choice of topics and the perspective on them, comes across as an unexpected introspection into his feelings and behaviour, which might be perceived as authentic reflection.

These three different response modes surfaced again during the interview when the pupils looked back on the instrument. In general, the tenor of the assessment turns out to be critical: pupil E. said, with a grin, that he did not get the point; he just did it, so it was done. N. added that the booklet served to write down the weekly goals, which she had in mind anyway, and she thought of it as "already something like wasted time". After a moment's reflection, M. paraphrased the purpose of the booklet as "to reflect on what we've done, and you can then take it to the coaching session". She added that there was no need for the booklet at all, "except when the good questions came. Like how I can improve". Her statement indicates once again that she already had internalized the self-optimization code. Pupil T. answered that the booklet was "good feedback for the teachers". Thus, he deployed not only his willingness to scrutinize his feelings and motivations but also to disclose and to communicate them via the booklet with the teachers.

In summary, the use of the green booklet is designed to guide pupils towards becoming reflexive subjects. Scheduled at the beginning of the week, it manifests the importance of reflection as fundamental for, especially self-directed, learning and integrates it into daily classroom practices. Pupils are introduced to the practice of self-interrogation and are expected to adopt it. The booklet is superficially reminiscent of a diary in which the pupils record their experience of self-exploration. However, the materialization as a notebook – in which given questions are to be answered – already hints at schoolwork routines. The moulding of the instrument by school routines becomes even more obvious in its handling. The five-minute time limit to write "a few sentences" already reminds one of the school mode of "getting things done". Furthermore, the option that the reflection tool could be used for coaching or parent-teacher meetings implies that the addressee is not the pupil themself, but the teacher.

While the series of questions includes personal and subject-related issues, the topics selected by the teacher reveal a cybernetic logic: self-reflection is here instrumentalized as a technical instrument to blunt self-optimization. This logic is reinforced by pupil answers conveying straight expressions of self-incrimination and self-improvement. As discussed earlier, pupil entries thereby vary between identification with the self-optimization code and an approach to authentic introspection. The dominance of formal affirmations of self-optimization, however, raises doubts about their seriousness. This interpretation is reflected by the critique expressed by some of the teachers that pupils only mechanically fill out reflection forms. Therefore, it is hardly surprising that the use of the reflection instrument was, without any explanation, not resumed in the next school year.

Doing reflexivity: Pupils reflecting in the context of a "project week"

The second example illustrates the use of reflective exercises during a project week focused on ecology. Pupils engaged, outside of school, with topics such as climate change, up-cycling, and forestry. Again, the pupils were asked to reflect on their learning process during that week, by answering nine questions from an assigned catalogue: the relevance of the topic, task satisfaction, personal involvement, and cooperation within the group formed the themes of the questions. The questions showed a strong resemblance to the ones concerned with subjectivation used in the green booklets. However, there were no self-evaluation questions such as those about mistakes, personal weaknesses, and intended improvement. In contrast to the green booklet, the pupils answered the questions in the format of a more or less self-contained text, similar to a school essay. It is beyond our knowledge, whether this format was required by the teachers. However, it can be deduced from the material that the pupils had all the questions in bulk and that they had to answer them in writing. The questionnaire helped to break down the experience of the project week into different aspects and to guide the pupils through the writing process. Not everyone complied with the task, some pupils wrote an experience essay and ignored the questions completely. Other pupils adhered strictly to the questions, incorporating them word-by-word into their text and visually distinguishing their answers through underlining. Some pupils, finally, confidently integrated the perspective given by the questions into the logic of their own text.

Comparing the eleven texts with the entries in the green booklets, we notice some striking differences: the texts dedicated to the project show a tendency to narration. The reflection on subjective well-being, the expectations and the significance quickly lead to descriptions of the various programme activities of the project week. The pupils highlight their experience, and its narration overshadows the original intent of the questionnaire – namely, encouraging the pupils towards reflection. Furthermore, some texts, while remaining in line with the narrative format, also display signs of authorship. The claim to authorship is recognizable in the title ("A Reflection by Noa Müller") or at the end, similar to the credits of a film ("End – by Mia Gerber"). The texts are furthermore characterized by the use of highlighters for emphasis, such as punctuation marks ("We built a chair!") or intensifiers ("totally important", "really fun"). All in all, it can be concluded that the focus of those texts is not the evaluation of work behaviour and the meeting of school norms. The only question that points in this direction is the one about group work: "What will I do so that we can have a good work atmosphere in the group?" The following quotation is an example of a lengthy response, which first looks back on the joint experiences before ending with a wilful intent:

> The group work triggered in me a certain urge to learn something new and it was fascinating that some members of the group really engaged with the topic, and some just didn't engage with the topic and didn't show any interest, but they didn't have any either, which was, in my opinion, quite a pity because the topic is very important for us and our future. In order to have a good work atmosphere I will actively engage with the subject and not sit there bored or half-asleep.

This statement can certainly be interpreted as a commitment to ecological awareness and thus be recognized as a proof of a socially desirable response. It cannot be dismissed that the pupil intends to present herself as a committed and interested pupil, concerned with what is sustainable and who performatively distinguishes herself from less desirable pupil subjects. At the same time, however, the passage reveals an authentic flavour, which might derive from its formal structure. The socially desirable habitus, personal concerns, and legitimation of these very norms are mentioned here in a very lengthy, breathless sentence deprived of punctuation. The relevance of the topic "for our future" justifies the intention of appearing as a woke, interested pupil. Even though the argument might be strategically motivated, it does not exclude its authentication by the process of writing it down.

The reflection on group work, motivated by the corresponding question, was answered by several pupils. The experiences that were reflected upon and the conclusions drawn from them noticeably differ from pupil to pupil. Here the citational character is less obvious than it is in the answers from the green booklets. While the pupil cited above addresses the problem of unequal engagement in group work, another mentions the issue of frequent speakers and notes "that some kids almost didn't get a chance to speak". An improvement is also suggested by this pupil: "Regarding this point one should make sure that next time, everyone has access to approximately equal speaking time". And finally, a third pupil laconically states: "Working in a group was easy, but you have to discuss a lot to make it work".

We conclude that such considerations on the part of pupils may certainly be identified as reflexive engagement with school experiences. They emerge as short moments during which introspection and confession meet. Albeit the guiding questions set the tone, the answers, unlike those in the green booklets, can be recognized as at least partially independent reflections. Also in this exercise, reflection takes the form of a written monologue that is guided by a questionnaire. However, the code that is activated is one of narrative reporting: pupils are addressed as writers who are required to relate to what they have learned. Thereby, the occasion, the focus, and the form of questions make for a certain leeway thanks to which the pupils can position themselves. The reflections on that project week bring forth pupil subjects that have something to say. And this is in a double sense of the word: they have experienced something that is worth talking or writing about, and what they have to say has relevance.

Conclusion

If reflection is to be understood as a method in which a subject bends back towards itself and positions itself in relation to its actions and preferences, then a broad spectrum of such practices can be observed in the field of education. As the discussed experiences in one school demonstrate, pupils are able to relate to their learning process and performance, as well as to their behaviour and the corresponding behavioural norms. However, if we summarize what we observed at the school, it is striking to see how prevalent specific practices are. Overall, evaluative self-interrogation predominates in the teachers' questions as well as the pupils' answers: pupils are encouraged to locate errors and formulate resolutions to improve their learning and behaviour. This logic of self-optimization is formally reflected in the pupils' standardized response behaviour. What follows reminds one more of the quality of reflex than of reflexivity (Edwards et al., 2010, p. 525): the pupils' formula-like citation of school norms serves both the performance of expected behaviour and the attempt to keep certain demands at bay. It is therefore comprehensible that many of the pupils are critical of this reflective practice and perhaps show a certain resistance to the school's subjectification processes.

Nonetheless, other forms of self-reflection were observed, during which pupils, albeit fragmentarily and casually, find their way towards authentic expression. In these moments, pupils not only repeat expected school norms but at least rudimentarily engage in introspection into their interests and preferences. The opposing experiences at the school allow to draw conclusions regarding the conditions that need to be in place for pupils to live through true experiences of self-reflection in the school: if reflection is detached from concrete subject-related content and prescribed in a decontextualized setting, it tends to become formalized and formalistic. The school form overrides the content and by doing so, the logic of adaptation and optimization, which is inherent in the concept of learning per se, takes on a life of its own. As a result, learning primarily becomes a technology of improvement and optimization, no matter in what and with regard to which goal. Reflection in the form of interrogating intentions of self-improvement and of an institutionally desired behaviour and habitus turn into rituals of verification (Power, 1999). Thereby, the process of writing serves as the reinforcement of formalization. The integration of self-reflection into broader evaluation and feedback loops subjugates reflection to the logic of assessment, which remains one of the main features of the grammar of schooling. If reflective practices, regardless of their concern with either self-development or self-optimization, are integrated into the all-encompassing framework of assessment, they are turned into performances and are evaluated as such. As a consequence, the reflective effort exhausts itself by absorbing the preferences of the evaluating institution.

If, in contrast, self-reflection is perceived in the sense of the autonomy concept as taking distance from oneself and critically engaging with one's own desires, inclinations, and attitudes (Dworkin, 2015, p. 14), then these reflective practices first have to be granted a space where they can be voiced. This space needs to exist without subjecting the individuals to an external agent of assessment – also in, and particularly in schools. There obtains a need for a space in which the pupils' reflection on their learning and their development would be stimulated not by questionnaires and written answers, but by dialogical conversations. Reflective practices would then facilitate the emergence of a space for a self that does not want to be judged but is rather respected and taken seriously in the way that it portrays itself at a particular moment in its development: always provisional, often contradictory, and sometimes suboptimal.

Notes

1 In the lower secondary school, pupils attend the seventh to ninth school year and are between 12 and 15 years old (according to the official new counting, which includes the two years of kindergarten, it corresponds to the ninth to eleventh grade).
2 The project is funded by the Swiss National Science Foundation (SNSF; Nr. 100019_173035) and supported by the Universities of Teacher Education Bern and Vaud. The project is led by Judith Hangartner, Regula Fankhauser (Bern), and Héloïse Durler (Vaud).
3 Fieldwork in this case study was done by Angela Kaspar. Names have been changed and context information has been left general or modified to protect the anonymity of research participants.
4 The oral and written quotations in Swiss German or German standard language have been translated by the authors.

References

Altrichter, H. (2000). Handlung und Reflexion bei Donald Schön. In G. H. Neuweg (Ed.), *Wissen - Können - Reflexion. Ausgewählte Verhältnisbestimmungen* (pp. 201–222). Innsbruck: Studien-Verlag.
Beck, U. (2007). *Weltrisikogesellschaft. Auf der Suche nach der verlorenen Sicherheit.* Frankfurt a.M.: Suhrkamp.
Beck, U., Giddens, A., & Lash, S. (1994). *Reflexive Modernization: Politics, tradition and aesthetics in the modern social order.* Stanford, CA: Stanford University Press.

Beck, U., & Holzer, B. (2004). Reflexivität und Reflexion. In U. Beck & C. Lau (Eds.), *Entgrenzung und Entscheidung* (pp. 165–192). Frankfurt a. M.: Suhrkamp.
Chak, A. W. S. (2006). Reflecting on the self: An experience in a preschool. *Reflective Practice*, 7, 31–41.
Dworkin, G. (2015). The nature of autonomy. *Nordic Journal of Studies in Educational Policy*, 2, 7–14. https://doi.org/10.3402/nstep.v1.28479
Edwards, R. (2008). Actively seeking subjects? In A. Fejes & K. Nicoll (Eds.), *Foucault and lifelong learning: Governing the subject* (pp. 21–33). London/New York: Routledge.
Edwards, R., Ranson, S., & Strain, M. (2010). Reflexivity: Towards a theory of lifelong learning. *International Journal of Lifelong Education*, 21(6), 525–536. https://doi.org/10.1080/0260137022000016749
Fejes, A., & Dahlstedt, M. (2013). *The confessing society. Foucault, confession and practices of lifelong learning*. London and New York: Routledge.
Forster, E. (2014). Reflexivität. In C. Wulf & J. Zirfas (Eds.), *Handbuch Pädagogische Anthropologie* (pp. 589–597). Wiesbaden: Springer Verlag für Sozialwissenschaften. https://doi.org/10.1007/978-3-531-18970-3_54
Foucault, M. (2000). Die Gouvernementalität. In U. Bröckling, S. Krasmann, & T. Lemke (Eds.), *Gouvernementalität der Gegenwart: Studien zur Ökonomisierung des Sozialen* (pp. 41–67). Suhrkamp.
Gläser-Zikuda, M., & Hascher, T. (2007). *Lernprozesse dokumentieren, reflektieren und beurteilen: Lerntagebuch und Portfolio in Bildungsforschung und Bildungspraxis*. Bad Heilbrunn: Klinkhardt.
Hangartner, J., Fankhauser, R., Budde, J., Forkby, T., & Alstam, K. (2022). How the self-governing imperative alters the classroom as a public space. In B. Hühnersdorf, G. Breidenstein, J. Dinkelaker, O. Schnoor, & T. Tyagunova (Eds.), *Going public? Erziehungswissenschaftliche Ethnographie und ihre Öffentlichkeiten* (pp. 135–148). Wiesbaden: Springer VS. https://doi.org/10.1007/978-3-658-34085-8_9
Hangartner, J., Kaspar, A., & Fankhauser, R. (2019). Selbständigkeit als Antizipation der Arbeitswelt in der Schule. *Schweizerische Zeitschrift für Soziologie*, 45(3), 299–316. https://doi.org/10.2478/sjs-2019-0014
Helmke, A. (2003). *Unterrichtsqualität erfassen, bewerten, verbessern*. Seelze: Kallmeyer.
Helmke, A. (2009). *Unterrichtsqualität und Lehrerprofessionalität: Diagnose, Evaluation und Verbesserung des Unterrichts*. Seelze: Kallmeyer.
Hilbe, R., & Herzog, W. (2011). *Selbst organisiertes Lernen am Gymnasium. Theoretische Konzepte und empirische Erkenntnisse*. Bern: Mittelschul- und Berufsbildungsamt.
Martens, M. (2018). Reflektieren als unterrichtliche Aufgabe: Zur Passung von Lehr- und Lernkompetenzen im individualisierten Unterricht. In K. Rabenstein, K. Kunze, M. Martens, T.-S. Idel, M. Proske, & S. Strauss (Eds.), *Individualisierung von Unterricht. Transformationen - Wirkungen - Reflexionen* (pp. 88–102). Bad Heilbrunn: Klinkhardt.
Matter, C., & Brosziewski, A. (2014). Routinierte Reflexion: Zur Individualisierung pädagogischer Reflexionsprobleme. *ZSE: Zeitschrift für Soziologie der Erziehung und Sozialisation*, 1, 23–37.
Menzel, C., & Rademacher, S. (2012). Die 'sanfte Tour'. Analysen von Schülerselbsteinschätzungen zum Zusammenhang von Individualisierung und Kontrolle. *sozialer sinn*, 13(1), 79–99.
Neuweg, G. H. (2010). Fortbildung im Kontext eines phasenübergreifenden Gesamtkonzepts der Lehrerbildung. In F. H. Müller, A. Eichenberger, M. Lüders, &

J. Mayr (Eds.), *Lehrerinnen und Lehrer lernen. Konzepte und Befunde zur Lehrerfortbildung* (pp. 35–50). Münster: Waxmann.

PHBern (2012). *Orientierungsrahmen.* Bern: Pädagogische Hochschule. (https://www.phbern.ch/ueber-die-phbern/hochschule/portraet/orientierungsrahmen; Access: 18.07.2022).

Power, M. (1999). *The audit society: Rituals of verification.* Oxford: Oxford University Press.

Rabenstein, K., & Reh, S. (2007). Kooperative und selbstständigkeitsfördernde Arbeitsformen im Unterricht. Forschungen und Diskurse. In K. Rabenstein & S. Reh (Eds.), *Kooperatives und selbstständiges Arbeiten von Schülern. Zur Qualitätsentwicklung von Unterricht* (pp. 23–38). Wiesbaden: Verlag für Sozialwissenschaften.

Reckwitz, A. (2002). Toward a theory of social practices: A development in culturalist theorizing. *European Journal of Social Theory*, 5(2), 243–263. https://doi.org/10.1177%2F13684310222225432

Reckwitz, A. (2009). Praktiken der Reflexivität: Eine kulturtheoretische Perspektive auf hochmodernes Handeln. In F. Böhle & M. Weihrich (Eds.), *Über Entscheidungen und Entscheidungsmöglichkeiten in der reflexiven Moderne* (pp. 169–182). Wiesbaden: VS.

Rieger-Ladich, M., Friebertshäuser, B., & Wigger, L. (2009). Reflexive Erziehungswissenschaft: Stichworte zu einem Programm. In M. Rieger-Ladich, B. Friebertshäuser, & L. Wigger (Eds.), *Reflexive Erziehungswissenschaft. Forschungsperspektiven im Anschluss an Pierre Bourdieu* (pp. 9–19). Wiesbaden: Verlag für Sozialwissenschaften.

Rolfe, G., & Gardner, L. (2006). 'Do not ask who I am...': Confession, emancipation and (self)-management through reflection. *Journal of Nursing Management*, 14, 593–600.

Schön, D. (1983). *The reflective practitioner: How professionals think in action.* London: Temple Smith.

van Manen, M. (1995). On the epistemology of reflective practice. *Teachers and Teaching: Theory and Practice*, 1, 33–50.

Wiesenthal, H. (2009). Rationalität und Unsicherheit in der Zweiten Moderne. In F. Böhle & M. Weihrich (Eds.), *Handeln unter Unsicherheit* (pp. 25–47). Wiesbaden: Verlag für Sozialwissenschaften.

Wrana, D. (2006). *Das Subjekt schreiben. Reflexive Praktiken und Sujektivierung in der Weiterbildung - eine Diskursanalyse.* Baltmannsweiler: Schneider Verlag Hohengehren.

8
GROUP PEDAGOGY AND THE ACQUISITION OF AUTONOMY IN LEARNING

Marie-Sylvie Claude and Patrick Rayou

Autonomy, groups, and contracts

Dominique Glasman (2016, p. 9) has remarked that "everything is done today as if the concept of autonomy was so pervasive and pivotal that all education could, in one way or another, be linked to it".[1] As a consequence, French curricula now revolve around this skill said to give pupils the ability to engage in school activities, to act, to communicate with others, and thus gradually exercise their freedom and their status as responsible citizens (Patry, 2018). As a keystone of the educational system, the acquisition of autonomy is often implemented by teachers who wish to be innovative through the pedagogical strategy of "learning pods" which organizes the work of pupils in small groups. Through careful scrutiny of the plurality of contracts underlying this method, this chapter proposes to determine whether such pedagogy promotes sought-after autonomy and in what manner.

The injunction to encourage autonomy is a consequence of the curricular reorganization movement that has affected schools throughout the West. According to Basil Bernstein (2007), this movement is revealed by the adoption of "invisible pedagogies" by the new middle class in order to organize the transition to a less direct and more symbolic form of social control. To achieve this objective, the kindergarten and primary school systems develop situations in which the teacher's main role consists in setting up a learning environment that the pupils, who are granted a great deal of autonomy, may rearrange and explore. These principles imply major reorganizations, not only in terms of the layout of the classroom but also in the relationships with the pupils, the common rules in the school, or the elaboration of knowledge (Lahire, 2001).

However, the enactment of this new paradigm placing "the child at the centre" (Lahire, 2001; Rayou, 2000) is not devoid of contradictions. Indeed, the injunction to being autonomous implies that the teacher will find validation mostly among the pupils who have been prepared to freely want what the educational institution expects of them. Obviously, such expectations remain devoid of meaning for all those who do not possess the resources necessary to understand what is implicitly or explicitly required of them (Durler, 2015). Assuming that the socially defined conditions required by autonomy are experienced by all may well conceal relationships of domination that go against the ideal of emancipation that it symbolizes (Périer, 2014). In particular, there is a great risk that the mere fact of giving pupils tasks to work on, an indisputable part of his or her autonomy, does not allow him or her to co-construct knowledge: the child who acts is not necessarily and spontaneously an author (Quentel, 2014).

The activists involved in New Education pedagogical methods have attempted to rethink the shape of schools (Vincent, 1994) and of learning methods through the prism of autonomy. In the early 20th century, the idea of *self-government* federated numerous groups into the formation of the International League of New Education founded in 1921 (Wagnon & Patry, 2019). This notion entered the educational field thanks to the idea of personal study and self-study on the one hand, and on the other hand, it came across as a means of self-governance involving a collective approach (Patry, 2018). Pedagogues such as Roger Cousinet (1968) then developed methods of free group work stemming from a principle of self-education. The contemporary cooperative pedagogies resulting from this movement insisted on the fact that in shared activity, people actually work together; they are no longer anonymous individual entities subjected to lectures. In doing so, they resort to an anthropological principle developed by Lev Vygotskij (2018, p. 307), according to which human consciousness "emerges, grows, and is transformed via communication among people, meaning that one's own consciousness does not grow in one's mind until exchanges with a finished product are possible; consciousness expands and derives its basic functions from a process of communication". These cooperative pedagogies sustain the project of making pupils more autonomous by confronting them to the existence of knowledge and skills that are not innate but instead form an inheritance which requires the help of others in order to be appropriated or even expanded. Therefore, they aim at promoting social relations but also academic learning. However, they have a hard time transcending the individualistic approach to self-education in the case of learning, mobilizing instead the collective for the regulation of relations and conflicts among the members of such schools (Patry, 2018).

The success of group pedagogies has more to do with the fact that it favours maintaining control of the class and of the attention of pupils than with the conviction that the pupils would learn better on their own in groups (Reverdy, 2016). Philippe Meirieu has thus drawn attention to the fact that group work, relying on the hypothetical identification of each individual with the "good pupils", very often sidesteps the question of learning. If learning is, as is often the case, geared at "production", then group work makes it possible to avoid a "waste of time", which would be detrimental to efficiency; if learning is geared at "fusion", then group work silences the expression of dissenting opinions, which would threaten its unity and identity. In these two deviations, which negate the deep processes involved in learning, the group becomes an end in itself, and the objective of acquisition is overshadowed by the task to be accomplished, which is nevertheless only a means to achieve the former (Meirieu, 1997). Such a warning is, in fact, often dismissed. Our hypothesis is that practitioners have a partial or unclear image of contract pedagogy, which has spread in the wake of the trend of placing the pupil at the centre of the educational system. Therefore, we intend to analyse the interactions involved in academic learning and the effects they produce (or are supposed to produce) in terms of contracts. "We thus speak of pedagogical contract, social contract, communication contract, didactic contract" (Reuter, 2010, p. 55). As for us, we retain three different but intertwined types of contracts from this explicit or implicit system of reciprocal expectations among the actors involved in school: a social contract, which situates the teacher among his peers, defines his relationships with the pupils, induces collective behaviour, and contributes globally to finding a way of living together at school; an educational contract, which aims at developing the critical skills contributing to the pupils' empowerment; and a didactic contract which, for a given discipline – literature in our case – contributes specifically to this objective. In our opinion, putting students to work in groups does not *ipso facto* lead to the development of the desired autonomy because it brings into play a plurality of contracts that must be distinguished and articulated at once.

A survey

We tested this hypothesis by studying the setting up of a work group *dispositif* in French class for year 9 pupils (14–15 years old) enrolled in a secondary school located in the centre of a town[2] in the Paris region. The teacher, whom we shall call Mrs Arnoux,[3] belongs to a small group of six teachers in that school claiming to be committed to innovative pedagogical methods. Over the course of two school years, we gathered elements to understand Ms. Arnoux's professional choices thanks to an initial one-hour biographical interview, several class observation sessions, and regular informal discussions. Then, we filmed a class devoted to the study of poems from the 19th and 20th centuries whose common point was their commitment to a political cause.[4] Each of the six groups made up of four to five pupils dealt with a different poem, following the same instructions. We recorded and transcribed the teacher's interventions and the discussions within the groups, thanks to a recorder placed on each desk. We also collected the material handed out to the pupils and their written productions. Two weeks later, we conducted another one-hour interview with the teacher, during which we confronted her with the various elements we had collected. We also conducted 18 individual interviews of about 30 minutes each with the pupils, whom we also confronted with the remnants of what they had written and said during the session. We analysed the material in order to find out whether the pupils are autonomous and to what extent and how the three contracts we defined (the social, educational, and didactic contracts) are articulated in this respect.

A social contract

Making pupils work in groups belongs to a teacher's individual choice for their classes, but such choice necessarily falls into one of the two "sides" making up today's teaching community. Indeed, while the pedagogical noosphere and the central institution promote pedagogical objectives meant to break away from the recommendations and practices that prevailed until the end of the 1980s, they provide limited means of achieving them (Saujat, 2010). Relying on group work for pupils is an important common denominator among teachers like Ms. Arnoux, who define themselves as innovators and take the injunction to develop the autonomy of their pupils very seriously. She is critical of those among her colleagues whom she considers to be professionally conservative. For them, "the pedagogical innovation of the century is the lecture-discussion or even better the lecture-discussion with 2 or 3 good pupils". They produce "standardized" pupils, some of whom ask her, at the beginning of the year, "if it's a problem if on page 125 they can't remember exactly if the character took the road on the right or the left!" Her own reading exams "never include questions on that sort of thing!"

Group work is thus based upon a first contract which may be described as social, insofar as it federates a community of colleagues who claim to have given up the lecture format; besides, it is also a commitment toward the pupils they mean to accept in all their differences. The latter, far from being obstacles, are perceived as means to buttress their own emancipation. In return, the pupils allow for a peaceful management of the class sequences. Despite their heterogeneity, "they cope relatively well, there are no conflicts or arguments".

Most of the pupils who were interviewed agree with this cohesive function of group work, which they claim to prefer to ordinary teaching methods. For Maxime, "it works well". Erwan believes that the strength of the group is to make pupils who do not necessarily have the same ideas work together:

> In a group where we all have the same opinion, things will go faster, but it won't necessarily be better, because we all have the same opinion and we

won't be able to improve the written work. But in a group in which each person has their own opinion, then we can have a discussion and thus we are able to improve our work by relying upon all our different opinions. (…) And the teacher specifically tries to team up pupils who have a spirit of initiative with pupils who only half want to work, in order to have balanced groups.

Of course, situations of tension may occur. For Mia, if her friend Léa wants to say "this" and she wants to say "that", there is a "risk of conflict", but it is preferable because it enables them "to write good texts". And according to Maxime, when placed with pupils who are "always contradicting others", the group regulates itself: "we'll take a vote, we'll see who gains most support and then the majority wins". Such organizational routines allow them to collaborate. To the demanding duty of secretary, some like Walid prefer the role of time manager "because there is not much to do!" However, if these divisions of labour are accepted because they pacify the situation, they worry pupils like Guerric:

> I like group work, but we can't ever claim it as our own. We cannot ever say: "I remember that, that's really what I thought". "Those were my ideas, they…". Each student has a task in fact, it is as if something was being passed around, each one has their task, and in the end, it's not really group work.

Likewise, Walid laments the fact that the teacher satisfies herself with ensuring the internal harmony of the groups and does not intervene as to the content of the work being done:

> It's like when she's called over and she says, "Do as you please". No really, when I asked her, she told me: "you can put down several themes". She didn't tell me: "or not, or not".

Forsaking the lecture format to privilege work in learning pods clearly allows this teacher to choose her side within her professional group while steering her class in a way that seems more satisfying to her and her pupils. The teacher and pupils say they are happier in school than they used to be and enjoy it more than they did the more traditional frontal teaching modalities in a classroom set up with rows of desks.

An educational contract

However, the teacher's various commitments to her pupils and peers are also based on an educational goal emphasizing the development of young people's intellectual autonomy. She believes that most of them are "formatted for lecturing". While her stated goal is to make sure "that they understand they're citizens", they feel that they have to endure society: "I would like them to understand that they are actors, that they are part of society, that they can be actors in it". She worries about what they will be able to do afterwards because "they are not autonomous at all for high school, they are not taught autonomy". Yet such is the educational virtue of the group. When she watches the recorded sequence, Ms. Arnoux is satisfied:

> They work on the text, they ask themselves the question: do we use the word "verse" or not? It's nice to see. For me, they are really at work then. They grapple with a text about which they really speak about the work they are doing. That's for sure.

Although the pupils usually "never put anything of themselves in the texts", she hopes that, beyond this obvious collaboration, they can make sense of what they do, that they discover that the power of literature "is to show how the same feelings move us all through the centuries". The group can help one understand this, because "questioning the world and questioning yourself…and looking at others…for me that forms a whole". Besides, "when looking at others, at some point empathy comes out…. And once empathy is out, you're saved".

The version of the educational contract put forward by the pupils validates the postulate that it does trigger and sustain their work since according to them, group work involves pooling together resources which make for the acknowledgement of each of them and the enrichment of all. The idea expressed by Vanessa is thus very widespread: "You don't only have your own idea, you have the ideas of others". It is obvious however that the group can accommodate some "free riders" like Ahmid who had not read the text beforehand. He "didn't listen too carefully either" but "wrote a little bit of what the pupils wrote". This raises questions about the ability of the implemented *dispositif* to achieve its learning objectives beyond the handing in of a product and the preservation of group unity, as underlined by Meirieu. Yet in addition to the satisfaction of working with peers comes the satisfaction of being able, thanks to the group, to hand in productions that are as thorough as possible, because it seems obvious that whatever knowledge comes from several people is greater than what comes from an isolated individual. When Ms. Arnoux told Erwan's group that "some elements were missing, so we put asterisks here and a little further down, and then we filled out the blanks", it is not certain that this quantitative vision of school work, which group work may lend credence to, is likely to help French pupils who have proved that they excel at gathering information in international surveys but struggle with more qualitative tasks, such as judging a point of view or putting aside their own opinion (Rémond, 2006).

The pupils we observed clearly adopted an attitude of social collaboration, not necessarily of intellectual cooperation (Connac, 2009) because the logic of producing a standardized piece of writing induces a division of labour, encouraged by the distribution of roles (of secretary, master, master of time, master of noise, etc.) defining high and low-level tasks. "Everyone had their own little task" chirps Lydia.

> Afterwards, we put everything together to have a complete essay. There were a few dissenting opinions, but they concerned the nature of the figures of style and we looked them up in the notebook, especially to find out if the rhyming pattern was based upon enclosing or cross-rhymes.

The educational virtues of group work are obvious in the regulation of their own behaviour by the pupils, but they seem less blatant when it comes to the development of their intellectual autonomy. Several pupils, like Mia, tell us that they appreciate it, but they are not necessarily intellectually comfortable because a form of self-censorship may seem necessary to preserve the unity of the group:

> When we do group work, we don't necessarily have the same ideas, so we are obliged to share our ideas with others, and we don't necessarily want to write what we had in mind.

Luca believes that he did not help the others: "they already knew everything". He just copied what they said. Taking into account the social and educational aspects of group work is clearly not enough to ensure the desired autonomy, and in some cases, it perpetuates ways of maintaining pupils in the unimaginative scholarly patterns so criticized by teachers.

In order for the educational contract to function, as Madame Arnoux insisted she wanted it to in the interview, i.e., to encourage, through the teaching of her subject, the intellectual emancipation of all pupils, it would be necessary for the didactic contract to provide a framework for reading activities that would indeed make for such liberation. We shall provide a more developed analysis of this third contract because it seems to us that its conception and articulation with the two others allow us to better explain some of the limitations of the chosen *dispositif* as regards the construction of autonomy within the context of work in small groups.

A didactic contract

During the interview, Ms. Arnoux explained her didactic objectives. Do the activities carried out by the pupils during the session we observed allow them to achieve such objectives?

Aiming at specific subject-related knowledge

First of all, the teacher said that she wanted to train readers capable of reading literary texts in their own way:

> When you teach French, you've got to respect the text and its readers (…). They will never learn to like [texts] if you monitor them all the time…if I had told them: "no, you absolutely have to put this in" (…) you have to suck up to me and write what I expect…, it would not be acceptable.

Striving to achieve the subject-related skill of independent reading is in keeping with her educational project of emancipation for the young people entrusted to her: she wants to teach them to craft by themselves a personal interpretation of the texts which may differ from hers and which is likely to contribute to their personal growth. Ms. Arnoux explained, "The text challenges them. (…) they are sensitive". The intuitions of her pupils are valued as working material. Such a conception is in line with the paradigm of the subject-reader as theorized by some of the researchers working on the didactics of literature today: the pupils are enticed to draw upon their subjective resources, their genuine reactions, and their emotions to sustain their interpretation of a text (Langlade & Rouxel, 2004). They are thus able to construct their own *reader's text* (Mazauric et al., 2011), a term designating the mental reconfiguration resulting from the singular reading that each reader makes of a given text. This way of reading privileges the appropriation of the text by the student: "he or she thus appropriates a literary work, they put their own spin on it, thus creating a trace that can be retained in their memory" (Shawky-Milcent, 2016, p. 36). When he or she is able to read a text in a manner that is really their own and differs from that of the teacher, the autonomous reader thus contributes to the emergence of the adult they are becoming.

Besides, Madame Arnoux has another didactic objective for her pupils who need "to gradually learn the skills involved in writing a text commentary", an exercise that they will be confronted with when they take the *baccalaureat* exams two years later.[5] She wishes to anticipate the preparation of this final examination because they will be expected to engage by themselves in "a textual research process". According to her, this calls for an initiation to the adequate "tools" they will need as early as the *Troisième* or year 9, particularly as regards the "identification of stylistic elements". She is therefore looking to foster autonomy and the ability for her pupils to carry out an analytical reading of the text on their own, so as to infer meaning from the observation of textual form. This is another way of tackling textual analysis: its articulation with the subjective reading that it aims at is often considered desirable by teachers but very difficult to achieve because it demands that the pupils learn to rely on their personal reactions to the text while mobilizing specialized knowledge and skilled approaches in order to achieve the very standardized production that school exercises require (Claude, 2020).

In addition to the objective of encouraging reader autonomy, understood as the ability to appropriate the text for personal development, comes the objective of achieving autonomy as a future *baccalaureat* candidate, understood as the ability to produce a text commentary on their own. This double objective mirrors the curriculum: on the one hand,

> the teaching of French in cycle 4 constitutes an important step in the construction of autonomous thinking based on the correct and precise use of the French language, the development of critical thinking and of qualities of judgment that will be necessary in high school.

On the other hand, the pupils must be taught to "read and understand a variety of texts independently".[6] Mrs. Arnoux considers it necessary to move beyond this last point and to introduce the pupils to the *baccalaureat* exercises, even if she emphasizes the fact that "it is complicated to fulfil all the objectives". Does the class we observed make it possible to do so?

The instructions

The groups of pupils are slated to make an oral presentation during the next class, respecting the following instructions:

> You will share the following roles: master of time, one or two secretaries and master of noise responsible for calling to order the members of the group who raise their voices.
> You will have 45 minutes to prepare an analysis of this text, respecting the following outline:
> A general presentation of the characteristics of your poem.
> The presentation of two to three themes addressed by the author, explaining how he or she has drawn on them, dealt with them, as well as the messages he wants to convey.
> Link the text to the poet's activism by drawing on the research you did beforehand.

The first entry consists in an operational framework aiming at making sure that the pupils work independently – i.e., without asking the teacher how to organize themselves. The cognitive framework is to be found in the next lines. The "general presentation" expected of the pupils amounts to identifying the formal characteristics of the poem, using guidelines that the pupils have in front of them (defining the types of verse, the rhyming pattern, and some stylistic devices). The next paragraph requires them to "find 2 to 3 themes" and analyse the way they are dealt with. Ms. Arnoux explained to us in an interview that "in the end, this amounts to preparing them for an organized text commentary": the canonical exercise for the *baccalauréat* includes an introduction presenting the text, followed by an organized development which is often thematic. However, nothing in the instructions specifies that, in order to develop the themes, one must make sure that "characteristics of the poem" yield meaning as expected in the commentary exercises: it is up to the pupils to understand this. Moreover, Ms. Arnoux's second aim which targets the production of a personal, emancipatory interpretation, seems to be downplayed since it is necessary to find "the messages he [the author] wants to convey" as if the text contained hidden meaning to be revealed rather than co-constructed. Such a guideline does not encourage intersubjective exchanges bearing on potential interpretations. It is therefore to be feared that although this framework makes it possible for the groups to be steeped in actual work, it does not necessarily guarantee that the pupils will achieve the intended learning objectives. Let's look at the interactions in one of the groups.

Interactions about Souvenir de la nuit du 4 by Victor Hugo

As a reminder, this poem is a pamphlet against Louis-Napoleon Bonaparte, the future Napoleon III, whose *coup* on December 2, 1851, provoked a popular uprising that was violently repressed. The body of her grandson, killed by a stray bullet, is brought back to a destitute old woman.

The following short excerpt is representative of the exchanges recorded in the group during the first 20 minutes of the study session. Throughout, the pupils focus on the characteristics of versification[7]:

- *There's only flat rhymes*
- *…flat…enjambments…(…)*
- *I wrote: "all the rhymes of this poem are flat", I put a /s/ (…)*
- *So, there's also the words…*
- *But we already said: "in it, we find".*
- *Write: there are also (…)*
- *They are all alexandrines…*
- *The verse all have 12…*
- *Its meter (…)*
- *Is made up of alexandrines.*

The pupils are concerned with the accuracy of their prosodic observations and the precision of wording; they try to avoid repetitions ("there are also") and to edit the spelling, which may seem surprising since an oral presentation is expected of them. They correctly identify the rhyme scheme (flat), the meter (alexandrine), and a metrical device, the enjambment. The regulations within the group allow for the relevant substitution of the word verse by the word meter. On the other hand, they fail to elaborate on the notion of alexandrine since the writer chooses to write that the verse is "made up of alexandrines", whereas the correct formulation ("they are alexandrines") is not retained. Moreover, the conversation does not involve any attempt at giving meaning to these formal characteristics. Work on the themes takes place later, without any link with the initial identifications. We can therefore consider that according to this exchange, the objective of preparation for the text commentary is very partially achieved since only the elements that may be used in an introduction are expressed. However, the way meaning is produced is not investigated. As for personal reactions to the text, they are given no place whatsoever.

A little later, during the second half of the allotted time, pupils focus on "finding 2 to 3 themes" and agree on the fact that "realism" is one of them, along with violence.

- *The themes developed are...*
- *Realism...uh...violence (...)*
- *Because the poor kid didn't do anything in the first place*
- *Yeah.*
- *The poor kid.*
- *OK, so I'm writing down realism...*
- *(...) Basically, it's Napoleon III's fault, he ordered troops to kill like...*
- *It's violence (...)*
- *Realism.... Violence... because... Violence because...*
- *I put "because".*
- *His skull was split open like a log*
- *Ah...*
- *One could put a finger in the holes...*
- *The wounds...*
- *For there are passages...don't use "shocking"...*
- *Abominable!*
- *She is happy*
- *Abominable passages...you spell abominable with two bs?*

One of the pupils tries to engage the group in the construction of meaning by pointing out the injustice of the death of an innocent person. A few exchanges show their sensitivity to the description of the wound.[8] But the work of interpretation is interrupted twice by the desire to fulfil the instructions. The suggestion of the word "abominable" rather than "shocking" satisfies the group without exploring the reasons for preferring the term nor seeking what, in the text, produces horror. The denunciation of the violence of the authorities is not made explicit, although one of the pupils alludes to the troops of Napoleon III. Their concern for the wording ("for" instead of "because") and the spelling (one or two /b/ to "abominable") takes over. The exchanges are not so much about the meaning of the text, but more about the way of writing what has not been discussed. Personal reactions to the poem are expressed fleetingly, notably about the child's fate with the empathetic repetition of "the poor kid", but far from producing intersubjective exchanges about interpretation, the interactions stifle them because they are concerned with dealing properly with the instructions. This does not lead to a convincing preparation for the text commentary exercise, since very few effects of meaning are tackled. Does the teacher's arbitration make it possible to reframe the pupils' work on a cognitive level?

The teacher's arbitration

When confronted with the transcript of these interactions in an interview, Ms. Arnoux said,

> To me, they are really at work there (...) What they don't say is why it's an enjambment, how does the enjambment produce something...if we were to take the time to revise...well, it's my dream to have the time to revise, but you know how it goes, right.

In order to manage what little time they have, she prioritizes the project of making them work in groups and autonomously so that they regulate their own behaviour. But from a didactic point of view, we may consider that she gives up her initial objective of literary reading since the meaning produced by the formal characteristics, which are at the heart of the subject, take second place, at least for the initiation to a method of reading to prepare for the text commentary.

In fact, when arbitrating the work of that very group, she draws the pupils' attention to a political interpretation of the text but does not impose it on them:

> It's up to you to choose, but we have a child who dies for political reasons that are beyond him and in which he plays no part, but as a result Victor Hugo's poem is itself political. So you can also choose, or not, to talk about it. Because after all, it's a very rich poem, you don't have to talk about everything.

One might think, although this might seem surprising, that she considers that the interpretation of the political message is not unavoidable for this text studied by ninth graders, that it is possible to make another interpretation. But she explains in the interview that she makes this choice for another reason:

> They have years of passivity behind them, so if you want to get them to grasp the message, even imperfectly, if they miss something that is normally obvious (...) I'd rather they feel satisfied with themselves rather than

think: "we completely missed what was important" (...) when they've worked really well.

She thus puts the educational contract before the didactic contract: it is especially important to change the passive attitude learned from attending her colleagues' classes and to restore their self-confidence. This activity can be analysed as a priority in her project on subject-based knowledge, and it is possibly independent from their learning strategy.

Interviewing pupils in the group

Three weeks after the session, the pupils were confronted with the transcripts of their interactions and with the text they wrote to prepare for their oral presentation; they had very fleeting memories of the poem and of the work they did.[9]

Fabio, whom the teacher considers a struggling student, finds it hard to recognize "Souvenir de la nuit du 4" among the six poems in the corpus. He recalls that "we had to find stylistic things". Pressed by the investigator to talk about meaning, he says, "There was a murder and at one point in the thing, there is a lady, I don't know who it was, who says that they could have killed her instead". When questioned about the identity of the murderers, he answers that he does not remember. He said that since he did not play the role of editor, he "didn't have much to do, just to copy". He, therefore, did not identify the oral exchanges as an opportunity to elaborate an interpretation.

Solène, ranked as a good student, remembers the title of the poem and the themes suggested by the group, which were "injustice and violence", but thinks that the poem was about a child "writing to his grandmother or something like that". She says, "it wasn't a very happy text", but she does not mention the child's death. She remembers more about the instructions to follow: "we had to follow the order of the text (...) we had to highlight the main ideas in the text". Having played the role of secretary, she recalls the stress of having to finish within the time limit, especially since the group "took a lot of time to organize their ideas". She insists on her efforts to avoid repetition ("I was often told that in my essays, I keep repeating words"), clearly not identifying the writing to be produced as notes for preparation for an oral.

Also considered a good student, Irène conversely speaks quite clearly of her understanding of the text:

> We said to ourselves: "It's not right, the granny is not well, she's crying, and the little boy, he died like that". Because it was really violent, I remember, there were many wounds (...), there was blood on his temple. And that's when we understood that we didn't have to find the rhyming pattern but that we had to go deeper into the story.

She explains that the teacher's intervention reinforced her idea that interpretation should prevail over the description of form: "then I heard the word politics, and there I understood, I understood that it was not only about enjambments!" Yet this does not appear at all in the group's notes for the oral preparation, which only includes a point-by-point, written development following the instructions. The session thus produced very uneven learning results from one member of this group to another, which is confirmed at the class level: only one of the 18 pupils we met went as far as Irène in interpreting the poem on which her group was working.

From a didactic point of view, the work thus carried out does not seem to prepare all the pupils to write an autonomous academic commentary, nor does it train them as autonomous readers capable of relying upon the reading of literary texts to support their personal development.

Conclusion

Our interviewee rightly sees the class dialogue *dispositif* as a possible substitute for the lecture. Like the Easter eggs hidden in the garden, it often rests on the knowledge that the pupils, although active in the search for its elements, apprehend as already constructed and to be assimilated without understanding that the knowledge that really makes them autonomous is the one that helps them solve a problem (Fleury & Fabre, 2005). Is group work the key to pupils' intellectual autonomy? Not necessarily, as we see in this case and in other situations in the global survey we are conducting on this theme.

Ms. Arnoux says she is "less tired" since she started resorting to group work. Her pupils, for their part, unanimously prefer this method. If Akim, for example, had had to do this work on poetry on his own, he would "not have been able to stand it" because he "doesn't like it much". Solen finds it "more fun to work in a group". However, Maxime is more reluctant: "Sometimes I've been in groups where I was only with people I liked, but then, we didn't even read the poetry". This reciprocal approval of the methodology adopted probably ensures a greater commitment to studying that more traditional systems are struggling to achieve today. It can also sustain the educational ideals for preparing the citizens of tomorrow in the very classroom, through respect for others and collaboration. But if the specific role of the school is to help pupils have access to culture by appropriating its works (Bruner, 2008) in order to make them capable, according to the ambition of the Enlightenment (Kant, 1991/1784), to find their way in life through thinking, then downplaying the didactic part of the contract seems harmful.

While one of the pupils in the group analysed in this chapter took advantage of this work to turn it into a springboard enabling her, on the day of the interview, to propose a reading based on the feeling of injustice she had experienced, enriched by the political dimension of which she was beginning to become aware, this was not the case for her classmates. The didactic contract can then become differential (Schubauer-Leoni, 1996; Rochex & Crinon, 2011), whether it amounts to enabling the pupils to carry out an academic text commentary exercise independently or to become independent readers capable of turning the reading of literature into an authentic experience of personal development, as the teacher of our study wishes it to be.

The case study we worked on shows that the intellectual autonomy of pupils is not automatically produced by self-regulated, small-group work. We have tried to explain this by distinguishing between three contracts (i.e., three modes regulating the interactions among participants) which seem to overlap or even to prevent one another from functioning when they should ideally be articulated: the didactic contract allowing for the construction of subject-based knowledge could then contribute to the educational contract favouring the intellectual emancipation of the pupils and, simultaneously, the social contract consisting in making schooling a nice common experience. Training teachers to use these tools for analysing school transactions would, in our opinion, help them to think of the three contracts simultaneously in such a way as to truly train pupils to be autonomous.

Notes

1 This chapter, including the original French citations, was translated by Elisabeth Lamothe.
2 Town centres in France are generally inhabited by middle- to upper-class families; the study site is located in a socially heterogeneous environment.
3 All names are pseudonyms.
4 Aragon, "Strophes pour se souvenir", *Le Roman inachevé*, 1956. Aragon, "Je vous salue ma France", *Le Musée Grévin*, extrait du poème VII, 1943. Eluard, "Courage", *Au rendez-vous allemand*, 1945. Eluard, "Liberté", *Poésie et vérité*, 1942. Hugo, "Souvenir de la nuit du 4", *Les Châtiments*, 1853. Pasternak, "Le prix Nobel", *L'Éclaircie*, 1959.
5 For this certification exercise, "the candidate composes an assignment that presents in an organized manner what he or she has retained from his or her reading and justifies his or her interpretation and personal judgments with precise analyses of the document". MEN, Bulletin officiel spécial n° 7 du 30 juillet 2020. (French Ministry of Education, Special official publication n° 7 dated July 30, 2020).
6 MEN, Bulletin officiel n° 30 du 26-7-2018 (French Ministry of Education, Official publication n° 30 dated July 26, 2018).
7 We find it impossible, when listening to the recording, to identify with certainty the different interlocutors, which is why we do not specify their names.
8 "On pouvait mettre un doigt dans les trous de ses plaies.
Avez-vous vu saigner la mûre dans les haies ?
Son crâne était ouvert comme un bois qui se fend".
"You could put a finger in the holes of his wounds.
Have you seen blackberries bleed in the hedges?
His skull was split open like a splitting wood".
9 We were able to interview only three of the four students who belonged to the group.

References

Bernstein, B. (2007/1975). Classe et pédagogies: Visibles et invisibles. In J. Deauvieau & J.-P. Terrail (Eds.), *Les Sociologies, l'école et la transmission des savoirs* (pp. 85–112). Paris: La Dispute.

Bruner, J. (2008). *L'éducation, entrée dans la culture. Les problèmes de l'école à la lumière de la psychologie culturelle.* Paris: Retz.

Claude, M.-S. (2020). Le commentaire littéraire vu par des élèves et des enseignants: Une progression empêchée? *Repères, 62*, 17–32. https://doi.org/10.4000/reperes.3099

Connac, S. (2009). *Apprendre avec les pédagogies coopératives, démarches et outils pour l'école.* Issy-les-Moulineaux: ESF éditeur.

Cousinet, R. (1968). *L'éducation nouvelle* (3rd éd.). Lausanne: Delachaux et Niestlé.

Durler, H. (2015). *L'autonomie obligatoire. Sociologie du gouvernement de soi.* Rennes: Presses Universitaires de Rennes.

Fleury, B., & Fabre, M. (2005). Psychanalyse de la connaissance et problématisation des pratiques pédagogiques. La longue marche vers le processus "apprendre". *Recherche et formation, 48*, 75–90. https://doi.org/10.3406/refor.2005.2064

Glasman, D. (2016). Préface. In P. Foray (Ed.), *Devenir autonome. Apprendre à se diriger soi-même* (pp. 9–10), Paris: ESF.

Kant, E. (1991/1784). *Réponse à la question: qu'est-ce que les Lumières?* Paris: Garnier-Flammarion.

Lahire, B. (2001). La construction de l'"autonomie" à l'école primaire: Entre savoirs et pouvoirs. *Revue française de pédagogie, 135*, 151–161. https://doi.org/10.3406/rfp.2001.2812

Langlade, G., & Rouxel, A. (Eds.). (2004). *Le sujet lecteur: lecture subjective et enseignement de la littérature.* Rennes: Presses Universitaires de Rennes.

Mazauric, C., Fourtanier, M.-J., & Langlade, G. (Eds.). (2011). *Le texte du lecteur.* Bruxelles: PIE-Peter Lang.

Meirieu, P. (1997). Groupes et apprentissages. *Connexions, 68*(1), 3–29.

Patry, D. (2018). L'autonomie: L'incontournable de toutes les pédagogies actuelles? *Tréma, 50*, 1–17. https://doi.org/10.4000/trema.4237

Périer, P. (2014). Autonomie versus autorité: Idéal éducatif ou nouvelle forme de domination? *Recherches en éducation, 20*, 42–51. https://doi.org/10.4000/ree.8093

Quentel, J.-C. (2014). L'autonomie de l'enfant en question. *Recherches en éducation, 20*, 23–32. https://doi.org/10.4000/ree.8075

Rayou, P. (2000). L'enfant au centre, un lieu commun pédagogiquement correct. In J.-L. Derouet (Ed.), *L'école dans plusieurs mondes* (pp. 245–274). Paris-Bruxelles: INRP-De Boeck.

Rémond, M. (2006). Éclairages des évaluations internationales PIRLS et PISA sur les élèves français. *Revue française de pédagogie, 157*, 71–84. https://doi.org/10.4000/rfp.433

Reuter, Y. (Ed.). (2010). *Dictionnaire des concepts fondamentaux des didactiques.* Bruxelles: De Boeck.

Reverdy, C. (2016). *La coopération entre élèves: des recherches aux pratiques.* Dossier de veille de l'IFÉ, n° 114, Décembre. Lyon: ENS de Lyon. https://www.researchgate.net/publication/311724773_La_cooperation_entre_eleves_des_recherches_aux_pratiques, (02.09.2022).

Rochex, J.-Y., & Crinon, J. (Eds). (2011). *La Construction des inégalités scolaires.* Rennes: Presses Universitaires de Rennes.

Saujat, F. (2010). *Travail, formation et développement des professionnels de l'éducation: Voies de recherche en sciences de l'éducation.* Note de synthèse pour l'Habilitation à Diriger des Recherches. Université Aix-Marseille.

Schubauer-Léoni, M.-L. (1996). Etude du contrat didactique pour des élèves en difficulté en mathématiques. Problématique didactique et/ou psychosociale. In C. Raitsky & M. Caillot (Eds.), *Au-delà des didactiques, le didactique. Débats autour de concepts fédérateurs* (pp. 160–189). Paris, Bruxelles: De Boeck.

Shawky-Milcent, B. (2016). *La lecture, ça ne sert à rien. Usages de la littérature au lycée et partout ailleurs.* Paris: Presses Universitaires de France.

Vincent, G. (Ed.). (1994). *L'Education prisonnière de la forme scolaire? Scolarisation et socialisation dans les sociétés industrielles.* Lyon: Presses Universitaires de Lyon.

Vygotski, L.S. (2018/1931–1934). *La science du développement de l'enfant.* Bern, Bruxelles, Berlin, New York, Oxford, Warszawa, Wien: Peter Lang.

Wagnon, S., & Patry, D. (2019). Le self-government: L'instauration d'un principe fédérateur de l'Éducation nouvelle (1900-1930)? In V. Castagnet & C. Barrera (Eds.), *Décider en éducation. Entre normes institutionnelles et pratiques des acteurs (du XVe siècle à nos jours)* (pp. 139–154). Lille: Presses Universitaires du Septentrion.

9
PRACTICING SOCIAL DISTINCTION WHEN SUPERVISING PUPILS' AUTONOMOUS PROJECTS

Stéphane Vaquero

Since the 2000s, all the pedagogical reforms implemented in the French secondary education system have established a series of pedagogical *dispositifs* around the pupils' timetables and organized them in a manner that makes them mandatory yet distinct from disciplinary courses.[1] Among the main study tracks to be found in French high schools, the "*Travaux Personnels Encadrés*" (supervised personal projects, abbreviated as TPE in the rest of this chapter) are the best-known examples of the situation due no doubt to their longevity (they existed from 2002 to 2020) and because they are, in the eyes of pupils, the "first exam towards the high school diploma". For two hours on a weekly basis, from September to February, pupils work in groups and choose a topic related to current events, their interests, or their hobbies. Their work can take many forms, such as written reports, models, videos, or fine arts projects.

In France, the word *dispositif(s)* is commonly used to refer to such classes; however, it is not clearly defined ("*dispositifs pédagogiques*", "*dispositifs interdisciplinaires*", "*dispositifs par projets*", for example). In its sociological use, a pedagogical *dispositif* is defined by two dimensions, the material and the cognitive. A *dispositif* is first of all a set of rules, a specific organization of school time and space (Foucault, 2001, p. 299; Peeters & Charlier, 1999; Terrail & Collectif, 2005, p. 32); it may apply to specific pedagogical backing or types of teaching aids (here, the use of "logbooks" by the pupils, the possibility to create "something different" rather than a written work; it may be also a defence in front of a jury), something that has the "capacity to vary from usual school system productions", to use the words of Anne Barrère, "by resorting to different groupings, either by the simultaneous intervention of several teachers or external contributors, or by the existence of interdisciplinary actions, or even by following a different temporality" (Barrère, 2013). In its

DOI: 10.4324/9781003379676-12
This chapter has been made available under a CC-BY license.

cognitive dimension, a *dispositif* relies on a relatively specific type of pedagogical discourse, a "grammar that is intrinsic to it" which formalizes the way in which knowledge may be thought about, restituted, recontextualized, and assessed (Bernstein, 2007, pp. 59–73). The TPE-type *dispositifs* include both aspects. The pupils must organize themselves into groups, plan their work ahead, and conduct research to tackle their subject, and the teachers must supervise and guide them, but they must not "teach". Because they are working on "concrete" topics, they must rely on a type of discourse that may be likened to "horizontal discourse" (Bernstein, 2007, p. 227), i.e., both understandable by all, devoid of explicitly mobilized concepts but also reflecting the "everyday" hobbies or preoccupations of pupils. For this reason, we propose to call them "horizontal *dispositifs*".

Although these *dispositifs* are based upon the principle of "work done autonomously" by the pupils (Durler, 2015), the observation of sessions over a long period of time shows that the pupils are far from working alone: there are many informal discussions between pupils and teachers, which are not really perceived as part of the pedagogical relationship. Above all, the link between the frequency and nature of these conversations and the perception of the degree of "autonomy" of the pupils concerned is complex. Are the pupils considered to be autonomous only those who manage to work alone? Conversely, are pupils who work without a teacher's assistance ultimately seen as "autonomous" in their TPE project? To what extent, during these informal conversations, do the teachers "sell out" information (Bourdieu & Passeron, 1964, p. 111) by showing some pupils, rather than others, how to provide "proof of their autonomy" in the context of the TPE? Does it concern the best pupils or those who are most in need of supervision and pedagogical guidance? All those questions raise the issue of the levelling or unequal effects of these *dispositifs*, both in how teachers assess the situation and in the nature of the knowledge derived from such pedagogical relationship. Two structural questions stem from the issue of autonomy in horizontal *dispositifs*. The first is the transformation of knowledge and school discourse induced by this type of pedagogical relationship. Indeed, for the sociologist Basil Bernstein, since the 1960s, these *dispositifs* have marked the transition from education in depth to education in breadth (Bernstein, 1997, p. 160). Secondly, they raise the issue of the power relations and symbolic domination that may result from the uses of this type of discourse in the same way as the forms of power resulting from the mastery of the "social scriptural form" (Lahire, 2021).

The following demonstration is based upon 80 hours of ethnographic observation of weekly TPE sessions involving 272 pupils, as well as a series of comprehensive interviews with 24 teachers who supervised these sessions, and on the production of "ethnographic statistics" that make it possible to position the detailed observations within the social and academic realm. Among them, the academic profile of the pupils is evaluated on the basis of the general grade averages obtained in secondary school (grades 7 and 9, i.e., the first and third years of secondary school, then at the General Certificate of Secondary Education level, or grades 10 and 11). Their social origin is assessed thanks to the numerical coding of the occupations of both parents, resulting in a "parental code" (Cayouette-Remblière & Ichou, 2019). Finally, the TPE productions, as well as the teachers' appreciation, were coded and analysed, using 30 score variables.[2] The database is called, in this chapter, the "base TPE".

Finding a topic, getting together as a group

During the first TPE session in September, the teachers set out the rules for the *dispositif*: the pupils have 18 weeks and a two-hour weekly slot to do research and produce a project on a subject of their choice, related if possible to current events, to their hobbies or their artistic practices. Each group, which is made up of two to four pupils, is supervised by two teachers specialized in the two disciplines involved in the subject. If possible, the project should be based on scientific experiments or on any other research or artistic process.

Cultural affinities in the choice of subjects

From the very first minutes of the first session, pupils must therefore prove their ability to be "autonomous", from the "political" angle as much as from the "expressive" angle (Durler, 2015; Lahire, 2007). They must first demonstrate their ability to organize into work groups, to imagine a "feasible" subject, to plan and anticipate a research methodology, or even a protocol if the project consists of an experiment or works to be analysed. They must also prove that they have enough "imagination" to find a subject that is original, has never been dealt with before, and is therefore likely to "surprise" the jury. Particularly because they are formulated at the very beginning of the school year, these expectations are perceived as pertaining to the "personal" qualities of the pupils, in the form of a "gift" (Bourdieu & Passeron, 1970; Mauger, 2011) that should be encouraged, but which is not related to academic learning.

Observations show that in this context, the pupils who manage to capture the attention (and the time) of teachers are in fact those who manage to mobilize, in an implicit manner, the techniques which come very close to the "social scriptural form" (Lahire, 2021) necessary to present and defend their subject: they talk about it in a detached manner (Bautier & Goigoux, 2004) and even for those who chose the scientific fields, manage to organize their ideas into a narrative, to create a plot, to give an aesthetic form to their subject, in order to articulate current topics and academic notions, even if the links between them are often hazy or merely rhetorical. They rely on their academic and cultural capital to prove that they are "inspired" during those first exchanges and to grab the teachers' attention. The teachers, because they are not obliged to spend an equal amount of time with each group, are more likely to stay with pupils with whom they have things in common, either in the choice of subject or in the adopted approach.

The way in which Garance (whose parents are both secondary school teachers), Alice (father in the military, mother unemployed) and Juliette (father working in health care/social services, mother both a painter and art teacher) engage with their subject and present them shows how they use their social, academic and cultural resources to capture the attention of Évelyne D. (art teacher)[3]:

> As early as September 23, the three pupils who decided to work on TV news broadcasts and the manipulation of images decide to produce a "satirical TV newscast". They did research in the media library, enriching their perspective with cultural references that were both very legitimate (two out of four were contemporary art references) and eclectic (the third was a reference to the movie Matrix). When they explain that they want to "work on the vision of society as presented on television" by combining philosophy and the visual arts, they highlight the artistic references in their logbook and specify that working on visual arts will not be a problem because Juliette's mother is herself a visual arts teacher; Alice dispels any misgiving by saying that her brother makes videos and that he has the necessary skills and equipment to film a fake newscast.
> *(September 29, 2014 observation session)*

Even more so than their ability to work alone or find inspiration, these pupils reveal above all a form of cognitive and cultural complicity (Bonnéry, 2014) with the teachers for whom the articulation between concrete and academic elements is part of the usual cognitive routine (Barrère, 2002). Paradoxically, these pupils who are perceived as "autonomous" find themselves steadfastly supported by conversations with the teachers: as they find the topic interesting, they "begin to play the game" and come up with thoughts, ideas, or references while developing the approach they would adopt if they had to deal with the subject. Since the pupils involved in this type of exchange tend to be the pupils who are most accustomed to writing techniques, they take advantage of these informal exchanges to write down their teachers' ideas as they come so they can appropriate them as if they were their own, which reinforces their image of "autonomous" pupils.

Shifting the focus back onto academic subjects

Conversely, other groups struggle to present a "catchy" topic. Sometimes they wait to find the perfect formula spontaneously (Baudelot, 1965), they write very little in their logbook and say that they have no ideas. Because they anticipate that discussions with these pupils may be fraught with misunderstandings, teachers tend to retreat behind the rule of "independent work" to justify not engaging with them:

> Frank R. (physics teacher) walks by past two pupils slumped over their desks without talking to them. Their pencil cases are in their schoolbags and they have spent the session "doing research" on electronic cigarettes without taking notes.
> The pupils whose ambition is to work on telescopes call on Guillaume O. (math teacher) to approve their topic. He doesn't know what to answer and pouts while looking askance at me, barely concealing the fact that he is not interested in the subject. He ends up answering that it is all right, while he watches the other groups file out of the room.
> Agnes T. (literature teacher) sits down next to Kouassi and Abou to talk with them, but within seconds, she turns around to two other pupils, Joanne and Berenice, who say they want to work on the artistic representations of war. They quickly talk about "a specific work or an artistic school, for example in literature, in painting, or representations of war by the surrealists, in poems and painting for example" and Agnès suggests that they do research on Breton, Guilbeaux and Sauvage. Kouassi and Abou, sitting nearby, are mere spectators of the discussion.

For the teachers, the "struggle" of finding a subject is a real test for the pupils who are considered as "flimsily committed" to their studies; it is a period during which they must prove their "perseverance" and their "commitment" to work without any help. The interviews conducted with these pupils or the perusal of their logbooks show that they do have "ideas", but that the pedagogical framework and the linguistic expectations of the teachers do not provide the adequate conditions for them to formulate their ideas (Labov, 1978). Moreover, the habit of thinking of their hobbies as really "all-out activities" (Barrère, 2011), without observing them from an external or analytical angle has convinced the pupils that they have nothing to say about what they enjoy doing in their leisure time. Thus, Jordan (whose father is a product technician and mother works as a childminder), Sydney (whose mother is unemployed), and Clémence (father in the military, mother unemployed) thought of working on ragga-dancehall, a dance that all three practise before having misgivings as to whether that could be a subject for a TPE project ("We do dance, but this dance is not...it's not classical dance or jazz.... Maybe it's...it's a cultural thing but we don't really know"). By saying that "dancing makes us feel good [...] teachers can't understand", Sydney even underlines the resistance and autonomy of popular and youth cultures that, according to her, cannot and should not be dissolved in school culture.

After three or four sessions marked by "struggle" and above all a lack of pedagogical supervision, these groups end up discussing other matters during the TPE time slot and come across, indeed, as less "committed" to their project. The teachers then resorted to a radical break in the "game" of autonomy and imposed upon them a subject that was often very similar to the school curriculum, the aim being to give them easy access to material (textbooks, internet sites) and thus be able to supervise their progress easily. Thus, after having tried to choose a subject on video games, Sydney, Jordan, and Clémence were "taken in charge" by Monique R. (history and geography teacher), who described these three pupils as an "emergency group". She decided in mid-October "not to let go of them until they gave up the idea of video games for a more feasible subject". In a very authoritarian tone and within five to seven minutes, she steers them towards another subject: starting with video games, she directs them towards the question of violence, then racism and propaganda, and since she considers that the propaganda of the Nazi regime is too complicated to deal with, she suggests that they deal with the Vichy regime propaganda and refers them to the history textbooks.

A heterodox appropriation of the dispositifs *geared at achieving autonomy*

Other pupils engaged in a "heterodox appropriation" (Millet & Thin, 2012) of the TPE sessions in the sense that they wished above all to do research "for themselves", without taking part in the process of explanation and demonstration that was implicitly required of them. They are very involved in the *dispositif* without necessarily perceiving that the aim is above all to put into words their personal reflection or research process, rather than to "really" produce knowledge. Their approach consists in adopting an "ethico-practical" aim and not a secondary or aesthetic aim (Bourdieu, 1980; Lahire, 2021). Such a posture can be found in two cases. Some people wish to defend a point of view that directly affects them in their social life. For example, Jeanne (father employed by local authorities, mother working in rental management) wanted to work on the theme of "work and alienation" because she considered this subject to be "close to her concerns" ("*I talked to my mother about it, frankly she thought it was good. And since we hear about work every evening…*"). Julie (lives alone with a mother who is a painter), who was influenced by her experience in a vocational high school in "fashion" which made her aware of the low wages in the industry, wanted to work on "economic slavery in contemporary societies". Others wish to engage in an experimental approach to obtain "real" answers to their questions. Such is the case of three pupils who are passionate about aeronautics and want to build a rocket or three high-level athletes who want to research the effects of overtraining. This approach could be described as "autonomous" since the pupils themselves find a topic and want to conduct research on it. Simply because no narrative is crafted upon it, it escapes the control of teachers and can be called an "invisible autonomy" in the eyes of the school institution. In the end, either these groups are reorganized, in the same way as groups deemed to have no ideas, or they set themselves aside to conduct their research away from the teachers, for as long as possible, without asking themselves how to eventually present their work.

Socially and academically differentiated postures

Table 9.1 groups together the three aforementioned cases, which we shall call "frequent exchanges centred on ideas", "occasional exchanges centred on control" and "work done 'by oneself'" and enables us to situate them in the social and academic landscape of the 272 pupils observed. Table 9.1 presents the general average of the junior high and high school pupils (out of 20 points), a "social score" allowing us to assess their social origin, the frequency of exchanges with the teachers during the TPE sessions, the frequency with which the pupils mobilized extracurricular resources to propose a project, how linked the subject was to school curricula, how easily they chose the subject, and how "original" or "ordinary" it was according to the teachers.

TABLE 9.1 Socio-academic indicators in relation to pupils' TPE results (n = 272)[1]

	Frequent exchanges with teachers	*Occasional exchanges with teachers*	*Work done by oneself*
Academic performance (average grade) in secondary school (/20 points)	14.1	13.1	13.0
Parents' social score	0.4	0	−0.4
Extracurricular resources mobilized in TPE	0.7	−0.1	−0.1
Link between TPE subject and school curriculum	−0.2	0.2	−0.4
Easy choice of TPE topic	0.5	−0.1	−0.1
Topic often dealt with (−) or rarely dealt with (+)	0.7	−0.1	−0.3

Note for reading the chart: Pupils who exchange frequently with their teachers have an overall average school performance index of 14.1/20 in lower and upper secondary school, while their synthetic index of social origin is the highest of the three pupil categories (0.4).

[1] The synthetic indicators in the table are score variables. The parents' score is based on the occupation of both parents and the other variables (extracurricular resources, topic's choice, originality of topics) are based on an analytic evaluation of the 272 pupils' TPE productions. For each production, each variable was rated on a scale number and these numbers have been transformed as centre-reduced values (zero mean and standard deviation = 1) for easier comparisons between different variables. It explains why the values are near 0. An exception, the performance indicator is composed of the pupils' average results (of 20 points) during the secondary school.

The differences shown in Table 9.1 could be explained by extracurricular reasons, such as the cultural capital (Bourdieu, 1979) acquired at home: pupils who choose the most "original" subjects could be considered to do so because of their cultural practices because they frequently go to cultural or artistic places (Octobre et al., 2010), which enables them to come up with subjects. Conversely, other pupils could be seen as unable to formulate original ideas because they live in families that are culturally "deficient" (Thin, 1998). However, we must steer clear of a "miserabilist" interpretation (Grignon & Passeron, 1989) according to which this alleged lack of ideas or originality would be the result of a cultural or linguistic deficiency among working-class families. On the contrary, the institutional and social frameworks set up by the *dispositif* are responsible for allowing or preventing certain pupils from handling these different types of discourse, either orally or in their productions (Labov, 1978). Autonomy, commitment, or originality are not qualities that are "already there", intrinsic to the pupils, but they are built into the pedagogical exchanges, even the most informal ones, beyond the first sessions aimed at finding a topic.

Work during the sessions

During the following sessions, from November to January, the level and type of pedagogical support greatly depended upon the demonstration of autonomy and commitment that the pupils were able to muster during the first sessions. The conversations are focused either on cognitive tasks or on the control of the work being done and even if the two are not exclusive of each other, this still has an impact on the amount of support given during the research and on the scripting of argumentation, as well as on the style of writing and the degree of elusiveness granted or not to the pupils.

The co-construction of knowledge or control of academic commitment

If pupils have been able to formulate and verbalize "good ideas" and show proof of self-control in planning their work, then teachers consider that it is not necessary to check on them, remind them of deadlines, or control their logbooks. This does not mean, however, that they do not interact with them: on the contrary, they go and see them to remain informed of the progress of their work, or simply out of curiosity. But since they do not feel obliged to control or supervise them, they take advantage of these moments to "play the game" of reflection about subjects that are of interest to them, and without meaning to, they co-construct the reflection and production with the pupils. They often think aloud, give their opinion, and dole out bibliographical references or methodological advice. Such is the case, for example, of Guillaume (math teacher), who is a computer programming enthusiast and who, during each session, spends between 10 and 15 minutes with a group of four pupils who have decided to model the spread of the Ebola virus by creating an algorithm. Such supervision provided to the pupils who are considered to be the most autonomous reinforces their commitment to their work since they not only receive very specific work or reading advice but also know that each week they can discuss the progress of their work with their teachers.

On the other hand, for the groups that failed to come up with an interesting topic, the nature of the conversations is different. Because of the very general topics linked to the school curriculum that they are obliged to deal with (such as the propaganda press under Pétain), their work essentially consists in compiling factual elements from textbooks or internet sites, in order to elaborate their project. However, this does not encourage teachers to "think" with them: they know perfectly well the subjects dealt with since they are part of the school curriculum and consider this work to be "repetitive" and "boring", even though they are the ones who have proposed the subjects for the pupils. In this context, exchanges between pupils and teachers are quite rare, and when they do take place, they focus primarily on checking and verifying the work done, respecting the timetable, the number of pages written in the logbook, and the absence of "cheating" signs or copying and pasting; in short, a whole range of "Taylorian skills" based on respecting procedures (Anderson-Levitt et al., 2017) but which do not make it possible for the cognitive and cultural elements expected in TPE to be explicit. The teachers also provide very little bibliographical information that could be useful to the pupils because they are not interested in the subject and because they consider the documentary research as primarily a "test". There was little encouragement to analyse the texts found by the pupils, who needed to be guided in this work, nor did they explain how to use them or how to discriminate between the types of sources.

The way Pierre F. (history-geography teacher) describes how he reorganized the work of Maxime (father blue-collar worker, mother salesperson) and Tony (father bar manager, mother nurse) illustrates this process. Both pupils were working on the American civil rights movement. Not really knowing what was expected of them, they observed their classmates working on books and manuals, and deduced that the "game" in TPE must consist in dealing with texts, something they did not usually do in class. Thus, they found an article written in English[4] and spent a considerable amount of time painstakingly trying to translate it, without really understanding the purpose of the task. Pierre F., who was already not very enthusiastic about a subject that he considered "repetitive" and "not very original", went to see Maxime and Tony at the beginning of the session and saw them translating the article. He did not give them any indication or tell them that they were wasting their time. It was only three weeks later that, faced with the predictable failure of these two pupils, Pierre F. decided this group was "not making any progress". Besides, the two pupils did not respect the instructions because they were gearing up for a "presentation" that is not valued in the framework of TPE:

> So I see them during the first session all alone: they had only one magazine, in English, and they go about translating it. And there are two of them! And after two hours I ask them "what have you done?" – "Well, we are translating!" After three weeks, we ask them to come around for an interview, we asked them "now you're going to tell us where you are at". They came, without so much as a piece of paper, without a pen. And when they explained to us what they had done, it basically boiled down to: "I/ Martin Luther King, and II/ Malcolm X"! I said, "No, boys, that's a presentation, it's not a problem statement!"
> *(Pierre F., history-geography teacher, November 25, 2013)*

The groups who wish to carry out scientific experiments "for themselves" come up against other material or logistical difficulties, also linked to the weak supervision of TPE projects. Indeed, since it is a "*dispositif* requiring autonomy", teachers consider that it is up to the pupils to define and carry out experiments. However, throughout their schooling, the former have only been faced with scientific experiments scripted for pedagogical purposes (Bonnéry, 2009), without managing the logistical dimension, and in any case, the pedagogical configuration of the TPE sessions does not allow them to engage in such an approach. Indeed, the teachers have to supervise too many groups simultaneously, the lab assistants cannot order all the material necessary to "really" carry out each experiment, and besides, the pupils lack the technical and scientific knowledge necessary to anticipate how the experiment will be carried out and to interpret the results:

> This is the kind of group…it was "we'd like to do this, we'd like you to help with the protocol." They got to the physics lab, they never had anything planned, so they asked the lab assistants to bring them what they needed, and that's it…now we have objective elements to say that they didn't…[…] well, we try to tell them nicely, but they don't listen to the advice we give. For example, we told them to take a cardboard box and try to determine the volume of the object thanks to the waves, which is what happens when you do a pregnancy ultrasound. And they never wanted to do it. So, all they did was pass stuff around [waves] but it was pointless!
> *(Paul G., earth and life science teacher, interview, April 24, 2015)*

The teachers expect, above all, an intellectual approach in planning the experiments and consider that if logistical problems interfere with the research process, it is because of the "lack of autonomy" (organizational side) of the pupils, combined with a "lack of hindsight" (cognitive side) in thinking. More fundamentally, the desire to conduct a "real" experiment betrays the fact that these pupils misunderstand the implicit expectations of TPE projects: they want to put forward a practical mastery of the "concrete" and not a scholastic staging of the "pseudo-concrete" expected within the school environment (Baudelot & Establet, 1971, p. 143).

Are pupils exempted from mastering school knowledge?

The proofs of autonomy given during the first sessions finally determine the level and nature of academic expectations applying to the pupils. Those who were able to formulate a "good" topic at the beginning of the year are presumed, without having to demonstrate it, to be "good" pupils. Comforted by the commitment or originality they showed at the beginning of the year, teachers never ask these pupils to "do research" to prove their mastery of academic knowledge. On the contrary, they come up with bibliographical references considered not as sources of information or constituted knowledge but as literary, artistic, or current affairs material that should be analysed.

This assumption that they have academic mastery is reinforced by the fact that during the TPE sessions, pupils never have to precisely mobilize the knowledge they are supposed to master: since teachers do not expect proof of this, they allow and encourage them to adopt a "non-academic", "personal" writing style, to find their "style":

> Three literary track pupils came up with the idea of writing the love letters that WW1 soldiers with facial injuries send to their wives, at first without talking to their history-geography and literature teachers. With the help of a member of the group's brother, who is a screenwriter, they write these letters and practice acting them out during their TPE hours. At the beginning of the reading, Monique R. (history-geography teacher), Rachel M. (philosophy teacher) and Claudie A. (literature teacher) were very interested in the story. Monique comes and listens very carefully. Monique sits at the table of the three pupils, does not give advice but asks questions. With a certain emphasis, she takes up, verbalizes and validates the process, punctuating the reading with repeated encouragement, "yes, yes, good, very good, that's very good". The other teachers echo this encouragement.
>
> *(Logbook, November 29, 2013, Literary Track pupils)*

These three pupils are allowed to handle a certain type of discourse deemed "expressive," to write those love letters at the same time as that they are allowed to forego conducting historical research on World War I. Even so, the evasive reference to facts suggests that they have a grasp of the historical context even though they are never asked to do so, either during the session or when presenting their work. Similarly, the work of a group of pupils making an animated film depicting a soldier in a pasteboard setting is highly appreciated by their teacher, even though their logbook shows that they did no documentary research:

> So there was a symbiosis between the art work and the story. They came to ask me how to represent the Nazis, so I told them why not represent them simply by the sound of boots, music…they did that with modelling clay. They made the battle of Stalingrad with pieces of cardboard, it was magnificent.
> *(Interview with Monique R., history-geography teacher)*

More generally, these pupils are allowed to interpret and test hypotheses and are never suspected of cheating or not playing the game. Thus, they can easily take up arguments found in the course of their research and extrapolate a few situations to make assertions about reality, even if they remain very approximate. Three science track pupils, for example, rely upon their mastery of narrative skills to draw general conclusions about the physiological conditions that make it possible to have strength when serving a ball at tennis: they simply stage a few photos and radar measurements, combined with elements copied from the internet, but do not provide any proof of causality. This type of discourse is often implicitly normative and relies upon rhetorical and graphic techniques (use of graphs, photos, captions, or comics), suggesting mastery of academic knowledge, without ever proving it. This has an effect on the writing style since with the successive authorizations given to them by the teachers, these pupils who are deemed to be "inspired" and "lively", are also authorized to develop a type of discourse that allows them to "be right" without demonstrating mastery of school knowledge.

Conversely, the pupils judged to be "not so autonomous" at the beginning of the year are required to demonstrate their mastery of academic knowledge. Considering that the spontaneous approach of these pupils is not sufficient to deal with the various materials or concrete topics in TPE, the teachers ask them to do research before being allowed to give an opinion or to demonstrate their "style". Simply in the absence of methodological guidance, this work turns into a vast enterprise of copying generic ideas and factual knowledge, which is nevertheless necessary to produce a minimum of work. The conversations with the teachers hinge again on control and supervision rather than on advice, hindering the possibility for these groups to test themselves in writing that was considered personal ("We're not allowed to copy and paste! We are obliged sometimes to take ideas but we have to rephrase them"). In the end, these groups take responsibility for their own "lack of ideas", "lack of desire", "lack of inspiration", and yield to the idea that their work does not resemble the "great stuff" that their peers are doing, even though in fact they have often done more documented work, and more autonomously so, than the most valued groups.

Table 9.2 presents four variables that make it possible to objectify the effects of these different types of supervision on the final production and the way it is assessed. The pupils with the most supervision in the TPEs, who were also the best pupils and the most socially endowed, were also the ones who most often resorted to humour, pastiche, or parody. They use their logbooks as a means to do work, not as a means for teachers to check if their work was done. But above all, these pupils are clearly judged to be the most "original" (score of 1.2 as opposed to −0.1 or −0.3 for pupils with little supervision or working "by themselves"), and they obtain the best grade by far for their TPE project with an average of 18.3/20, as opposed to 13.5 and 13.4/20, respectively, for the other two student profiles.

The pupils who have the social, academic, and cultural resources to be autonomous during the first sessions benefit, paradoxically, from a framework that enables them to better meet the explicit expectations of the TPEs, to learn to produce the type of discourse expected of them, enabling them to prove

TABLE 9.2 Socio-scholastic indicators and pupils' TPE results (n = 272)[1]

	Frequent exchanges with teachers	Occasional exchanges with teachers	Work done by oneself
Academic performance (average grade) on secondary school (/20 points)	14.1	13.1	13.0
Social score for parents	0.4	0	−0.4
"Style", humour, pastiche, parody	0.9	−0.1	−0.5
Evaluation of "originality" by the teachers	1.2	−0.1	−0.3
Grade received in TPE (/20 points)	18.3	13.5	13.4

Note for reading the chart: Pupils who frequently exchange with their teachers are the ones who most often use humour (0.9), and who are most often valued for their originality (1.2); these pupils obtain an average grade of 18.3/20 in TPE.

[1] The synthetic indicators in the table are score variables. The parents' score is based on the occupation of both parents and the other variables ("style", humour, evaluation of "originality" by teachers) are based on an analytic evaluation of the 272 pupils' TPE productions. For each production, each variable was rated on a scale number and these numbers have been transformed as centre-reduced values (zero mean and standard deviation = 1) for easier comparisons between different variables. It explains why the values are near 0. An exception, the performance indicator is composed of the pupils' average results (of 20 points) during the secondary school.

that they are "different" and "original" in their approach and contents, in addition to obtaining better results.

Conclusion

Thus, in this type of arrangement, the injunction to autonomy paradoxically conceals a socially and academically differentiated supervision by the teachers which is sometimes very strong. The most socially and academically privileged pupils end up being the most strongly supervised ones in the cognitive dimension of the work and thus they learn to be both "committed" to the work and "original" in their productions. Conversely, for pupils who are academically weaker and come from working-class backgrounds, these "*dispositifs* for autonomy" are also *dispositifs* meant for testing academic commitment, at the same time as they are very faintly supervised from the cognitive point of view. This first conclusion supports the research that has shown since the 1960s that implicit pedagogy and the implementation of activities without explicit goals increase social differences in learning and tend to essentialize so-called personal qualities in pupils (Bautier, 2005; Bernstein, 1975; Bonnéry, 2007; Deauvieau, 2009).

However, these systems do not only create differentiation in relation to knowledge or learning that is "already there": they are also places where a whole range of knowledge, ways of formulating ideas, writing and reporting on daily experiences, current events, cultural practices or leisure activities are created, where pupils must be capable of showing curiosity (and arousing that of teachers) in a large number of areas, without, however, providing an "expert" vision on them. However, as we have seen in the course of this study, these rhetorical and scriptural techniques are not "socially weightless": they are forged by the most socially and culturally endowed teachers who use these *dispositifs* to "break the routine" of the lessons and to mobilize and put forward their cultural capital, and by the pupils who also have a high level of cultural, academic and social capital. In this sense, the academic learning produced and transmitted within these *dispositifs* creates social differentiation because of the pedagogical work that is carried out there but also because it transforms knowledge.

Notes

1 This chapter, including the citations from texts and interviews, was translated by Elisabeth Lamothe.
2 The numerical data are centered-reduced, with the exception of the TPE grades and school averages, which are left at 20 points for better readability. This operation consists in transforming each series of values so as to obtain a zero mean and a standard deviation of 1. This process explains the small amplitude of the data but offers the advantage of making it possible to compare variables.
3 All names are pseudonyms.
4 Let us remember that they are francophone pupils.

References

Anderson-Levitt, K., Bonnéry, S., & Fichtner, S. (2017). Introduction du dossier. Les approches dites "par compétences" comme réformes pédagogiques "voyageuses". *Cahiers de la recherche sur l'éducation et les savoirs, 16*, 7–26.
Barrère, A. (2002). *Les enseignants au travail: Routines incertaines.* Paris: L'Harmattan.
Barrère, A. (2011). *L'éducation buissonnière: Quand les adolescents se forment par eux-mêmes.* Paris: Armand Colin.
Barrère, A. (2013). La montée des dispositifs: Un nouvel âge de l'organisation scolaire. *Carrefours de l'éducation, 36*(2), 95–116. https://doi.org/10.3917/cdle.036.0095
Baudelot, C. (1965). La rhétorique étudiante à l'examen. In P. Bourdieu, J.-C. Passeron, & M. de Saint Martin, *Rapport pédagogique et communication* (pp. 71–84), Cahiers du Centre de Sociologie Européenne. Paris/La Haye: Mouton.
Baudelot, C., & Establet, R. (1971). *L'école capitaliste en France.* Paris: François Maspero.
Bautier, É. (2005). Mobilisation de soi, exigences langagières scolaires et processus de différenciation. *Langage et société, 111*(1), 51–71. https://doi.org/10.3917/ls.111.0051
Bautier, É., & Goigoux, R. (2004). Difficultés d'apprentissage, processus de secondarisation et pratiques enseignantes: Une hypothèse relationnelle. *Revue française de pédagogie, 148*(1), 89–100. https://doi.org/10.3406/rfp.2004.3252
Bernstein, B. (1975). *Classes et pédagogies, visibles et invisibles.* Centre pour la recherche et l'innovation dans l'enseignement. Paris: OECD.
Bernstein, B. (1997/1967). Écoles ouvertes, société ouverte? In J.-C. Forquin, *Les sociologues de l'éducation américains et britanniques: Présentation et choix de textes* (pp. 155–164). Paris/Bruxelles: De Boeck Université.
Bernstein, B. (2007). *Pédagogie, contrôle symbolique et identité: Théorie, recherche, critique.* Québec: Presses de l'Université Laval.
Bonnéry, S. (2007). *Comprendre l'échec scolaire: Élèves en difficultés et dispositifs pédagogiques.* Paris: La Dispute.
Bonnéry, S. (2009). Scénarisation des dispositifs pédagogiques et inégalités d'apprentissage. *Revue française de pédagogie, 167*(2), 13–23. https://doi.org/10.4000/rfp.1246
Bonnéry, S. (2014). *De l'étude des inégalités scolaires à celle de la domination scolaire. Pertinence de la dimension méso-sociologique en sociologie de l'école. Vol. II, Note de synthèse* [Habilitation à diriger les recherches]. Paris 8 - Circeft-Escol - EA4384.
Bourdieu, P. (1979). *La distinction: Critique sociale du jugement.* Paris: Les Éditions de Minuit.
Bourdieu, P. (1980). *Le sens pratique.* Paris: Les Éditions de Minuit.
Bourdieu, P., & Passeron, J.-C. (1964). *Les héritiers.* Paris: Les Éditions de Minuit.
Bourdieu, P., & Passeron, J.-C. (1970). *La reproduction: Éléments pour une théorie du système d'enseignement.* Paris: Les Éditions de Minuit.
Cayouette-Remblière, J., & Ichou, M. (2019). Saisir la position sociale des ménages: Une approche par configurations. *Revue française de sociologie, 60*(3), 385–427. https://doi.org/10.3917/rfs.603.0385
Deauvieau, J. (2009). *Enseigner dans le secondaire: Les nouveaux professeurs face aux difficultés du métier.* Paris: La Dispute.
Durler, H. (2015). *L'autonomie obligatoire.* Rennes: Presses Universitaires de Rennes.
Foucault, M. (2001). *Dits et Écrits, tome 2: 1976–1988.* Paris: Gallimard.

Grignon, C., & Passeron, J.-C. (1989). *Le Savant et le populaire. Misérabilisme et populisme en sociologie et en littérature*. Paris: Seuil.

Labov, W. (1978). *Le parler ordinaire: La langue dans les ghettos noirs des États-Unis*. Paris: Les Éditions de Minuit.

Lahire, B. (2007). Fabriquer un type d'homme "autonome": Analyse des dispositifs scolaires. In B. Lahire, *L'esprit sociologique* (pp. 322–347). Paris: La Découverte.

Lahire, B. (2021). *Culture écrite et inégalités scolaires. Sociologie de l'"échec scolaire" à l'école primaire*. Lyon: Presses Universitaires de Lyon.

Mauger, G. (2011). Sur "l'idéologie du don". *Savoir/Agir*, *17*, 33–43. https://doi.org/10.3917/sava.017.0033

Millet, M., & Thin, D. (2012). *Ruptures scolaires: L'école à l'épreuve de la question sociale*. Paris: Presses Universitaires de France.

Octobre, S., Détrez, C., Mercklé, P., & Berthomier, N. (2010). *L'enfance des loisirs. Trajectoires communes et parcours individuels de la fin de l'enfance à la grande adolescence*. Paris: La Documentation Française.

Peeters, H., & Charlier, P. (1999). Contributions à une théorie du dispositif. *Hermès, La Revue*, *25*(3), 15–23. https://doi.org/10.4267/2042/14969

Terrail, J.-P., & Collectif (2005). *L'École en France: Crise, pratiques, perspectives*. Paris: La Dispute.

Thin, D. (1998). *Quartiers populaires—L'école et les familles*. Lyon: Presses Universitaires de Lyon.

SECTION III
Autonomy concerns in the context of educational reforms
Inclusion and digitalization

10

INSIDE THE "COCOON" OF SPECIAL EDUCATION CLASSES. WHEN AUTONOMY SERVES AS A GOLD STANDARD FOR REORIENTING PUPILS

Laurent Bovey

Transforming schools in order to make them more inclusive is now on the agenda of most educational systems (UNESCO, 2016).[1] Such a situation obtains in the Canton of Vaud in Switzerland, which is currently undergoing a so-called inclusive reform of its education system by encouraging schools to close special education classes and to include and retain as many pupils as possible in regular classes (DFJC, 2019). This reform involves a reorganization of the *dispositifs* made available to students designated as having special educational needs and thus impacts their schooling. The aforementioned reform also changes the work of special education teachers, who are expected to devote more time to the detection of learning difficulties and to the selection of pupils. My doctoral work (Bovey, 2022) seeks to demonstrate that in order to be reintegrated into a regular classroom, special education pupils have to meet certain academic criteria, but above all, they must prove that they master soft skills such as patience, emotional control, and autonomy. This research focuses on the selection process resorted to by special education teachers to decide which students may go back to a regular classroom and which ones should remain in special education classes or schools. This chapter is specifically dedicated to showing how autonomy is used as a standard and a selection criterion.

This paper is divided into five sections. The first section presents the context of the Vaud canton and the organization of schooling for pupils designated as having special education needs. The second section tackles the theoretical framework and the research methodology this chapter is based on. The third section focuses on the "cocoon" image associated with special education classes among most school actors. These classes are said to allow pupils to work without pressure, to learn better in smaller groups, and to be spared the hardships of academic competition. I will show that since the implementation of the so-called inclusive school reform, the *dispositifs* associated with special education are far from being cocoons, but actually make the pupils face the challenge of selection again. The term "*dispositif*" used in this chapter is meant to include all places or forms of support sharing the common characteristic of having "a capacity to inflect the usual school norm characterized by the simultaneous presence of schoolchildren and of a teacher in the given space of the classroom" (Barrère, 2013, p. 100). The *dispositifs* offer an "alternative" to the usual functioning of the school, by allowing for changes in traditional teaching practices (Kherroubi, 2004) and modifying the teacher's tasks (Cauterman & Daunay, 2010). Using the example of Sylvain, a pupil who was being considered for placement in a more competitive class, the fourth section discusses the work of preparation done by special education teachers to enable pupils to return to a regular classroom. The pupils' autonomy proves to be an essential criterion used to assess whether or not they may be reintegrated and forms the basis of the "work of self-transformation" (Darmon, 2016; our translation) which is required of them. The fifth section presents the case of Esmeralda, a pupil bound for a future career in special education, who attempted to defeat the educational prognosis by refusing the school's authority, so as to undertake vocational training of her own choosing. I shall provide an analysis of the education system's negative reactions to what could be considered a demonstration of autonomy. Finally, my conclusion will return to the double statutory constraint to which schoolchildren in special education are now subjected and to the hold that such arrangements have on the most vulnerable pupils and young people.

Context: the school system in the Vaud canton

In spite of the agreement signed in 2007 by its 26 cantons to align educational practices, the Swiss federalist system entails cantonal sovereignty over such issues. Differences in curricula, disparities in the vocabulary resorted to, and the manner of counting special education pupils make it difficult to interpret statistics and complicate comparisons between cantons. The choice of the context of the Canton of Vaud[2] makes for an interesting field of research because it is characterized by a separative and selective[3] heritage on the one hand and by the wish to set up an inclusive school system on the other hand, notably through a reform reorganizing the special education system (DFJC, 2019). The Vaud school system thus finds itself at the heart of schooling and guidance issues for the children designated by the institution as having special educational needs. Each school (they total 93 throughout the canton) enjoys some leeway to function and manage its budget, and it may set up its own support and tutoring system for schoolchildren designated as having special educational needs.

In Vaud, schooling is compulsory for 11 years, from the first year of primary school to the 11th year (marking the end of secondary school). At the end of grade 8, students are selected and assigned to one of two tracks depending on their grade point average: the pre-"Gymnase" track[4] (VP) welcomes the best pupils on the academic level. These students will then be able to study for the *maturité* certificate and then move on to tertiary level studies (university, higher education); the general track (VG) welcomes pupils slated to attend general or business schools or to begin vocational training (called "apprenticeship"[5]). In addition to the regular school system, there are many special educational *dispositifs*: special classes which are administratively linked to schools but where pupils are physically separated, or special schools that take in schoolchildren "whose condition requires special training, particularly because of an illness or a mental, psychic, physical, sensory or instrumental disability".[6] There are also many *dispositifs* in place to support pupils within the regular schooling system: "interstitial" *dispositifs* (referring to establishments meant to host schoolchildren on an ad hoc basis for certain subjects) or tutoring *dispositifs* set up in the classroom by special education teachers or integration assistants. Figure 10.1 shows the statistics for pupils placed in a special education programme at the start of the 2019–2020 school year.

Following the international incentive to promote an inclusive education system (Armstrong et al., 2016), the Canton of Vaud, like other regions of the world, has changed the mode of operation of its school system. By virtue of the laws and commitments of the canton, integrative solutions are privileged over separative situations. In fact, in recent years, a large number of special

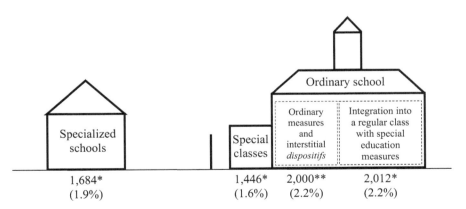

FIGURE 10.1 Percentage of pupils according to the special education system at the start of the 2019–2020 school year (Canton of Vaud – Switzerland).

* Official data from the Department of Education of the Canton de Vaud.
** Estimates based on questionnaires sent to school principals.

education classes have been closed or reorganized to allow as many pupils as possible to return to a regular class with special help.

Theoretical framework and methodology

This chapter is based upon the doctoral research I conducted between 2018 and 2020 amongst special education teachers and schoolchildren in the Canton of Vaud. Adopting an ethnographic approach, I conducted observation sessions and "informal interviews" (Skinner, 2012) over a period of two years in different special education environments (special education classes, special education schools, integration into regular classes, etc.). The objective was to understand how, under the effect of inclusive policies, special education *dispositifs* impacted the pupils' schooling and reconfigured the professional realm of special education. In addition to those observation sessions, a questionnaire was sent to school principals to identify the measures put in place in the canton; besides, semi-structured interviews with parents, school principals, and special education officials were conducted.

The analysis of this material is based upon the sociology of special education (Tomlinson, 2012) and the sociology of school *dispositifs* targeting the assessment of "organizational in-betweenness" and "institutional fragmentation" (Barrère, 2013, 2014) manifested by the existence of those *dispositifs*. From an interactionist perspective, my work accounts for the different turning points along the pupils' "moral careers" (Goffman, 1963) by seeking to understand what strategies they mobilize to keep their place and how they experience separation or reintegration. How do pupils understand these transitions? What status changes do schoolchildren experience during their schooling? How do they handle these different statuses (i.e., being a pupil from a special education class and being a "normal" pupil)? What leverage, if any, do they enjoy?

My dissertation also analyses the influence of *dispositifs* on the work of special education teachers and the reshuffling undergone by the profession in recent years: what effects do these *dispositifs* have on interprofessional collaboration? What tasks do special education teachers perform? The analysis of my observations led me to focus on how teachers "shape" their teaching strategies to help pupils and to create a positive "atmosphere" I chose to call a "cocoon", that is to say, a special and separate space supposed to protect pupils from academic competition.

From the cocoon to getting back to work

The recent reforms of the Vaud school system aiming at a more inclusive education have changed the landscape of the existing educational *dispositifs*, particularly by accelerating the closing of the special education classes that are still in operation. Those classes have a bad reputation; they are perceived by the pupils, the teachers, and the public as "ghettos" (Oberholzer, 2005) bringing together in one place all the schoolchildren considered to have behavioural or academic problems. The pupils who attend these classes hardly ever reach graduation and are less likely to begin vocational training later on (Eckhart et al., 2011). Paradoxically, special classes are also viewed by teachers and principals as "cocoons" that protect pupils from academic competition and stigmatization. The idea that special classes constitute a protective bubble was and still is widely held by the actors of the field (teachers, specialists, school boards). Thanks to those classes and their limited number of pupils, specialized teachers find the space and time to provide guidance and support to pupils whom they consider to be "mistreated" by the school system, to respect their learning rhythm, to remotivate them, and to restore their self-esteem and self-confidence (Pelgrims, 2003). In all the *dispositifs* I encountered, guidance and individualized tutoring make up an important part of the activity carried out by special education teachers. In my fieldwork, the *care* involved in the work (Tronto, 1998) manifests itself through the significant amount of time devoted to informal discussions about the children's school experience and private life, and also through linguistic and physical proximity. Special education teachers, for example, touch pupils more than their colleagues do in regular schools, thus overlooking the rules of professional "distance" and disregarding the potential accusations of sexual abuse that have plagued the education profession in recent years (Herman, 2007).

The twofold goal of separating pupils to protect them (the cocoon principle) and maintaining the competitiveness of mainstream classrooms (the separation principle) has been used in many countries to legitimize the implementation of structural differentiation, for much of the 20th century (Winzer, 2009). Following the introduction of inclusive policies in the 2000s, some of the special education classes were transformed into interstitial education *dispositifs* (see Figure 10.1) characterized by a time limit placed on how long pupils may attend these classes (one or two years) to prevent them from being sidelined. Such arrangements are more "porous" in that they allow students to study certain subjects in regular classes in order to facilitate their eventual reintegration. In short, special classes are no longer seen as alternative schooling arrangements in which pupils can spend their entire school years but are designed to serve more as temporary "airlocks" in which pupils await a new placement. These changes, therefore, have a significant impact on the school career of the students. Other special education classes have closed, and children have been reintegrated into regular classes with specialized tutoring.

These changes also have an impact on the way special education teachers support pupils. In addition to the fact that some teachers now work in regular classrooms (with the associated challenges of integration, negotiation, and collaboration) or in more flexible settings, the teachers' work has changed. A large part of the activity of special education teachers is now devoted to the selection of pupils: since reintegration is conditional, it is their responsibility to determine who can go back to a regular class and who must enrol in a special education school. Using the information contained in the pupils' "file" (assessments, diagnoses, observations, grades), the special education teachers select the most promising pupils and prepare them, making sure they have a chance to succeed in their temporary placement[7] in a regular class and eventually stay in it. Far from being a cocoon separate from the norms that apply to the regular classroom, special education *dispositifs* now "test" (Martuccelli, 2006) students by submitting them again to the academic competition from which they had been removed a few months or years earlier.

The case of Sylvain: A facade of autonomy

Special education teachers are responsible for preparing pupils to return to the regular classroom. We shall now turn to this work of preparation. It is indeed possible to understand, through the way in which teachers prepare, drill, coach, and lecture pupils, the stakes that the regular classroom represents for special education teachers. Their concern is to make sure that the students they send to a regular classroom on a try-out period are able to cope and manage on their own. Their reputation is at stake. Special education teachers thus put the pupils back to work and set up new goals for them to succeed in the placement. These "takeovers" (Durler, 2015) interestingly reveal that the expectations of the regular classroom become the norm, including for pupils who have been separated from it and who supposedly should not be subjected to it. In this way, interstitial arrangements constitute a test for pupils who must (once again) prove, at the risk of failing, that they possess the personal "qualities" necessary to attend a regular class. Among the skills worked on and assessed by teachers, we find classic academic skills such as mastering the multiplication tables in mathematics or the basics of conjugation in French. Other behavioural skills are worked on such as the ability to remain calm and to keep silent for a given period of time or to muster persistence when faced with a task. Among these skills, demonstrating that one is capable of carrying out school tasks alone is an important criterion taking up much importance in the teachers' discourse. Autonomy is a central assessment criterion, a "gold standard" to decide of a pupil's new orientation. In several of the classes I observed in the course of my research, the special education teachers sought to develop their pupils' autonomy, a skill most often defined as being able to carry out a required task alone but also being able to "control oneself" on behavioural and emotional levels. Interstitial *dispositif* teachers often reorganize the space and the syllabus to have pupils study in workshops during which they can complete worksheets or activities on their own (the solutions or answers are freely available). A large number of games to be played independently are available in these classrooms. In many of them, there are also devices designed to manage emotions or behaviour, all geared to making students more responsible and helping them gain self-control. The wish to develop student autonomy can also be traced in the teachers' discourse. The example that follows is taken from an observation made in a special education class numbering eight pupils experiencing significant academic difficulties (they were described to me by their teacher as suffering either from a language disorder, a personality disorder, or a developmental delay). The pupils were enrolled for a maximum of two years before being redirected to other pedagogical services. One student, Sylvain,[8] had reached the end of the two-year term in this class and had just learned that he was eligible for a try-out period in another special class with a higher level. This try-out, and the prospect of reintegration into a regular class the following school year, changed the way the teacher talked to him, essentially when it came to the topic of his behaviour in class. The comparison established by the teacher between Sylvain and his peers sheds light on what is expected of students bound for a more integrative system.

> The special needs teacher, Ms. Wicht, indicates that she is more or less tolerant with the students. By way of comparison, she shows me another student, Celil, and explains to me: "He is hyperactive and cannot control himself, it is a miracle that he should stay put now, in a moment he might be crawling on the floor. I can't punish Cecil like him all the time because he has no self-control whereas I have to be much more demanding with Sylvain because he's going on a try-out placement in another class soon".
> *(Excerpt from field diary)*

The fact that the teacher adjusts her level of tolerance depending on which student is involved is not an isolated phenomenon. The comparison between Sylvain and Celil is interesting. According to the teacher, Sylvain can (and should) control himself (and is therefore punishable), while Celil cannot. This type of distinction is comparable to what can be observed in other fields, and in particular in socio-educational institutions catering to people with intellectual disabilities. The staff distinguishes between residents who "control" their gestures and those who make inappropriate or violent gestures because of their disability. As far as the latter are concerned, professionals take it upon themselves to hold the disability responsible for their actions. By contrast, residents who are deemed to be responsible for their actions are morally condemned and punished (Bovey & Kuehni, 2019).

On several occasions during the time I spent observing the class, the teacher would rebuke Sylvain for his behaviour: "Sylvain, stop chattering, I can assure you that it won't be tolerated in the other class". The remarks also applied to learning: "Sylvain, you have to work alone and concentrate, it's important when you're over there". These remarks sound much like what Héloïse Durler (2015, p. 89) calls "lectures" or "takeovers" by teachers. While these lectures are meant to signify to the pupil that there are differences in expectations and levels between the two classes, they also denote a concern that the pupil may not be well prepared or adequate during their try-out period, a tell-tale sign that the teacher prepared her pupils poorly. For Ms. Wicht, the challenge is also to demonstrate to sceptical teachers at her school that the reintegration of her pupils is possible. The teacher devised a specific emergency programme for Sylvain: games which, according to her, make it possible to work on autonomy skills and more difficult math exercises. The objective is that he should be able to manage on his own when he is on placement so as not to overburden the teacher hosting him, the risk being that the latter, feeling overburdened by Sylvain's presence, might give negative feedback on the placement and refuse to keep him in his class. It is therefore necessary to make sure that Sylvain will be as discreet as possible. During my fieldwork, several teachers mentioned the fact that moral skills and behaviour are more important than the pupil's academic level.[9] Ms. Wicht is less concerned about his academic performance than about his attitude in class: "He takes off other children's hats, puts pencils in the hood of their coats, touches the bottom of his classmates". The teacher was worried that Sylvain would stand out.

Thanks to the observation of Sylvain's situation and to other similar situations analysed during my fieldwork, it is possible to make several remarks.

First of all, it should be noted that the deficiencies and weaknesses which had been identified in the pupils' learning abilities earlier in their schooling (lack of autonomy, concentration problems, etc.) and that had tipped the scales in favour of placement in special education structures[10] were resorted to again by the teachers[11] as assessment criteria to identify potential "candidates" for reintegration into a regular class. In these situations, "student autonomy is both an objective and a demand, the problem often arising from the inversion of this temporality" (Maulini & Erceylan, 2020, p. 2). When it is thus prescribed and worked on in an urgent manner by special education teachers, autonomy serves more as an evaluation tool for selection than as a learning objective.

Secondly, autonomy is reduced to its narrowest definition here: it amounts to ensuring that students remain quiet and do not demand that teachers pay attention to them. The goal is to "fit in" during the try-out period without disturbing anyone. The teachers accept pupils who face challenges, but above all they want them to be "quiet". This figure of the "ideal client" (Becker, 1952) raises questions about how to support reintegrated pupils, what teachers expect of them, and the "ghost" role they would like them to play. The autonomy demanded of pupils serves only short-term interests, amounting to a facade of autonomy that seems very far removed from the objectives of freedom of action and emancipation that a more global autonomy or the development of social and political skills (or *agency*) would ensure. We see that the work involved to develop student autonomy is meant to fulfil the objective of maintaining school order through mechanisms labelled "work on the self" (Giuliani, 2020).

Despite the school's inclusive intentions, we observe that the teachers seek above all to transform pupils so that they can adapt and strive in a reintegration situation, not to transform the environment (which is the cornerstone of the inclusive school system, cf. Armstrong et al., 2016) to allow for the inclusion of students who do not correspond to school norms. It is therefore (always) up to the students to adapt in order to meet the standards of the regular class. The work involved to prepare the students can be read as "make-up" work. Because they are drilled to keep quiet, then the conception of autonomy here appears to be superficial and akin to the fabrication of a "sham" pupil meant to hide their true "nature" or identity. This "fraud" gives the impression that the special education teachers are concealing the true nature of their pupils, as one would conceal the origin of a stolen car. The ability to put on this facade is said to be a way for special education teachers to get their pupils across the line separating the special education classroom from the regular one and to ensure that the regular teachers they send their pupils to on placement do not spot the "deception" entailed. During another field research, a special education teacher talked about the relief she felt when the regular teacher assessed the placement of one of her pupils (described as hyperactive and unpredictable); she expressed her surprise, saying that "one couldn't tell he was a special education student". Boundary crossing had been successful.

Is it possible for pupils to escape this selection process? Do they enjoy any leeway? The following field diary excerpt partly answers these questions based on the situation of one pupil, Esmeralda, who tried to outsmart the school prognosis and "go it alone".

The example of Esmeralda: The irony of autonomy

> I meet Esmeralda in October 2019; she attends a "lieu Ressource" (dispositif in which students, alone or in pairs, leave the regular classroom to attend French or math classes with a special education teacher). She tells me about her background. Esmeralda was born in Portugal and arrived in Switzerland at the age of nine, without speaking any French. She went to intensive French classes for the first two years, but then difficulties in oral comprehension were detected. Esmeralda attended speech therapy for one year (when in 7th grade). Due to her academic difficulties and poor grades, she received specialized tutoring from the 9th grade onward. She tells me that it was complicated for her parents to accept the assistance of a special education teacher, "they wanted me to be normal". After high school, she would like to be a hairdresser (she was convinced by a traineeship at a hairdresser's) but would rather become a medical assistant.
>
> At recess, her special education teacher, Ms. Chappuis, completes her profile with more information. According to the education department official who "panicked" when she saw Esmeralda's report card (according

to her file, she suffers from a "massive" language disorder also called dysphasia), she should have been referred to a special institution or received 100% specialized teaching. Ms. Chappuis insisted that she remain in the regular classroom with tutoring. As there was no room in the institution anyway, she was placed on the waiting list. A game of "ping-pong" to establish a diagnosis ensued between the psychologists and the speech therapists; they lost a great deal of time trying to detect her language "disorders". With this in mind, the teacher requested that the school grant her an extension to give her a chance to catch up. According to everyone at the school (teachers, administration, school counsellor), Esmeralda will continue her post-compulsory education in transitional dispositifs for young people with difficulties, such as supervised training in sheltered workshops. At school, all are thus waiting for her to finish her education. However, Esmeralda would like to be a medical assistant (this, according to her teacher, makes the teachers and the guidance counselor smile, because "no one would bet anything on her").

In the spring of 2020, Ms. Chappuis contacted me again and told me that Esmeralda, without telling anyone, was likely to have landed an apprenticeship as a pharmacy assistant. During a traineeship there, the pharmacist found that she understood things and learned very quickly. On the manager's advice, she contacted the vocational officer[12] about her problems at school and her poor results. The commissioner told her that they would arrange to get funding from the disability insurance company so that she could complete her training.

(Excerpt from field diary)

Due to the school's passivity and defeatist discourse, Esmeralda adopted a strategy of reappropriation of her life (Goffman, 1968) by ignoring the school's predictions that she was slated to fail. By doing so, she showed that she no longer expected anything from school and that she could manage on her own. This type of strategy (using one's network, taking personal steps, asking for help) is more common in families endowed with more cultural capital (Ruiz & Goastellec, 2016) and is less common among pupils who find themselves at the end of their schooling stint in special education. According to Ms. Chappuis, the teachers, deans, and specialists were all surprised to learn that Esmeralda had taken those steps on her own. When the dean learned of Esmeralda's training plans, she smiled and told Ms. Chappuis that she would be no more than "a nice green plant in the pharmacy".[13] The surprise of the school protagonists was due to the pupil's supposedly poor cognitive and organizational abilities (she was diagnosed with massive dysphasia and doomed to remain in a specialized institution), and also caused by questions of legitimacy and by the daring that the pupil had demonstrated in asking by herself, without the school's approval, for support from various authorities (disability insurance, vocational officer) and for applying in a company (the pharmacy) which was not previously known to her. In this way, she thwarted all predictions about her (Delay, 2020): a girl of foreign origin, from a working-class family and in a special education *dispositif* does not take such initiatives.

The surprise (and cynicism) of the school protagonists in the face of Esmeralda's endeavour are interesting. The reaction betrays a certain paradox on the part of the school in its propensity to assess (and sanction) students on the criterion of autonomy, to make it a central reference in the education of students, as well as a sign of deviance (see Merl in this book) and at the same time to find surprising and even illegitimate the very actions revealing the qualities that the school expects from its students: responsibility, resilience, tenacity, maturity, projection into the future, motivation and a great deal of autonomy.

In the end, Esmeralda's "heroic" commitment did not have a positive outcome. I met her again a few weeks later. She told me that a few days before signing the apprenticeship contract, her employers (in the pharmacy) feared that she would not pass the theoretical courses and fail her first year. She then enrolled in a transitional *dispositif* meant to ease her into the professional world. In view of her "school record" (Payet, 1995), she was placed in a special class where special education teachers reinforced her basic skills and where vocational counsellors helped her find an apprenticeship and coached her to draw up a "realistic" career plan (Delay, 2020).

In the light of Esmeralda's situation, it seems difficult for students to escape the grip and control exercised by the school institution through such mechanisms. This story reveals institutional procedures that may be described as insidious, straddling both a "tragic" and "ironic" side, so much so that "the education deployed by public institutions would continue to rhyme with domination" (Laforgue, 2019).

Conclusion: School control and the dual constraint of special education

This chapter highlights the effects that an inclusive school reform may have on special education pupils when it comes to reintegrating them into mainstream schooling. Such reintegration is not a given; it is conditioned by the acquisition of academic skills and, above all, behavioural ones. The status of these students reveals a double constraint: they have, because of their diagnosis and their school career, the status of "handicapped" pupil with its attendant social stigmas, and at the same time, they are forced to play the role of normal pupils by being subjected to the norms of the ordinary class. This situation constitutes a twofold challenge for special education students, as was the case for Sylvain and Esmeralda.

This new phenomenon consisting in selecting pupils in special education environments involves the formal or informal setting up of objectives to determine who can study in a regular class and who cannot. This selection system highlights an important paradox: while the school seeks to make students autonomous, it is not ready to "let go" of them. We have seen with the story of Esmeralda that the school is not prepared to deal with a special education student going it alone and taking responsibility for her own destiny. Her demonstration of autonomy was considered to be illegitimate by the school institution. In recent years, the introduction of tutoring strategies and tools for monitoring pupils (such as case management or individual coaching) has largely permeated school policies. Although this support strategy allows political authorities to leave no young person without a solution – an honourable policy if ever there was one – it has become very difficult for children and young people to forgo the monitoring of their decisions. There are many other ways for young people and families to do things independently from institutions and to bypass school policies. Some parents endowed with a certain amount of social and financial capital decide to take their children out of regular schools and put them in private schools.[14] Other families mobilize their "network" of acquaintances to find alternative paths to professional training, and still others decide to return to their country of origin in the face of academic failure and the narrowing down of possibilities.

We saw in Sylvain's situation that although the required autonomy could be qualified as a "facade", it appeared to be a determining and normative criterion for the continuation of his school career. We also saw in Esmeralda's situation that the injunctions to autonomy were paradoxically counterbalanced by a permanent control and monitoring of the students and young people that can be described as the "hold" of the systems and institutions. This control over individuals – which goes beyond the perimeter of the school – led some sociologists to use the term "total institution" used by Erving Goffman (1961) to highlight the restriction of freedom and the hold that institutions exercise over individuals. Such is the case, for example, of sociologist Hugo Dupont (2021) who noted a recent reconfiguration in the way children and young people with disabilities are supported by institutions. He proposes the term "total support" to qualify a

> new institutional form that has managed to preserve its normative ambition. The word "support" allows us to acknowledge the change in institutional form by taking into account the fact that social concern for vulnerable people has led to individualized support, along with a form of horizontalization due to the breakdown of the services dedicated to them.
>
> *(p. 190)*

Thus, the following observation is increasingly valid: the most vulnerable pupils and young people on the academic and social level are sooner or later reclaimed by the institutions through new coaching *dispositifs* (Oller, 2020) or professional and social integration *dispositifs* in which special education teachers, social workers, and coaches "(re)teach" them to develop a realistic life project and to take responsibility for their own lives: their autonomy is in safe custody.

Notes

1 This chapter, including the original citations in French, was translated by Elisabeth Lamothe.
2 The canton of Vaud is a French-speaking canton with 90,582 students at the start of the 2019–2020 school year for a general population of 815,300. Both in terms of size and number of inhabitants, the Canton of Vaud is one of the largest in Switzerland.
3 The Canton of Vaud has long been amongst those practicing early student selection into separate study tracks (in 2000, 6% of the pupils were enrolled in a special class or institution). It also practices early selection at the age of 11–12 by directing students into separate study courses at the beginning of compulsory secondary school.
4 Gymnase corresponds to the upper secondary school level (15–18 years old). It is the equivalent of the Lycée in France, the American High School or the end of the Secondary School in the UK.
5 In Switzerland, a large proportion of young people (nearly two-thirds) enrol in a vocational training program called "*apprentissage*" (apprenticeship) after completing compulsory school. Apprentices are employed for two or three years by a private company or institution and are trained by apprenticeship instructors while taking classes at a vocational school.
6 https://www.vd.ch/themes/formation/pedagogie-specialisee/institutions-et-ecoles-specialisees/.
7 The schoolchildren who are being considered for placement in a regular classroom usually spend a week or two in a class where there is a place for them and, if possible, where the teacher is willing to have them and is supportive (special education teachers often keep an informal list of classes where they can place students and where they cannot). At the end of the stint, the host teacher produces his assessment of the experience and gives prior notice as to whether or not the student should be reintegrated.
8 All names are pseudonyms.
9 French sociologist Hugo Dupont (2021) observed the same phenomena when conducting research and noted the existence of similar selection criteria: "Behavior, concentration, autonomy and sociability are scrutinized and become the criteria used to assess the legitimacy of the pupil's presence in class, […] with academic level ranking second only" (p. 134).
10 These orientation criteria are described in the literature, e.g., Gremion-Bucher, 2012.
11 In the case of some hyperactive pupils, medication becomes a crucial issue in order to avoid crisis situations or excitement, especially during the placement. On two occasions in my fieldwork, special education teachers called the parents of pupils diagnosed with ADHD (attention deficit hyperactivity disorder) to ensure that they would take their medication before and during the placement.
12 For each training period, there is a professional commissioner (a professional in the trade) responsible for monitoring the training given to apprentices and the working conditions in the companies.
13 The dean made a pun on two French expressions based on the word "plant". She refers to Esmeralda as both a "belle plante", i.e., a beautiful girl, and a "plante verte" (green plant), which is another French expression referring to an idle, useless person who is at most a decorative "item". Special education students are sometimes referred to in this way. For example, in one school I visited during my research, a special class was informally referred to by the teachers as "la classe des plantes vertes" (the class for green plants) or "la classe des légumes" (the class for vegetables) in reference to the students' presumed low intellectual potential.

14 The Canton of Vaud is characterized by the high rate of students enrolled in private schools (7.7% for the canton of Vaud in 2020 compared to an average of 4.6% for Switzerland at large). Such numbers are conditioned by the existence of a significant number of international schools and private boarding schools. Nevertheless, the rate of enrolment in private schools remains relatively marginal compared to other countries (for example, the European Union average is 15%).

References

Armstrong, F., Armstrong, D. & Barton, L. (2016). *Inclusive education: Policy, contexts and comparative perspectives*. London: Routledge.

Barrère, A. (2013). La montée des dispositifs: Un nouvel âge de l'organisation scolaire. *Carrefours de l'éducation*, 36(2), 95–116. https://doi.org/10.3917/cdle.036.0095

Barrère, A. (2014). *Des dispositifs pour raccrocher à l'école: Enjeux, promesses, ambivalences…?* Conférence à la Haute école pédagogique du canton de Vaud. https://vimeo.com/137939007

Becker, H. (1952). Social-class variations in the teacher-pupil relationship. *Journal of Educational Sociology*, 25(8), 451–465. https://www.jstor.org/stable/2263957

Bovey, L. (2022). *Aux marges de l'école inclusive. Une étude ethnographique des reconfigurations du rôle des enseignantes spécialisées et des carrières d'élèves dans les dispositifs de l'enseignement spécialisé vaudois (On the margins of the inclusive school. Students' careers and the teaching profession in the separation and reintegration systems of the canton of Vaud special education system)* [Thèse de doctorat, Université de Genève]. Geneva. https://archive-ouverte.unige.ch/unige:163152

Bovey, L. & Kuehni, M. (2019). Corps-à-corps dans le travail éducatif auprès des personnes en situation de handicap avec déficience intellectuelle. *La Nouvelle Revue du Travail* [en ligne], 14. https://doi.org/10.4000/nrt.4781

Cauterman, M. & Daunay, B. (2010). La jungle des dispositifs. *Recherches. Revue de didactique et de pédagogie du français*, 52, 9–23. https://revue-recherches.fr/wp-content/uploads/2014/06/009-023-Cauterman-Daunay.pdf

Delay, C. (2020). L'apprentissage pour "horizon" ou comment les élèves des classes populaires intériorisent le sens de leur orientation contrariée. *Formation emploi*, 2(2), 27–54. https://doi.org/10.4000/formationemploi.8118

DFJC - Département de la formation, de la jeunesse et de la culture. (2019). *Concept 360. Concept cantonal de mise en œuvre et de coordination des mesures spécifiques en faveur des élèves des établissements ordinaires de la scolarité obligatoire*. Lausanne, Suisse: Département de la formation, de la jeunesse et de la culture. https://www.vd.ch/fileadmin/user_upload/organisation/dfj/dgeo/fichiers_pdf/concept360/Concept_360.pdf

Darmon, M. (2016). *Becoming anorexic: A sociological study*. London: Routledge.

Dupont, H. (2021). *Déségrégation et accompagnement total. Sur la progressive fermeture des établissements spécialisés pour enfants handicapés*. Grenoble: Presses universitaires de Grenoble.

Durler, H. (2015). *L'autonomie obligatoire. Sociologie du gouvernement de soi à l'école*. Rennes: Presses universitaires de Rennes.

Eckhart, M., Haeberlin, U., Sahli Lozano, C. & Blanc, P. (2011). *Langzeitwirkungen der schulischen Integration. Eine empirische Studie zur Bedeutung von Integrationserfahrungen in der Schulzeit für die soziale und berufliche Situation im jungen Erwachsenenalter*. Bern: Haupt Verlag.

Giuliani, F. (2020). Revendication, réserve, ruse. L'engagement des écoliers "perturbateurs" face à l'exigence de réflexivité. *Revue des sciences sociales*, 64, 16–27. https://doi.org/10.4000/revss.5592

Goffman, E. (1961). *Asylums. Essays on the social situation of mental patients and other inmates*. Garden City, NY: Anchor Books.

Goffman, E. (1963). *Stigma. Notes of the management of spoiled identity*. Upper Saddle River: Prentice Hall.

Gremion-Bucher, L. (2012). *Les coulisses de l'échec scolaire. Étude sociologique de la production des décisions d'orientation de l'école enfantine et primaire vers l'enseignement spécialisé* [Thèse de doctorat, Université de Genève]. https://archive-ouverte.unige.ch/unige:22847

Herman, E. (2007). La bonne distance. L'idéologie de la complémentarité légitimée en centres de loisirs. *Cahiers du Genre*, 42, 121–139. https://doi.org/10.3917/cdge.042.0121

Kherroubi, M. (2004). Les activités pédagogiques hors classe au collège. In J.-F. Marcel (Ed.), *Les pratiques enseignantes hors de la classe* (pp. 19–30). Paris: L'Harmattan.

Laforgue, D. (2019). Le mandat éducatif des institutions publiques contemporaines. Quelles transformations? *Sociologies* [en ligne]. https://doi.org/10.4000/sociologies.10059

Martuccelli, D. (2006). *Forgé par l'épreuve. L'individu dans la France contemporaine*. Paris: Armand Colin.

Maulini, O. & Erceylan, S. (2020). *Que penser... de l'autonomie des élèves?* Université de Genève: Working paper. https://www.unige.ch/fapse/SSE/teachers/maulini/publ-2011.pdf

Oberholzer, V. (2005). L'enfance inadaptée ou la "part maudite" de l'École vaudoise. *A contrario*, 3, 80–106.

Oller, A.-C. (2020). *Le coaching scolaire. Un marché de la réalisation de soi*. Paris: Presses universitaires de France.

Payet, J.-P. (1995). *Collèges de banlieue. Ethnographie d'un monde scolaire*. Paris: Armand Colin.

Pelgrims, G. (2003). La motivation à apprendre des élèves en milieu scolaire: Des classes ordinaires aux classes spécialisées. In G. Chatelanat (Ed.), *Éducation et enseignement spécialisés: ruptures et intégrations* (pp. 215–240). Bruxelles: De Boeck Supérieur.

Ruiz, G. & Goastellec, G. (2016). Entre trouver et se trouver une place d'apprentissage: Quand la différence se joue dans la personnalisation du processus. *Formation emploi* [en ligne], 133. https://doi.org/10.4000/formationemploi.4663

Skinner, J. (2012). *The interview. An ethnographic approach*. London: Routledge.

Tomlinson, S. (2012). *A sociology of special education*. London: Routledge.

Tronto, J. (1998). An Ethic of Care. *Journal of the American Society on Aging*. 22(3), 15–20. https://www.jstor.org/stable/44875693

UNESCO. (2016). *Education 2030: Incheon declaration and framework for action for the implementation of sustainable development goal 4: Ensure inclusive and equitable quality education and promote lifelong learning opportunities for all*. UNESCO. http://uis.unesco.org/sites/default/files/documents/education-2030-incheon-framework-for-action-implementation-of-sdg4-2016-en_2.pdf

Winzer, M. (2009). *From integration to inclusion: a history of special education in the 20th century*. Washington, DC: Gallaudet University Press.

11
ON THE NORM OF INDIVIDUAL AUTONOMY IN SCHOOL

Thorsten Merl

Introduction

The philosophical idea of individual autonomy – understood as "the idea of self-determination or self-government" (Mackenzie & Stoljar 2000a, p. 5) – is not only a central aim for the school system, but it also constitutes the core of the concept of "*Bildung*". It thus heavily influences educational practices and can hardly be overestimated in its normative significance for how we think about pedagogy. The idea of self-governing subjects not only functions as an aim, but it also operates as a means of learning, specifically organizing learning in schools. By aiming at self-governing subjects and organizing education in school along this norm, it can *theoretically* be stated that pupils are constantly addressed as pupils who are, have to, or at least should be able to govern themselves. It is the research interest of this chapter to *empirically* analyse these performed expectations of individual autonomous pupils and their consequences in German secondary schools that consider themselves as inclusive. The focus on inclusive classes leads the research interest to analyse and scrutinize not only the expectation of individual autonomy but also to analyse its relation to disability in such classes.

The present analyses are based on the empirical data and key findings of a finalized ethnography of inclusive classes in Germany. While in earlier publications I focused on teachers' differentiation practices and how the said practices (re-)produce who is considered as sufficiently vs. insufficiently able (see Merl 2019, 2021), this chapter uses the existing evidence as a starting point for further reflections regarding the role that the concept of individual autonomy plays in these school classes' practices.

DOI: 10.4324/9781003379676-15
This chapter has been made available under a CC-BY license.

I will therefore (1) give a summary of the underlying poststructuralist and practice theories and Studies in Ableism that allow us to conceptualize individual autonomy as a specific ability expectation that is constitutively dependent on the notion of disability. I will then (2) relate this to the German school system and the meaning of inclusion in this system. After presenting briefly (3) the methodology of my ethnographic research, I will sum up some key findings that build the basis for (4) analysing how and to what extent individual autonomy can be understood as an implicit norm and (5) what is done to maintain this norm, although every day it becomes obvious that this norm does not suit all pupils in the class. The chapter concludes (6) by relating inclusion and autonomy as conflicting standards.

Autonomy and dis/ability: Theoretical foundations

Practice theories and poststructuralist theories build the theoretical basis for the present study (Schatzki 1996; Schatzki, Knorr-Cetina & Savigny 2001; Reckwitz 2016a; Butler 1997a, 1997b, 2011; Laclau & Mouffe 2001). They allow us to understand social practices as the place where (a given) social order and meanings are produced: "Social orders are thus the arrangements of people, artifacts, organisms, and things through and amid which social life transpires, in which these entities relate, occupy positions, and possess meanings" (Schatzki 2002, p. 22). I understand positions – i.e., "where an entity fits in a nexus" (ibid. p. 19) – in those social orders as *relational positions* that obtain their meaning "not positively, in terms of their content, but negatively by contrast with other items. ... What characterizes each most exactly is being whatever the others are not" (Saussure 1983, p. 161).

This relational perspective is also essential for theoretical perspectives in Disability Studies and Studies in Ableism (Waldschmidt 2007; Campbell 2009; Watson, Roulstone & Thomas 2012; Goodley 2014, 2016) that, amongst others, posit a constitutive relation between the concepts of autonomy, ability, and disability. The theoretical standpoint of this chapter thus requires us to understand and analyse performed doings, sayings, and their material relations as situated differences and positions that relationally produce meaning; i.e., produce someone and something *as* someone and something specific. Such a relational perspective on the emergence of meaning is at the same time a critique of ontological claims that situate the meaning of entities in itself rather than in relational positions that emerge from temporarily unfolding practices.

In opposition to structuralist theory, poststructuralist theories argue that the orders of differences are not fixed but are potentially subject to constant changes. Poststructuralist theories thus raise awareness about the openness of meaning and allow us to understand the fixation of discourses – e.g., by naturalizing differences – as constitutively fragile (Derrida 2001). This does not imply that social orders and discourses do constantly change; whether they change or persist is rather an empirical question.

Furthermore, poststructuralist theories provide a deeper understanding of the role discourses play in shaping social practices, social orders, and subject positions within these orders. Regarding the theoretical reflections of Reckwitz (2016b) discourses and practices are not different empirical entities. Discourses are also practices, i.e., discursive practices. The difference between practices and discursive practices lies in the epistemological interest: discourses, understood as "regimes of signification" (ibid. p. 53), reflect *orders of representation*. Discursive practices thus are "practices of representation, that is, practices in which objects, subjects, contexts are represented in a particular, regulated way and are first produced in this representation as specific, meaningful entities" (ibid. p. 62, my translation).

Discourses constitute objects as specific objects; they structure *how and as what entities can be perceived*. At the same time, "every object is constituted as an object of discourse, insofar as no object is given outside every discursive condition of emergence" (Laclau & Mouffe 2001, p. 107). In this perspective, subjects also are understood as entities that emerge from performative practices that are influenced by discourses. "Being" a subject is thus the result of a process of subjectivation, which

> denotes both the becoming of the subject and the process of subjection [...] Such subjection is a kind of power that not only unilaterally acts on a given individual as a form of domination, but also activates or forms the subject. Hence, subjection is neither simply the domination of a subject nor its production, but designates a certain kind of restriction in production.
>
> *(Butler 1997b, pp. 83–84)*

If we relate this concept of subjectivation to the common understanding of autonomy (i.e., someone who is an independent, self-governing individual, see Christman 2020), it becomes clear that the notion of independent subjects ignores that individuals only become subjects by processes of subjection. Depending on these processes – and therefore on the recognition of others – implies not being independent.

Butler, therefore, argues for a different understanding of autonomy as a result of processes of subjectivation. As Butler puts it, "[O]ne inhabits the figure of autonomy only by becoming subjected to a power, a subjection which implies a radical dependency" (Butler 1997b, p. 83). Autonomous agency thus is a certain way of living in the world; a subject must be enabled to live in this way. So, in contrast to the common understanding and critique of individualized concepts of autonomy, sociologically informed theoretical perspectives argue for a concept of "relational autonomy" (see Mackenzie & Stoljar 2000b; Oshana 2015). Those socio-relational approaches to autonomy are premised on the shared "conviction that persons are socially embedded, and that agents' identities are formed within the context of social relationships and shaped by a complex of intersecting social determinants" (Mackenzie & Stoljar 2000a, p. 4).

One can therefore argue that assumptions, claims, or expectations of individually sovereign subjects "must consequently be grounded in a kind of (self-) deception" (Geipel & Mecheril 2014, p. 41, my translation): claims of individually sovereign subjects inevitably suppress constitutive dependencies to stage oneself as individually autonomous. As Butler (2004, p. 77) argues, autonomy rather "is a socially conditioned way of living in the world". This perspective on the necessity to reject dependencies in order to maintain the possibility to believe in individual autonomy influences my further analysis. I will recall it specifically when showing how the delusion of autonomy is maintained in the practices of the schools observed.

As I stated earlier, meanings of entities arise from their relational position in a (discursive) order. One constitutive relation of differences for establishing and maintaining the notion of individual autonomy is the concept of dis/ability. "Since the late 1300s, 'ability' has signified a quality in a person that makes an action possible; in turn, someone who can execute an expected range of actions is able-bodied" (Campbell 2015, p. 46). Disability stands in a negative deviating relation to those expected abilities; it is understood "as a diminished state of being human" (Campbell 2009, p. 5). From the perspective of the Studies in Ableism, being able amongst others implies the notion of a "human (adult) subject [that] is assumed to be an independent centre of self-consciousness, who holds autonomy" (Campbell 2012, p. 213). Thus, a central "claim in disability studies reformulation is that 'autonomy' is itself [...] saturated with ableist norms" (Braswell 2011, cha. 6). It comes therefore as no surprise that accounts of "autonomy within liberal philosophy [...] have excluded people with intellectual disability from moral and political theories by denying their capacity for individual autonomy, seen as a chief marker of moral personhood" (Davy 2015, p. 132). Such an exclusion of those not fitting into the norm of individual autonomy is not a coincidence; it is necessary to maintain the notion of individual autonomy itself. For this notion, it is necessary to differentiate between people with and without intellectual disability and to exclude the former. Otherwise, we would have to admit that people aren't simply independent. This perspective not only relates the concept of individual autonomy to disability but also relates it to ability expectations.

Because it is discourses – and not just individual attitudes – that shape what counts as being able-bodied, it is important to understand this norm as *socially established*. What behaviour is perceived as an expression of ability or disability is socially established and precisely not an individual decision. This does not mean that such social norms can't change; it only implies that it is not possible to individually change them.

To recap: a notion of individual autonomy implies specific, socially established expectations of ability. Because these expectations hide constitutive dependencies and thus question the idea of autonomy, they can only be maintained if one hides these dependencies. We can understand this as a necessary delusion to maintain the idea of autonomy. Only if we downplay dependencies and thus deceive ourselves (and others) can we conceive of individuals as being autonomous. One aspect of this delusion can be found in the common understanding of abilities themselves as "a quality in a person" (Campbell 2015, p. 46) because it is not self-evident that the entity abilities relate to is a person (see Buchner, Pfahl, & Traue 2015). It could just as well be a collective entity that is perceived as able to make an action possible. Perceiving abilities only as individual abilities tends to suppress dependencies and thus consolidates notions of individuals as autonomous subjects.

Dis/ability and inclusion in the German school system

I will now put the previous theoretical thoughts in relation to the German school system and to its self-presentation as an inclusive school system. As is the case for many school systems worldwide, the German school system also distinguishes between general education schools and special education schools; while the former is designated in principle for all (sic!) pupils, the latter is designated for pupils with special educational needs. This differentiation is fundamentally based upon the individual and binary distinction between ability vs. disability (see Dederich 2009). This becomes clear in the fact that special education needs are constitutively based on categories of disability (see Sturm 2016, p. 108) and that the constitution of a "special education" system is historically based on the concept of disability (see Dederich 2009, p. 18). Furthermore, the wording (general vs. special as well as ability vs. disability) already indicates that we are dealing with a binary differentiation establishing a general norm and a deviation from this norm.

Being an individually autonomous pupil is a central ability norm in school: if for instance one looks more closely at what is meant by the term "learning disability" the connection to the norm of individually autonomous subjects becomes apparent. Based on a reconstruction of the learning disability discourse, Pfahl analyses that a learning disability is generally "conceived as a restricted capacity for autonomy inherent in the organism of the individual" (Pfahl 2011, p. 107, my translation). A learning disability is understood as a lack of "mastery over the mind and body" (Campbell 2012, 214) that is expected in schools; e.g., pupils are expected to be able to comprehensively control their own behaviour. So, the concept of *learning disability* not only depends on notions of individual autonomy as the underlying norm but is also commonly conceived as ontological. Of further interest here is the fact that a learning disability is defined not only medically but equally pedagogically and psychologically (ibid. p. 22). This explains why it is a form of disability that does not exist at all outside of school because it only exists in relation to schools' ability norms. What discursively is understood as (learning) disability is not only relevant for the formal status of pupils with special educational needs, but it also shapes what teachers expect from the able pupils and what behaviour or abilities they deem to be an expression of a learning disability. In other words, the learning disability discourse structures the perceptions and expectations of teachers regarding both pupils with and without special educational needs.

Due to the ratification of the UN Convention on the Rights of Persons with Disabilities, in Germany, the federal school systems implemented structural changes to establish as the norm the joint education of pupils with and without special educational needs in general education schools. This was intended to meet the legal demand for an equal right of participation in the education system for all pupils at the level of structural regulations. However, the differentiation among pupils with and without special educational needs remains as it was before, and it also remains possible for those pupils with special educational needs to attend special education schools, but it is now considered an exception that needs to be justified. The legal implementation of inclusion can therefore be understood as a change in school structure that in principle dispenses with forms of external/structural differentiation while at the same time maintaining this differentiation among pupils. According to this, the school law interprets inclusion as the placement of pupils who are classified as disabled in the general education schools.

The theoretical considerations have shown the constitutive relation between ability and disability and the understanding of learning disability as an expression of limited individual autonomy. I will now empirically analyse which abilities are expected in the teaching practice and to what extent these ability expectations refer to a norm of the individually autonomous pupil subject. I will then ask how constructions of disability as a deviation emerge in constitutive relation to this norm and how this norm is maintained. With this focus on expected abilities in schools rather than on disability, my research is grounded in studies of ableism (Campbell 2012; Goodley 2014; Buchner, Pfahl & Traue 2015; Köbsell 2015; Meißner 2015).

Becoming in/sufficiently able

The underlying study is an educational ethnography (Breidenstein 2008; Breidenstein, Hirschauer, Kalthoff & Nieswand 2013; Tervooren, Engel, Göhlich, Miethe & Reh 2014), specifically praxeography[1] for which I conducted participant observations in four school classes (grade 5 to 7) at three different secondary schools in North Rhine-Westphalia, Germany. I observed each class for four to six months with one to two days of observation per week. There I focused on teacher-pupil interactions. Furthermore, I collected artefacts and participated in teachers' meetings to understand how the teachers speak about their pupils outside the classroom. I recorded my observations in class with handwritten field notes. The teachers' meetings were audio recorded.

All schools, or at least all the observed classes, described themselves as inclusive, and furthermore, all schools teach pupils with and without special educational needs or disabilities. The four chosen schools are the result of the theoretical sampling research process in the Grounded-Theory-Methodology (see Clarke 2005).[2] This methodology permeates the entire research process. In addition, field notes that were especially rich in content have been analysed sequentially. For more details on the methodology, the research questions, and the heuristics of the study, I refer to other publications (see Merl 2019, 2021).

I will now summarize some key findings to build the basis for the then following analysis of autonomy as an underlying ability expectation (for more details see Merl 2019, 2021). In the inclusive classes, one differentiation among pupils could be observed in many different teachers' practices: teachers differentiate how they regulate pupils' (mis)behaviour along the distinction of whether a pupil is deemed sufficiently or insufficiently able in relation to the ability expectations. Those who are deemed able have to act accordingly, while those who are not may legitimately deviate. This can be exemplified by the following observation:

> During a class discussion on how to use the gas burner, Mr. Roland says: "Stop, stop a minute. Tom, can you do it or do you need a time out?" Tom: "Uh-uh, need a time-out". Mr. Roland: "Well, then take it". ... I hear a pupil utter a long, drawn-out "ey" and another pupil says rather more quietly: "I need a time-out, too". Someone else: "Me too". Mr. Roland says loudly "Shhhh. Andrea wanted to say something" and continues the class discussion. Tom leaves the class in the meantime.[3]

This example shows how a teacher interrupts the class discussion to offer one pupil a time-out under the condition that he is no longer able to behave as expected – in other words: if he is insufficiently able to meet the required abilities for this specific teaching format. Other pupils who want to have a time-out as well are not allowed to take one because they are deemed to be sufficiently able by the teacher; however, this remains implicit. So, it can be summarized that teachers differentiate their regulations of pupils on the basis of attributed abilities. With precisely this everyday differentiation, teachers establish who is sufficiently able and who is insufficiently able to participate fully in the classes. The same logic of differentiation can be found not only in daily time-outs but in many different regulation practices in the classroom (e.g., the seating arrangement; see Merl 2019). This is particularly relevant to show that it is a distinction that is performed generally by teachers in inclusive classes.

Based on this analysis of the practices of differentiation between pupils being made dis-/abled (Merl 2019), it is of interest here to see which abilities are expected and expectable and thus what it means to be able in the first place. In other words: in differentiations, as in the previous examples, ability norms are also (re)produced in the form of universal, actual requirements.

The implicit norm of autonomously acting subjects

What are the underlying ability expectations in those teachers' regulations of pupils' behaviour? First of all, it is important to note that the expected abilities vary according to the format of teaching and may also vary depending on the teacher. Through their regulations, teachers demand those abilities that appear to be necessary for the creation and maintenance of order: being quiet, sitting still, listening, not allowing oneself to be distracted by others are such behavioural and thus ability requirements. As such, they refer to the implicit expectation that pupils are able to comprehensively and independently regulate themselves. In my observations, this expectation of ability was never made explicit. Instead, it is an implicit expectation that those abilities simply exist in principle, which is why I name this an implicit ability norm.

If one furthermore considers that pupils who are deemed to be sufficiently able generally are sanctioned for their misbehaviour, another ability expectation is revealed: only if someone is considered responsible for their misbehaviour does it seem appropriate to sanction them for it. Thus, being sanctioned for misbehaviour implies not only the expected ability to self-regulate, but also the ability to take both the responsibility and the blame for one's misbehaviour.

These implicit expectations of comprehensive and individual self-regulation, as well as the ability to take responsibility, ultimately designate pupils as *sovereign or autonomously acting subjects* in principle. In other words, teachers' regulations implicitly expect pupils to be individually autonomous subjects who are able to regulate themselves constantly. This implicit expectation needs to be understood as an ideal norm about which the teachers themselves would probably argue that it is unlikely to be ever attained completely by their pupils. Nevertheless, it is this ideal norm that orients the teachers' regulation practices.

It is important to stress here that individual autonomy as an expectation in principle is deeply rooted in socially established and acknowledged teaching formats and in state-mandated curricula. However, it remains contingent and thus could also change. A shift in expected abilities in schools would at the same time mean a shift in terms of how pupils are considered sufficiently or insufficiently able (see Wolbring & Yumakulov 2015).

Maintaining the norm

Based on the previous analysis, I will now elaborate on how this norm of individual autonomy is maintained.

Acknowledging and hiding external influences on abilities

When teachers interpret why pupils are not able to fulfil some requirements, they identify family background as a reason, as the following examples demonstrate: in an ethnographic interview with one teacher, he explained to me that in his eyes, one pupil was not able to sit quietly in his chair and concentrate on his tasks (i.e., he is insufficiently able) because of his father's heart attack a few weeks before. In another ethnographic interview, another teacher explained to me that the reason why one pupil often is not able to concentrate on the given tasks is that their parents would spend every weekend at a campsite, drinking a lot of alcohol and neglecting their child. Another explanation for insufficient abilities given to me was that the parents of one pupil were addicted to drugs when he was in the first years of his life.

In all of these examples, the teachers' knowledge about family backgrounds is not only used to explain a pupil's insufficient abilities (and we can clearly see how social backgrounds here become relevant in the classroom) but also implies that teachers acknowledge that abilities can depend on external factors (i.e., factors over which a pupil has no control) and thus strictly speaking are *not* individual abilities.

However, these external influences are in a way irrelevant at the moment of the situational assessment of insufficient abilities in the classroom. For what counts situationally is the question of whether someone can meet the requirements or not – regardless of whether this is due to external factors or not. At the moment of the teachers' attribution of in/sufficient abilities, the generally acknowledged relevance of external influencing factors is thus situationally disregarded again. I argue that this is necessary in order to maintain the norm of *individual* autonomy that constitutively relies on the idea of individual abilities.[4]

Allowing deviation instead of questioning the expectation

Another way of maintaining the norm of pupils who are able to comprehensively control their own behaviour as expected by the teachers and for the entire duration of the school day is by allowing deviations under the condition that those who deviate are deemed to be insufficiently able. This is exemplified by the teacher who offers Tom an additional time-out. Tom needs to agree that he can't make it anymore and therefore needs to acknowledge that he is insufficiently able in order to be granted that additional time-out. Even though the teacher offers this time-out and thus legitimizes it, it remains a deviation from the still existing ability norm.

The central point here is that the norm of the individually capable subject can only be maintained at the cost of producing a deviation. If we look empirically at classroom practices, it becomes apparent that some of the pupils repeatedly fail to meet the requirements set by the teachers. It would therefore be quite conceivable to conclude from these repeatedly observable deviations that the "actual" requirements set by the teachers are inadequate because they cannot be met by everyone. The observed regulation practices proceed differently. Teachers explain deviating activities by the fact that pupils are insufficiently able. This functions as an explanation that locates the cause of the deviation individually in the pupils and thus not in the set requirements. The "actual" requirements and the norm of the ability for comprehensive self-regulation contained therein thus can remain unquestioned.

So, through the construction of this deviation, it is possible to maintain the norm that pupils are basically able to control themselves entirely, even though it becomes clear in everyday classroom practices that the norm is inadequate insofar as it does not correspond to the existing abilities of all pupils. Here again, I argue that this enabling of deviation is a means of maintaining an individualistic norm of ability.

Explaining ongoing deviations with disabilities

While the former arguments explain how in concrete situations deviations are legitimized *temporarily* when pupils are deemed insufficiently able and how this allows schools to maintain ability norms, I also observed that some pupils were continually deemed to be insufficiently able and exempted from the requirements.

Regardless of whether deviations are legitimized temporarily or continually, the function remains the same: by allowing deviation, teachers contribute to confirming ability expectations as a norm. But the temporality makes a difference insofar as one might expect that pupils could learn to meet the expected abilities in school and thus become sufficiently able over time. In order to legitimize an ability norm of individual autonomy even though teachers acknowledge that some pupils will also prospectively not be able to fulfil the schools' ability expectations, some kind of differentiation becomes necessary. This is when disabilities come into play. Disabilities construct restricted individual autonomy as an ontological naturalized difference. Thus, disability categories allow for a one-sided, individualizing explanation of ongoing deviations – and thus allow us to not question the underlying norm itself.

This shows that and how the concept of disability is a necessity in order to maintain the ability norm of *a subject that is capable of acting autonomously*.

Without the schools' production of pupils with special educational needs, the ableist expectations would necessarily be understood as inappropriate because they simply do not suit every pupil. As Waldschmidt and Schneider (2007) argue,

> Obviously, the demarcation category disability is "needed"... to maintain certain, culturally predetermined notions of corporeality and subjectivity. Above all, contemporary society needs this category as a deviation fact in order to be able to establish and secure something like "normality" in contrast.
> *(Ibid. p. 10, my translation)*

Conclusions

Based on the theoretical frameworks of practice theory and poststructuralism, the analyses and reflections of teachers' regulations practices show that inclusive schools implicitly expect pupils to be able to constantly regulate themselves independently of others. This expectation points to an ableist norm of pupils as in principle *sovereign or autonomously acting subjects*. Based on theoretical perspectives of Disability Studies and especially Studies in Ableism, my empirical analyses show three ways by which this ideal of individual autonomy is maintained: by hiding external influences on abilities, by allowing deviation instead of questioning the expectation, and by explaining ongoing deviations with disabilities.

Overall, the analysis of the implicit norm shows that the implemented so-called inclusive education in schools – here understood as teaching pupils with and without special educational needs together in the regular school system – does *not* lead to a questioning of the ableist norm of individual autonomy. This norm persists even though teachers and schools claim to be inclusive. Furthermore, the school system's logic to differentiate between able and disabled pupils – respectively to differentiate between those with and without special educational needs – as a means to maintain the ability norm of individual autonomy remains as it was in the former separated school system. What changed is *where* this differentiation takes place: it no longer takes place by separating pupils into different school types but by differentiating them within school classes in the general school system.

One central aim of the concept of inclusive education is to enable comprehensive participation for every pupil, regardless of their abilities. The analyses now demonstrate that so-called inclusive schools maintain individual autonomy as an ability expectation, even though it follows from this that some pupils cannot continuously participate in the lessons. This shows that the norm of individual autonomy is and remains deeply established even in so-called inclusive schools. Even though an equal opportunity to comprehensively participate in the classroom is one of the main aims of inclusion, the ableist norm of individual autonomy obviously is superior to this norm of inclusion.

Notes

1 Because the focus is not an ethnic group but practices (see Schmidt 2012).
2 Initial field observations took place in parallel in two maximum-contrast schools: a gymnasium that was forced to establish inclusive classes and a secondary school, which has itself chosen to be an inclusive school. In the latter, two classes were observed one after another to get a minimal contrast. In a second phase, a private school (founded by parents of children with disabilities as an inclusive school) was observed as another maximum contrast.
3 All names are pseudonyms.
4 To prevent potential annoyance: I don't argue that taking external factors as an influence on abilities into account is inadequate. I just argue that these influences are acknowledged and at the same time don't lead to questioning the continuing norm of an autonomous subject.

References

Braswell, H. (2011). Can there be a disability studies theory of 'end-of-life autonomy'? *Disability Studies Quarterly*, *31*(4). https://dsq-sds.org/article/view/1704/1754

Breidenstein, G. (2008). Schulunterricht als Gegenstand ethnographischer Forschung. In B. Hünersdorf, C. Maeder & B. Müller (Eds.), *Ethnographie und Erziehungswissenschaft: Methodologische Reflexionen und empirische Annäherungen* (pp. 107–120). Weinheim, München: Juventa.

Breidenstein, G., Hirschauer, S., Kalthoff, H., & Nieswand, B. (2013). *Ethnografie: Die Praxis der Feldforschung*. Konstanz: UTB.

Buchner, T., Pfahl, L., & Traue, B. (2015). Zur Kritik der Fähigkeiten: Ableism als neue Forschungsperspektive der Disability Studies und ihrer Partner_innen. *Zeitschrift für Inklusion*, *10*(2). http://www.inklusion-online.net/index.php/inklusion-online/article/view/273/256

Butler, J. (1997a). *Excitable speech: A politics of the performative*. New York: Routledge.

Butler, J. (1997b). *The psychic life of power: Theories in subjection*. Stanford, CA: Stanford University Press.

Butler, J. (2004). *Undoing gender*. New York; London: Routledge.

Butler, J. (2011). *Bodies that matter: On the discursive limits of "sex"*. New York; London: Routledge.

Campbell, F. K. (2009). *Contours of ableism: The production of disability and abledness*. Basingstoke: Palgrave Macmillan.

Campbell, F. K. (2012). Stalking ableism: Using disability to expose 'abled' narcissism. In D. Goodley, B. Hughes, & L. J. Davis (Eds.), *Disability and social theory: New developments and directions* (pp. 212–230). New York: Palgrave Macmillan.

Campbell, F. K. (2015). Ability. In R. Adams, B. Reiss & D. Serlin (Eds.), *Keywords for disability studies* (pp. 46–51). New York: New York University Press.

Christman, J. (2020). Autonomy in moral and political philosophy. *The Stanford Encyclopedia of Philosophy*. https://plato.stanford.edu/archives/fall2020/entries/autonomy-moral/

Clarke, A. (2005). *Situational analysis: Grounded theory after the postmodern turn*. Thousand Oaks, CA: Sage.

Davy, L. (2015). Philosophical inclusive design: Intellectual disability and the limits of individual autonomy in moral and political theory. *Hypatia*, *30*(1), 132–148. https://doi.org/10.1111/hypa.12119

Dederich, M. (2009). Behinderung als sozial- und kulturwissenschaftliche Kategorie. In: M. Dederich & W. Jantzen (Eds.), *Behinderung und Anerkennung* (pp. 15–40). Stuttgart: Kohlhammer.
Derrida, J. (2001). Signatur Ereignis Kontext. In *Limited Inc.* (pp. 15–46). Wien: Passagen.
Geipel, K. & Mecheril, P. (2014). Postsouveräne Subjektivität als Bildungsziel? Skeptische Anmerkungen. In B. Kleiner & N. Rose (Eds.), *(Re-)Produktion von Ungleichheiten im Schulalltag: Judith Butlers Konzept der Subjektivation in der erziehungswissenschaftlichen Forschung* (pp. 35–54). Opladen, Berlin, Toronto: Verlag Barbara Budrich.
Goodley, D. (2014). *Dis/ability studies: Theorising disablism and ableism*. Hoboken: Taylor and Francis.
Goodley, D. (2016). *Disability studies: An interdisciplinary introduction*. 2nd ed. London: Sage.
Köbsell, S. (2015). Ableism: Neue Qualität oder alter Wein in neuen Schläuchen? In I. Attia, S. Köbsell, & N. Prasad (Eds.), *Dominanzkultur reloaded: Neue Texte zu gesellschaftlichen Machtverhältnissen und ihren Wechselwirkungen* (pp. 21–34). Bielefeld: transcript.
Laclau, E., & Mouffe, C. (2001). *Hegemony and socialist strategy: Towards a radical democratic politics* (2nd ed.). London: Verso.
Mackenzie, C. & Stoljar, N. (2000a). Introduction: Autonomy refigured. In C. Mackenzie & N. Stoljar (Eds.), *Relational autonomy: Feminist perspectives on autonomy, agency, and the social self* (pp. 3–31). New York: Oxford University Press.
Mackenzie, C. & Stoljar, N. (Eds.). (2000b). *Relational autonomy: Feminist perspectives on autonomy, agency, and the social self*. New York: Oxford University Press.
Meißner, H. (2015). Studies in Ableism. Für ein Vorstellungsvermögen jenseits des individuellen autonomen Subjekts. *Zeitschrift für Inklusion*, 10(2). http://www.inklusion-online.net/index.php/inklusion-online/article/view/276/259
Merl, T. (2019). *un/genügend fähig: Zur Herstellung von Differenz im Unterricht inklusiver Schulklassen*. Bad Heilbrunn: Klinkhardt.
Merl, T. (2021). In/sufficiently able: How teachers differentiate between pupils in inclusive classrooms. *Ethnography and Education*, 16(2), 198–209. https://doi.org/10.1080/17457823.2021.1871853
Oshana, M. (2015). Is social-relational autonomy a plausible ideal? In M. Oshana (Ed.), *Personal autonomy and social oppression: Philosophical perspectives* (pp. 3–24). New York, NY: Routledge.
Pfahl, L. (2011). *Techniken der Behinderung: Der deutsche Lernbehinderungsdiskurs, die Sonderschule und ihre Auswirkungen auf Bildungsbiografien*. Bielefeld: transcript.
Reckwitz, A. (2016a). *Kreativität und soziale Praxis: Studien zur Sozial- und Gesellschaftstheorie*. Bielefeld: transcript.
Reckwitz, A. (2016b). Praktiken und Diskurse: Zur Logik von Praxis-/Diskursformationen. In: *Kreativität und soziale Praxis: Studien zur Sozial- und Gesellschaftstheorie* (pp. 49–66). Bielefeld: transcript.
Saussure, F. (1983/1916). *Course in general linguistic*. London: Duckworth.
Schatzki, T. R. (1996). *Social practices: A Wittgensteinian approach to human activity and the social*. Cambridge: Cambridge University Press.
Schatzki, T. R. (2002). *The site of the social: A philosophical account of the constitution of social life and change*. Pennsylvania State University Press.

Schatzki, T. R., Knorr-Cetina, K., & von Savigny, E. (Eds.) (2001). *The practice turn in contemporary theory*. New York: Routledge.

Schmidt, R. (2012). *Soziologie der Praktiken: Konzeptionelle Studien und empirische Analysen*. Berlin: Suhrkamp.

Sturm, T. (2016). *Lehrbuch Heterogenität in der Schule*. 2. (revised edition). München: UTB.

Tervooren, A., Engel, N., Göhlich, M., Miethe, I., & Reh, S. (Eds.). (2014). *Ethnographie und Differenz in pädagogischen Feldern: Internationale Entwicklungen erziehungswissenschaftlicher Forschung*. Bielefeld: transcript.

Waldschmidt, A. (Ed.), (2007). *Disability Studies, Kultursoziologie und Soziologie der Behinderung: Erkundungen in einem neuen Forschungsfeld*. Bielefeld: transcript.

Waldschmidt, A., & Schneider, W. (2007). Disability Studies und Soziologie der Behinderung.: Kultursoziologische Grenzgänge - eine Einführung. In A. Waldschmidt (Ed.), *Disability Studies, Kultursoziologie und Soziologie der Behinderung: Erkundungen in einem neuen Forschungsfeld* (pp. 9–25). Bielefeld: transcript.

Watson, N., Roulstone, A., & Thomas, C. (Eds.). (2012). *Routledge handbook of disability studies*. London: Routledge.

Wolbring, G., & Yumakulov, S. (2015). Education through an ability studies lens. *Zeitschrift für Inklusion*, 10(2). http://www.inklusion-online.net/index.php/inklusion-online/article/view/278/261

12
THE (DE)CONSTRUCTION OF THE AUTONOMOUS LEARNER IN A DIGITALIZED SCHOOL WORLD

Mario Steinberg and Yannick Schmid

Introduction

The current political and societal discourse on digitalization in education establishes an intimate relationship between digitalized educational settings and the autonomous, self-directed learner (Grimaldi & Ball, 2021). This unverified assertion is reinforced by the fact that the "digital revolution" in education is supported by a multitude of political and economic interests (Williamson, 2016, 2018; Ball, 2012; Münch, 2018). What all of the current discourses about digitalization in education have in common, however, is that they all anticipate – in different forms and shapes – the belief that digitalization is accompanied by fundamental disruptions in learning situations (Selwyn, 2013, 2016; Ball, Junemann & Santori, 2017; Ball, 2017). Digital technologies allow one to personalize learning content and goals, and to use algorithms to adapt to individual learning trajectories (Selwyn, 2016). Therefore, the prediction of a "digital revolution in education" (Steinberg, 2021a) is associated with a radical individualization of learning. The prediction is that this revolution is associated with sophisticated techno-solutionists utopias which go hand in hand with the individualization of teaching as well as autonomous and self-directed learning (Peschitola, 2021). As Grimaldi and Ball (2021, p. 394) point out,

> Digital technologies are discursively constructed as the solution to the (re)making of education as an effective means to address a vast and heterogeneous array of social and economic challenges, such as the production of a high-quality human capital, the elimination of poor educational performance by students in disadvantaged areas, the education for the poor in late

DOI: 10.4324/9781003379676-16
This chapter has been made available under a CC-BY license.

developing societies, special needs education, and more generally the personalisation of education.

(Grimaldi & Ball, 2021, p. 394)

This link between autonomous learning and digitalization in education is often routinely postulated without questioning any possible underlying implications (Ball, 2016, p. 5). As Grimaldi and Ball (2021, p. 401) outline, educational technology in practice can be continuously described along three principles that are discursively interconnected:

- Modularization and the dissolution of the classroom unit to create the greatest possible individualized learning structure.
- Neoliberal reorganization of learning through a radical shift towards individualization and self-direction.
- Paradoxical regulation of freedom through technology.

The common assumption is that by shaping the learning processes individually and in a self-organized manner, there is a chance of overcoming the "old school" system by "[…] delivering personalized, flexible and customized learning experiences" (Grimaldi & Ball, 2021, p. 395). With the help of digital tools, it seems possible to quickly assign tasks individually and to align them to a previously (algorithmically) measured learning level. This hegemonic discourse is meant to persuade teachers and principals to invest in digital learning technologies (Convery, 2009, p. 26).[1]

The recent works of critical scholars exploring digital technologies in education from a sociological point of view mainly focus on educational governance (Williamson, 2020a, 2020b, 2021; Hartong, 2019), on moral and philosophical questions (Selwyn, 2019; Williamson, 2020b; Lupton & Williamson, 2017), on their implications in the policy of educational institutions (Macgilchrist, 2019, 2021), or the emergence of new private actors and online learning platforms (Förschler et al., 2021). Current pedagogical research on the use of digital media in schools is mainly concerned with the development of and the improvement of pupils' learning process by digital devices (for a brief study overview, see Steinberg, 2021a, p. 111). These studies insufficiently take into account the transformational aspects that digital media have on classroom activities from an "actor-centred" micro-sociological point of view.[2] From this perspective, little attention has been paid so far to the question of how and whether digitalization[3] becomes part of daily school life and how school actors deal with the discursive demands of digitalization. What remains largely overlooked is thinking about how the figure of the digitally mediated autonomous learner is translated into everyday practices and whether the relationship between the teacher and the pupil is reshaped by the hegemonial discourse about autonomous learning in digital education.

With this contribution, we intend to show how different actors position themselves as regards the use of digital media in schools and how they deal with and interpret the figure of the "autonomous learner" in their everyday (school) practice. Theoretically, the analysis is informed by a strand of French pragmatic sociology called *sociology of conventions* (Boltanski & Thévenot, 2007; Boltanski & Chiapello, 2003; Leemann & Imdorf, 2019). This theoretical framework is based on the assumption that social situations are fundamentally contingent, which means that actors cannot anticipate either the consequences of their actions or the expectations of their counterparts with certainty. Accordingly, actors have to constantly justify their actions and decisions to themselves and others. By justifying their own standpoint and criticizing others, actors refer to one or more superordinate logics. These meta-principles are being defined as *conventions* (Diaz-Bone, 2011). Following this theoretical approach, digitalization and its promise of shaping and radically changing educational processes to steer them towards individual and autonomous learning can be seen as a *situation of testing – a "test of worth"* (Leemann & Imdorf, 2019, p. 34) for digital tools *in practice*. From this theoretical perspective, we are interested in finding out what conventions different actors activate to justify their view on the digitalization of school education and how they relate the figure of autonomous learner to it. In order to endow the empty signifier of digitalization in education with a life of its own, we will take a closer look at three stakeholders:

- "Innovative", technophile teachers
- School principals
- Teachers of a primary school, to explain – resorting to the sociology of conventions – how they deal with digitalization and the figure of the autonomous learner in everyday practice.

Discovering the autonomous learner from an actor's perspective

The empirical findings presented here are based on two case studies belonging to an ongoing research project (Steinberg, 2021b).[4] When presenting the results of the first case study, we discuss *four* teachers who place digitalization at the centre of their professional activities and who consider themselves, with their use of digital media in education, as being particularly "innovative". By doing so, we analyse how these actors align their actions with the discourses on digitalization and autonomous learning outlined earlier. In the second case study, we show how actors from an elementary school in German-speaking Switzerland handle digital media and its related claims. The main focus of this case study lies in the question of *if* and *how* the increased use of digital media impacts the justifications of everyday educational practice in the case of a primary school in the German-speaking part of Switzerland. In doing so, we present the interview excerpts of two focus group interviews (Merton, 1990) with five teachers from this school, focusing on their usage of digital media in everyday school life. In addition, the three principals from the same school discussed the same issues in two focus group interviews.

The collected data are analysed by using the Documentary Method following Ralf Bohnsack (2007, 2014). The goal of this methodical procedure is ultimately the reconstruction of the constructions of everyday life (Asbrand, 2011, p. 3) The data analysis shows how these actors justify their use of digital means in their specific school context: while the "innovators" are engaged in the discourse on technological innovation and credit its high potential with the ability to change the way schools operate, with the help of digital technology, principals, as well as teachers from the second case study presented here, are rather sceptical of the promises related to technology – one could possibly argue that they assess the situation more pragmatically.

The autonomous learner as part of a vision for a digitalized school of tomorrow

Those four teachers we shall call "innovative" see themselves as a kind of avant-garde of the digital revolution in education. They belong to a category of (former) teachers who now work as freelance consultants for big tech companies, such as Apple, Google, or Microsoft. These actors organize themselves in networks, holding informal and regular (online) meetings in which they discuss digital innovations in education. They also offer in-service and continuing education for teachers in school practice. The following statement from a network in Switzerland adequately illustrates the intentions of these actors: "Informed by research, strategic thinking about the future, integral frameworks and participative design, we contribute to creating transformative shifts in education from a place of inspiration".[5] In the following section, we give an insight into their justifications around the value of digital technologies and how they are related to the subject of self-directed digital learning.

The four teachers that we interviewed aspire to fundamentally change education through the imposition of new digital technologies. Far beyond equipping schools with digital tools, they strive for a profound change in teaching and learning. The following statement comes from an actor who is, like the other interviewees, engaged in different programmes of private teacher training. He formulates very clearly what others also said:

> For me, this electrification of education does not have much to do with digital change or digitality. What often happens now when I hear about tablet classes and such, what I often hear and observe now, is that people

say: "Yes, we now have to introduce digitalization in the school". That means we buy the appropriate software and the blackboard is now also an e-board and so on. But what they do is actually the same.

(Interview, innovator)[6]

Thus, for this actor, the implementation of digital tools without a change in the teaching and learning culture merely boils down to a process of translating the analogous "one-to-one" method onto the digital arena without thinking it along the lines of a cultural change. He describes this observation as follows:

What was done before with pens and ink is now simply transferred one-to-one to electronic devices along with the hierarchy, the linearity in working and learning, the deterministic structure, that is precisely defined for everyone and a system and a system in which every student is treated equally. There is no change in assessment procedures, which consist in testing everyone at the same time in the same subject and according to the same methodology, and sometimes the attempt even backfires, and it is even more controlled, actually even more centralized. That's just old school. That is the industrial age in my eyes.

(Interview, innovator)

From this point of view, digital tools are currently subordinated to the disciplinary logic of a traditional classroom, treating unequal pupils in a synchronized space-time matrix, which may even strengthen centralism and control, by teachers having access to all their pupils' screens in the classroom at the same time. Significant changes in school, according to this view, can only occur when pupils are no longer just lumped together via the same standardized method of teaching and with centralized tests, but when teachers take the individual student into account. Instead of reproducing traditional classroom practices with digital means, the interviewee suggests that digital tools should rather be used for a radical renewal of the classroom, transforming it into an open learning environment:

And for me, education in the digital age has a lot to do with individualisation, has a lot to do with network structures, independence of learning from place and time, and that is simply supported by these electronic media. But it is not done with electronic media in and of itself.

(Interview, innovator)

The interviewee explicitly calls for opening up the classroom to allow pupils to connect to the outside world and use the network for learning. He also calls for opening up the space and time of learning. This is a process which can essentially be supported by digital tools. Following this future imagination, pupils learn with the help of digital tools in a self-directed and autonomous way and in an open environment. This utopia drives innovators to strive for a better school.

The interviewed "innovative" teachers are basically putting the same arguments forward: they are convinced that in a digitalized world, educational institutions are no longer preoccupied with selection and differentiation along the lines of performance but are supportive of the interests and needs of each individual pupil as they are digitally mediated. The narrative of these actors reflects the discourse on digitalization mentioned at the beginning of the chapter. In short, the vision of good digital practice is built in opposition to the dominant manner of teaching and the use of digital media in schools. The vision of good digital practice is then drawn in contrast to the criticized practice. In the eyes of these actors, "true" digitalization in classrooms goes along with processes of individualization and increased autonomy for pupils. The main logic of these actors is to bring about innovation in education through a digital cultural change.

From the perspective of the sociology of conventions, we call this reference point a "world of inspiration" (Boltanski & Thévenot, 2007, p. 222). The justification of the inspirational world means that these actors fully commit to achieving the mission and overarching vision of digitalization. It is related to enlightenment, which eludes any external scrutiny and stands only for itself (Boltanski & Thévenot, 2007, p. 222). Relying on an inspirational order of reference, actors break out of the familiar world and radically question the established norms and traditions (Boltanski & Thévenot, 2007, p. 225). The main tenets of this world are *innovation*, *motivation*, *passion*, and *vocation*.

Important values are *creativity*, *discovery*, and *dedication* (Leemann & Imdorf, 2019, p. 10). The innovators have also identified that "true and good" digitalization – the existence of a "digital culture" in education – depends on fundamental disruptions in teaching and learning. Moreover, they claim that technology will deliver a solution to many fundamental social problems, such as adapting learning content to individual talents and thereby creating more educational equity (Nachtwey & Seidl, 2017, p. 20). These teachers criticize the inertia and persistence of school traditions that hinder the transformation toward a "true" digital culture in the classroom.

Processing the figure of the autonomous learner in a digitalized school practice

The data presented in the next two sections derives from group interviews with principals and teachers from a primary school in German-speaking Switzerland. The school was chosen because it claims to have fulfilled the requirements of the new curriculum with regard to digitalization. The research aimed at gaining insight into the possible divergence between the demands of the curriculum and actual school practice. The school closures as a result of the COVID-19 pandemic prompted us to supplement interviews already conducted with another round of data collection after the schools reopened. The aim of this approach was to learn about the conventions the actors refer to and also to see whether the references were challenged by the Corona crisis or whether they remained stable.[7] The classrooms in that school have been equipped with a comprehensive digital infrastructure (whiteboards/tablets) for about four years. Thus, the school can be viewed as rather experienced in handling digital media at the primary school level. In line with the revised curriculum, the concept of school digitalization demands that teachers resort to digital teaching and learning media in all school subjects. The school supports teachers via a short instruction period describing in rudimentary ways how teachers could use digital media in the classroom. However, as the interviewed actors reported, practical implementation is not further specified or controlled; rather, it is placed ultimately under the responsibility of each individual teacher to decide how to integrate digital tools into classroom practice.

Principals' reflections on self-directed learning in the digital age

First, the state of digitalization in the school was discussed with those three principals who are responsible together for the administration, finance, and management of the ICT facilities. In the focus group discussion, our interviewees recalled how they started to implement the digital curriculum in coordination with the local administration. Although the local authority defined a financial framework, it provided no further specifications concerning the digital setup of the school. Accordingly, the principals had considerable freedom in equipping the school with digital tools. However, for them, the installation of a digital infrastructure at the school was not – as they all emphasize it – an end in itself. Rather, they argue that digital technologies are only beneficial if they enhance teaching and learning. The principals consider that the way digital learning technologies are used in school is not, as expected, involved in a fundamental transformation of teaching practice. They explain this by pointing out that institutions such as schools are historically slow in implementing changes. This becomes obvious in the following statement, by which one of the interviewees reflects on the changes instigated by school closure during the COVID-19 pandemic:

> The school is always a dinosaur. If you implement something in school [...] then you can sit down calmly and wait for ten years [...]. And if others are naturally seven steps ahead of us in spirit, then this really is a digital revolution in education. But for us, this is far from being a paradigm shift in primary education, it is simply an aid to teaching. [...] So, there's a gap [...] It's not going to do that within two years, it's going to take 20, 25 years, if

at all. However, there is a gap between demand and school practice. You can't do that in two years, it will take 20, 25 years, if at all.
(Interview, principals)

The principal distinguishes school practice from external prescriptions and imagined (digital) futures: while digital technology is discursively constructed as disruptive learning technology, it is interpreted here as an "aid to teaching". In this framework, technologies thus quickly lose their revolutionary character. It is striking that the principals' discussion about digitalization should lead to an assessment of the development of self-directed learning at their school:

Self-directed learning [...] needs a setting, which is created by the teacher that helps and prepares that and I believe we are only just beginning the process at our school. There we have a lot of potential to grow.
(Interview, principals)

The group discussion – which focuses on digitalization – is taken as a matter of course by the interviewees to reflect on the development of self-directed learning and the individualization of teaching. Despite the fact that they obviously link digitalization to self-directed learning, the principals do not stress the way in which it is supported by digital tools, but highlight the idea that teachers are the essential means of initiation for self-directed learning. Moreover, they argue that self-managing competencies are always (in the digital age, as well as in the analogue age) part of the repertoire of a good pupil:

Because the competences which they have been learning belong less to the area of digital learning but more of the area of personal learning competences: being organized, learning how to manage their time, to hand in tasks in due time, to search for help when they need it and there is no teacher around.
(Interview, principals)

The principals' expectations towards improvement afforded by digital technologies are less concerned with pupils learning to handle the technologies than with their competences to guide their learning process. Furthermore, they argue that in order to develop these competences, however, pupils need to rely on adequate teaching practices. One of the interviewed principals expressed it as follows:

So, I think the relationship is what really counts in the end. No computer can make up for that. [...] In the end, and I think this is the crucial point, the teacher has to convey the learning content anyway and he still has to set goals and differentiate. [...] If the children like to learn, then it doesn't really matter whether it is digital or something else.
(Interview, principals)

The crucial point here is that the principals explicitly focus their argumentation on the *development of self-competences, innovation* in *teaching*, and *didactics* but at the same time – just as explicitly – deny the importance of the digital tools supporting this process. The statements, therefore, indicate that they value didactical individualization and self-managing competences more than its support through the use of digital tools. In this sense, the question of whether or not the figure of the autonomous learner is expressed through digital media is secondary for them.

The principals' focus on the teacher-pupil relationship can, with Boltanski and Thévenot (2007), be attributed to a domestic convention. When principals emphasize the importance of the relationship between teacher and pupil in the elementary school setting, they measure the quality of pedagogical actions by values such as *tradition, community, coexistence, trust, closeness* (Imdorf & Leemann, 2019, p. 10). This dominant convention, however, is counteracted by the reference to a project-based polis (Boltanski & Chiapello, 2003) in which the new spirit of capitalism manifests itself. According to this convention, actors possess greatness and the flexibility to adapt their behaviour to changing situations (Boltanski & Chiapello, 2003, p. 466). This convention emerges from the principals' emphasis on the importance of "personal learning competence" and is latent when they express the overall pedagogical goal of making self-directed learning possible (whether it is with or without the help of digital technologies). With this claim, school practice is implicitly justified with the preparation of flexibilization and subjectivation in (later) work relations (Münnich, 2017, p. 386).[8] It seems that principals formulate the same criticism of existing pedagogical practices as the innovators. They also seem to value the importance of self-managing competences for pupils. In contrast to the innovative teachers, the principals do not use justifications regarding the use of digital technologies to promote the autonomous learner. Rather, they criticize the fact that digital technologies are not supporting this process on their own and therewith relativize the usefulness of digital tools. Applying our theoretical perspective on the narration of the principals, the project-based polis is implicitly intertwined within a domestic world. Taking this argument further, one could argue that this is the implicit expression of the integration of a project-based polis into the domestic world that is established historically as a key logic in (primary) education (Derouet, 2019, 57). By doing so, the principals seem to integrate *innovation* into *tradition*.

Control in the digitalized classroom setting

After presenting the opinion of principals, we describe now how teachers who work at the same school use these digital tools on a daily basis and how they reflect on them. The group interview included both experienced and novice teachers; among them, some are self-proclaimed experts in the use of digital media and have a lot of technical knowledge, while others do not use digital media as much and have only little technical knowledge. Our research interest was to analyse how practices are justified in the group of teachers. We first asked teachers to describe how they use digital technologies in their classrooms.

The teachers report using digital technologies as devices supporting their teaching by using them so as to prevent disruptions and distractions in the classroom in an efficient and long-lasting manner. The dominant themes thereafter were issues of control. The teachers discuss the supervision of pupils when they work with their tablets, compared to traditional classroom settings:

> *I1:* You also have that in class, even if you don't have digital media [...].
> *I2:* You walk around and see what they are doing.
> *I3:* Yes, that's right. We are actually responsible for them, or to make sure that they don't do things they are not allowed to do, so we have to control them.
>
> *(Interview, teachers)*

The teachers legitimize their control of the pupils' digital practices. This control seems to be deeply inscribed in the functioning of schools, which does not actually change through the digitalization of classrooms. As the following short dialogue makes it obvious, teachers see paternalistic control as a means to lead the pupils to autonomy:

> *I5:* We are actually responsible for them, to make sure that they don't do stuff they are not allowed to do, so we have to control them.
> *I4:* Yes, autonomy has to be learned, [...], otherwise they are overwhelmed later on.
>
> *(Interview, teachers)*

Even though teachers see a general need to control what pupils do, the digital classroom provides new ways of controlling pupils:

> *I1:* We have the classroom app where you can see who is doing what, i.e., which iPad is doing what. And my pupils don't know yet how I see it, because I've never had to lock the iPads, but I've already heard from others where it's happened; the reactions were quite interesting (laughs)
> *I2:* My pupils know that it's me, but I think it's great because it's enough if I have my iPad on, I don't even have to look at it, but even if I have it on, I always see when someone glances at me, then I always know they're doing something they shouldn't be doing. Then I quickly go and look at the classroom app (laughs) – and then the look is enough. You go: Mhm, mhm – and then it's fine again.
>
> *(Interview, teachers)*

The teachers demonstrate how the mere option of a controlling gaze by the teacher via the tablet leads the pupils to adjust their behaviour. Digital surveillance in the digitalized classroom is a way to discipline the pupils without even being present. In the words of Foucault (2014, p. 224), the digital classroom setting thus becomes the "perfect disciplinary apparatus [...], the one that allowed a single gaze to see everything". From a central observation point (the so-called master-tablet), the teacher can "record all activities, [...] perceive and judge all errors" (Foucault, 2014, p. 224, our translation). According to the interviewed teachers, classical sanctions (such as taking equipment away, or giving extra work as punishment, etc.) become largely superfluous in the digital classroom – the teacher's disciplinary gaze (Foucault, 2014, p. 224) is sufficient to create an "*efficient working climate*" (teacher in group interview), as the interviewees unanimously point it out. From their standpoint, learning autonomy can only be achieved within boundaries set by the teachers and under their guidance.

The presented analysis shows that for teachers, traditional school values do not lose their importance in the digital age. Lessons must be run as efficiently as possible, disruptions should be avoided or stopped as early as possible, and teachers should know and control what pupils do. The possibilities offered by digital teaching tools come in handy. Digital media and the demand for self-directed learning both result in a system of social control that integrates pupils into panoptic monitoring. Our analysis suggests that the figure of the autonomous learner is given by these teachers only as much space as is compatible with established school norms. From a theoretical point of view, the interviewed teachers refer primarily to an "industrial convention" (Boltanski & Thévenot, 2007, p. 276), in which the traditional values of teaching, such as discipline, hierarchy, efficiency, are prominently emphasized (Boltanski & Thévenot, 2007, p. 278). The evaluation of the usefulness of new media and the figure of the autonomous learner in this convention are decisively based on productivity and efficiency. In this world, the social relations between teachers and pupils are characterized by hierarchical relationships and are organized, measurable, functional, and standardized (Boltanski & Thévenot, 2007, p. 278). Therefore, digital technologies are used to stabilize this order. The figure of the autonomous learner is exposed to these very norms, within which he has to move and perform – in a system of complete control by the teacher.

Conclusion: The processing of the autonomous learner in a digitalized school world

The three perspectives presented allow us to assume the analytical relations between digitalization and the figure of the autonomous learner. Our analysis suggests that the discourse which intimately connects the use of digital tools in the school setting to autonomous learning is not readily translated into classroom practice and is interpreted differently by school actors. The self-proclaimed innovative teachers who were interviewed emphasize the value of digital technologies for disruptive change towards individualized teaching and self-directed learning. In their digital imaginary, learning outcomes are increased, and social problems are solved through digital educational technology. On the other hand, the principals of the primary school emphasize personal learning competence as an essential attribute for any (successful) pupil – whether he works with digital tools or not. Referring to a project-based convention, principals emphasize the value of self-directed learning to foster the active, flexible, and responsible lifelong learner. However, their justifications make no explicit reference to educational technologies, but highlight the value of the personal relationship between teachers and pupils. Therewith they integrate a project-based polis into a domestic convention.

Conversely, an industrial convention is the guiding logic of teachers in the same school. The teachers focus on the most efficient possible design of lessons through technology. Their narrations are concerned with social control, and they transform the digital classroom into a panoptical coercive institution. It is reasonable to assume that schools are slow in transforming classroom practices (as the interviewed principals also suspected it).[9] Our conventional analysis undertaken in one school suggests one should be cautious about expecting a transformation of conventions towards a strong anchoring of the autonomous learner by digital tools. It seems to be well-established, historically grounded conventions, not new media per se (as the discourse initially suggested it), which shape teaching practices.

Interestingly, the teachers we approached integrate digital tools into conventional ways of teaching. To the extent that new media become part of the historically embedded set of conventions, it is possible that the discursively formulated claim – digital tools enable teachers to respond to each individual pupil and to promote autonomous learning – turns into something unexpected; in the discussed example, it leads to increased panoptic control in the classroom. Overall, we see signs that strong conventional orientations define the way pupils are thought about by teachers. Digital technologies are then swallowed up and integrated by established dominating conventions working in schools.

Notes

1 In order to promote the vaunted benefits of digitalization and its contribution to the radical transformation of learning to teachers and school administrators, education fairs have established themselves in the international context (Player-Koro, Bergviken-Rensfeldt & Selwyn, 2018).
2 However, there are few examples for ethnographic studies in a German-speaking context focusing on the development of media competences (Lange, 2020; Rode & Stern, 2017), sociological studies exploring media use in so-called tablet classes

(Steinberg, 2021a), critical studies exploring the opportunities afforded by digital media in schools (Silseth & Erstad, 2022), or studies empirically exploring the "learning lives" of pupils shaped by digital media (Erstad, 2012).
3 The terms "digital", "digitalization", "digital media", or "new media" are widely and simultaneously used in this chapter. This should in no way be misunderstood as analytical vagueness. Rather, it is a deliberate expression of the fact that the intentional content of these terms is not uniformly defined, neither for the interviewees nor in the documents studied; digitalization rather seems to take on the form of a "black box" in the empirical data studied.
4 The main focus of this PhD project lies in the question of how the hegemonic social and political discourses around digitalization in education are reflected in everyday pedagogical practice – how actors in the multi-level system of education interpret them in their practice. In other words, how they become effective and how actors themselves shape the discourse of digitalization in education. We gratefully acknowledge the financial support from the OA-fund of the Zurich University of Teacher Education supporting this publication.
5 https://educreators.net, 09.09.2021, our translation.
6 The interviews were held in German and are translated by us.
7 However, the conventions in the justifications remained constant in the reflections during this time (Steinberg & Schmid, 2020). This also points to the persistence of logics of justification in educational settings.
8 By promoting the importance of self-directed learning for the pupils and didactical differentiation as a key task for the teachers, they also seem to refer to an anticipation of the working world (Hangartner, Kaspar & Fankhauser, 2019), even in elementary education.
9 This has also already been shown for vocational education and training (Leemann, 2019).

References

Asbrand, B. (2011). *Dokumentarische Methode*. Retrieved from: http://www.fallarchiv.uni-kassel.de/wp-content/uploads/2010/07/asbrand_dokumentarische_methode.pdf, 09.09.2021.
Ball, S. J. (2012). *Global Education Inc.: New policy networks and the neoliberal imaginary*. London: Routledge.
Ball, S. J. (2016). Neoliberal education? Confronting the slouching beast. *Policy Futures in Education, 14*, 1046–1059. https://doi.org/10.1177/1478210316666425
Ball, S. J. (2017). *Foucault as educator*. Cham: Springer.
Ball, S. J., Junemann, C., & Santori, S. (2017). *Edu. Net: Globalisation and education policy mobility*. London: Routledge.
Bohnsack, R. (2007). Dokumentarische Methode und praxeologische Wissenssoziologie. In R. Schützeichel (Ed.), *Handbuch Wissenssoziologie und Wissensforschung* (pp. 180–190). Konstanz: Halem.
Bohnsack, R. (2014). *Rekonstruktive Sozialforschung. Einführung in die qualitativen Methoden*. Opladen and Toronto: Barbara Budrich.
Boltanski, L., & Chiapello, É. (2003). *Der neue Geist des Kapitalismus*. Konstanz: UTB.
Boltanski, L., & Thévenot, L. (2007). *Über die Rechtfertigung. Eine Soziologie der kritischen Urteilskraft*. Hamburg: Hamburger Edition.
Convery, A. (2009). The pedagogy of the impressed: How teachers become victims of technological vision. *Teachers and Teaching: Theory and Practice, 15*(1), 25–41. https://doi.org/10.1080/13540600802661303

Derouet, J. L. (2019). Die Soziologie der Konventionen im Bereich der Bildung, Wissenschaft, Politik und Gesellschaftskritik in Frankreich am Übergang vom 20. ins 21. Jahrhundert. In C. Imdorf, R. J. Leemann, & P. Gonon (Eds.), *Bildung und Konventionen. Die "Economie des conventions" in der Bildungsforschung* (pp. 47–84). Wiesbaden: Springer VS. https://doi.org/10.1007/978-3-658-23301-3

Diaz-Bone, R. (2011). Einführung in die Soziologie der Konventionen. In R. Diaz-Bone (Ed.), *Soziologie der Konventionen. Grundlagen einer pragmatischen Anthropologie* (pp. 9–41). Frankfurt a.M: Campus.

Erstad, O. (2012). The learning lives of digital youth – beyond the formal and informal. *Oxford Review of Education, 38*(1), 25–43. https://doi.org/10.1080/03054985.2011.577940

Förschler, A., Hartong, S., Kramer, A., Meister-Scheytt, C., & Junne, J. (2021). Zur (ambivalenten) Wirkmächtigkeit datengetriebener Lernplattformen: Eine Analyse des "Antolin"-Leseförderungsprogramms. *MedienPädagogik: Zeitschrift für Theorie und Praxis der Medienbildung, 44,* 52–72. https://doi.org/10.21240/mpaed/44/2021.10.28.X

Foucault, M. (2014). *Überwachen und Strafen. Die Geburt des Gefängnisses.* Frankfurt a.M.: Suhrkamp.

Grimaldi, E., & Ball, S. J. (2021). The blended learner: Digitalisation and regulated freedom – neoliberalism in the classroom. *Journal of Education Policy, 36*(3), 393–416. https://doi.org/10.1080/02680939.2019.1704066

Hangartner, J., Kaspar, A., & Fankhauser, R. (2019). Selbstständigkeit als Antizipation der Arbeitswelt in der Schule. *Swiss Journal of Sociology, 45*(3), 299–316. https://doi.org/10.2478/sjs-2019-0014

Hartong, S. (2019). The transformation of state monitoring systems in Germany and the US: Relating the datafication and digitalisation of education to the Global Education Industry. In M. Parreira do Amaral (Ed.), *Researching the global education industry* (pp. 157–180). London: Palgrave.

Jobér, A., & Player-Koro, C. (2019). *Education trade fairs, Digitalisation and education. NERA conference paper.* Retrieved from http://muep.mau.se/handle/2043/29978, 18.03.2020.

Lange, J. (2020). Medienkompetenz als unbekannte Praxis. Ethnographische Perspektiven auf Digital Natives. *Zeitschrift für Grundschulforschung, 13*(1), 15–29. https://doi.org/10.1007/s42278-019-00068-1

Leemann, R. J. (2019). Educational Governance von Ausbildungsverbünden in der Berufsbildung – die Macht der Konventionen. In: R. Langer & T. Brüsemeister (Eds.), *Handbuch Educational Governance Theorien* (pp. 265–287). Wiesbaden: Springer VS. https://doi.org/10.1007/978-3-658-22237-6_13

Leemann, R. J., & Imdorf, C. (2019). Potential der Soziologie der Konventionen in der Bildungsforschung. In C. Imdorf, R. J. Leemann, & P. Gonon (Eds.), *Bildung und Konventionen. Die "Economie des conventions" in der Bildungsforschung* (pp. 3–47). Wiesbaden: Springer VS. https://doi.org/10.1007/978-3-658-23301-3

Lupton, D., & Williamson, B. (2017). The datafied child: The dataveillance of children and implications for their rights. *New Media & Society, 19*(5), 780–794. https://doi.org/10.1177/1461444816686328

Macgilchrist, F. (2019). Cruel optimism in edtech: When the digital data practices of educational technology providers inadvertently hinder educational equity. *Learning, Media and Technology, 44*(1), 77–86. https://doi.org/10.1080/17439884.2018.1556217

Macgilchrist, F. (2021). What is 'critical' in critical studies of edtech? Three responses. *Learning, Media and Technology*, *46*(3), 243–249. https://doi.org/10.1080/17439884.2021.1958843

Merton, R. K. (1990). *The focussed interview*. New York: The Free Press.

Münch, R. (2018). *Der Bildungsindustrielle Komplex*. Weinheim: Belz.

Münnich, S. (2017). L. Boltanski & E. Chiapello: Der Neue Geist des Kapitalismus. In K. Kraemer & F. Brugger (Eds.), *Schlüsselwerke der Wirtschaftssoziologie* (pp. 385–392). Wiesbaden: Springer VS. https://doi.org/10.1007/978-3-658-08184-3_42

Nachtwey, O., & Seidl, T. (2017). *Die Ethik der Solution und der Geist des digitalen Kapitalismus* [The Ethic of Solutionism and the Spirit of Digital Capitalism]. Frankfurt a.M: Institut für Sozialforschung an der Johann Wolfgang Goethe-Universität. Retrieved from: https://www.ifs.uni-frankfurt.de/wp-content/uploads/IfS-WP-11.pdf, 18.03.2020.

Peschitola, M. (2021). Re-imagining digital technology in education through critical and neomaterialist insights. *Digital Education Review*, *40*, 154–171. https://doi.org/10.1344/der.2021.40.154-171

Player-Koro, C., & Beach, D. (2017). The influence of private actors on the education of teachers in Sweden. A networked ethnography study of education policy mobility. *Acta Paedagogica Vilnensia*, *39*, 83–96. https://doi.org/10.15388/ActPaed.2017.39.11476

Player-Koro, C., Bergviken-Rensfeldt, A., & Selwyn, N. (2018). Selling tech to teachers: Education trade shows as policy events. *Journal of Education Policy*, *33*(5), 682–703. https://doi.org/10.1080/02680939.2017.1380232

Rode, D., & Stern, M. (2017). Praktiken der Objektivierung und Subjektivierung. Eine praxeologische Perspektive auf Medienkompetenzerwerb im Tanzunterricht. In *Jahrbuch Medienpädagogik 13* (pp. 231–243). Wiesbaden: Springer VS.

Selwyn, N. (2013). *Distrusting educational technology: Critical questions for changing times*. London: Routledge.

Selwyn, N. (2016). *Is technology good for education?* New Jersey: John Wiley & Sons.

Selwyn, N. (2019). What's the problem with learning analytics? *Journal of Learning Analytics*, *6*(3), 11–19. https://doi.org/10.18608/jla.2019.63.3

Silseth, K., & Erstad, O. (2022). Exploring opportunities, complexities, and tensions when invoking students' everyday experiences as resources in educational activities. *Teaching and Teacher Education*, *112*, 1–11. https://doi.org/10.1016/j.tate.2022.103633

Steinberg, M. (2021a). Zum Umgang mit Digitalisierung im Schulunterricht. Auf Spurensuche in einer Schweizer Tabletklasse. *Pädagogische Korrespondenz*, *62*(1), 111–124.

Steinberg, M. (2021b). Transformation durch Bildungsdigitalisierung? Zur Governance der digitalen Schulwelt. *Sozialwissenschaftliche Rundschau*, *61*(4), 431–450.

Steinberg, M., & Schmid, Y. (2020). "Wenn wir jetzt nichts machen, dann lernen die ja nichts – und dann haben wir sofort angefangen zu arbeiten." Wert und Rechtfertigung der Nutzung neuer Lehr- und Lernmedien in der Primarschule, vor und nach den pandemiebedingten Schulschließungen. In *Philologie im Netz*, *24*, 448–462.

Williamson, B. (2016). Political computational thinking: Policy networks, digital governance and 'learning to code'. *Critical Policy Studies*, *10*(1), 39–58. https://doi.org/10.1080/19460171.2015.1052003

Williamson, B. (2018). Silicon startup schools: Technocracy, algorithmic imaginaries and venture philanthropy in corporate education reform. *Critical Studies in Education*, *59*(2), 218–236. https://doi.org/10.1080/17508487.2016.1186710

Williamson, B. (2020a). New digital laboratories of experimental knowledge production: Artificial intelligence and education research. *London Review of Education*, *18*, 209–220. https://doi.org/10.14324/LRE.18.2.05

Williamson, B. (2020b). Bringing up the bio-datafied child: Scientific and ethical controversies over computational biology in education. *Ethics and Education*, *15*(4), 444–463. https://doi.org/10.1080/17449642.2020.1822631

Williamson, B. (2021). Making markets through digital platforms: Pearson, edu-business, and the (e) valuation of higher education. *Critical Studies in Education*, *62*(1), 50–66. https://doi.org/10.1080/17508487.2020.1737556

INDEX

academic failure 42
activity regulation 68–69
actor's perspective 208–209
alphabetical principle 32
Apprentissage et pratique de la lecture (Learning and Practicing Reading) 46
autonomous learner, fabrication of 1–2; critique of autonomy-oriented learning environments 9–11; deconstructionnnnnn 206–221; French/German research traditions 11–16; translation of concepts of autonomy 6–9
autonomous workshops 29–33; knowledge mobilization 30–31; near absence of support for pupils 32–33; worksheets 31–32
autonomy: autonomous school activities 25–40; autonomous workshops 29–33; autonomy as essentially contested concept 3–6; autonomy-oriented learning settings as *dispositif* 2–3; critiques 9–11; as essentially contested philosophical concept 3–6; facade 182–185; getting pupils to take responsibility for their learning 107–124; group pedagogy 141–157; irony of 185–188; norms of 192–205; lack of 168, 184; learning settings oriented to 2–3; mindfulness meditation and 91–104; pedagogy of 61–74; self-reflection and 125–140; sovereign or autonomously acting subjects 199, 202; special education classes 177–191; term 2; thwarted 117–119; translations of concepts of 6–9; *Travaux Personnels Encadrés* (TPE) and 158–173
autonomy-oriented learning environments, critique of 9–11

baccalaureat 148–149
becoming in/sufficiently able 197–199
Bernstein, Basil 13, 26–31, 42, 109, 141; analyzing autonomous school activities: framing, concept 28–29; invisible pedagogy 27–28
Big Tech 98
Bildung 192
Bissex, Glenda L. 45
Bohnsack, Ralf 209
Boltanski, L. 214
Bovey, Laurent 177
Buddhism 96–98
Butler, Judith 12, 193–195

castaway 51–53
Chartier, Anne-Marie 45
choices, offering 112–115
"Classes and Pedagogies: Visible and Invisible" 27
classes flexibles 11
Claude, Marie-Sylvie 141
co-construction 165–168

cognitive autonomy 44–49; French appropriation 46–48; psychogenetic theory of ethnocentric reading 44–46
compulsory autonomy 119
concernment 113
confrontation, pupils 115–117
contracts 141–143
Council of Europe's Modern Language Project 7
Cousinet, Roger 142
COVID-19 212
curriculum 41–44, 118, 163, 166, 212; for compulsory education 125; of French *école maternelle* 49–54; language in 42; penetrating 47; pupil autonomy in 77–78; rewriting of 54; specific subject-related knowledge and 149; from universal psychogenesis to 44–49

Dangwal, R. 8
deconstruction, autonomous learner 206–208; control in digital classroom setting 214–217; digitized school of tomorrow 209–211; discovering autonomous learner from actor's perspective 208–209; processing figure of autonomous learner 211–212; reflections on self-directed learning 212–214
deviations: allowing 200–201; explaining 201–202
didactic contract, group pedagogy 147–148; instructions 149–150; interactions 150–152; interviewing pupils 153–155; subject-related knowledge 148–149; teacher's arbitration 152–153
didactics, autonomy: case studies 78–89; contrasting 86–89; cycle 1/2 classes 82–86; primary school 79–82; concepts in differentiated classroom settings 77–78; multigrade class differentiation 76–77; in multigrade classrooms 75–90; from teaching to learning 75–76
digitized school of tomorrow, vision of 209–211
dis/ability 193–196
discipline of the self 94–96
dispositif: alternative 178; of autonomous learner 9, 129; autonomy-oriented learning settings as 2–3; invented spelling 41–60;
learning arrangements as 108–110; pedagogical 44, 119, 158; term 3
Documentary Method 209
Durler, Héloïse 1, 13, 15, 107, 183

école maternelle 25–27, 41–42; autonomous workshops in 29–33; individual Montessori-type activities 34–38; invented spelling and 41–60
Écrire et Rédiger 48
éducation nouvelle 6
education: activity regulation 68–69; adult 7, 127; different uses of "meta" 69–72; digital 208; inclusive 2, 107, 179–180, 202; maintaining school order 66–68; numerical strip 62–64; secondary 42, 107, 158; self-education 142; special 16, 50, 96, 177–192, 196–197; student error conceptions 64–66; teacher 9, 98, 125, 127
educational cosmopolitan enclave 102
educational reform, approaches to 6–9
élève autonome see autonomous learner, fabrication of
emancipatory counter-cultural movements 7
emergent literacy 45
essentially contested concept, autonomy 3–6
ethnocentric reading, psychogenetic theory of 44–46
ethnography 12, 16, 128, 192, 197, 200; fieldwork 15, 92, 129–131, 181, 184; participant observation 12, 129; perspectives 128–129
expressive model 41
external influences, acknowledging/hiding 200

Fankhauser, Regula 1, 125
Ferreiro, Emilia 45
Fietcher, Ursula 75
flipped classroom 111
forme scolaire 3
Foucault, M. 3, 12, 93–95, 99–100, 129
framing, concept 28–29
Francophone research traditions 11–16
French and German research traditions 11–16
functional deceleration 101

Gachet-Delaborde, M. 32
general competences *(Überfachliche Kompetenzen)* 77

genius young reader 45
German school system 196–197
Germanophone research traditions 11–16
ghettos 181
Girinshuti, Crispin 1, 107
Glasman, D. 141
governmentality 12, 129
government, techniques of 93, 99–100
green booklet 132–135
Grounded-Theory-Methodology 198
group pedagogy: contracts 141–143; didactic contract 147–155; educational contract 145–147; social contract 144–145; survey 143–144

Hangartner, Judith 1, 125
heterodox appropriation 163–164
heterogeneity, term 77–78

ideal client 43
implicit norms 199
inclusive reform 177
individual autonomy 192–193; becoming in/sufficiently able 197–199; implicit norms 199; maintaining norms 200–202; norms of 192–205
individual Montessori-type activities 34–38; commitment of students 37–38; monitoring 36–37; quantitative/qualitative differentiation 34–36
instructions 149–150
International School 92–94, 99
invented spelling 41–44; cognitive autonomy 44–49; didactization of paradigm of 46–48; explaining concept 43, 47–52; transposition into actual curriculum 49–54
invented writing (*écriture inventée*) 43
invisible pedagogy 27–28, 38, 43, 109, 141, 163

Joigneaux, Christophe 25, 32, 61

Kabat-Zinn, Jon 96–98
Kant, E. 4, 6

Lahire, Bernard 13, 25
learning disability, concept 196–197
learning journal 130–131
lifelong learning 127
lower secondary school, autonomy in 110–111

Martens, M. 128
McNay, L. 102
Menzel, C. 128
Merl, Thorsten 192
meta, different uses of 69–72
metagraphic interview 47
mindfulness meditation 91–94; discipline 94–96; *see also* technology of the self; growing interest in 96–98; pedagogical intentions of 100–102
Mindfulness-Based Stress Reduction Programme 98
Ministry of National Education 41, 46
mobilization 112
modernity, reflexive 126–128
monitoring 36–37
Montmasson-Michel, Fabienne 41
multigrade classes 14, 75–88

Naço, Ditjola 125
Netterm, Julien 61
New Education 142
new education movement (le mouvement d'"éducation nouvelle") 108–110
new middle classes 27–28
norms, maintaining 200–202
numerical strip, uses of 62–64

OECD 1

parents, recourse to 119–121
pedagogy, autonomy 61–62; activity regulation 68–69; different uses of "meta" 69–72; maintaining school order 66–68; numerical strip 62–64; student error conceptions 64–66
personalized learning 8; worksheets 31–32
Piaget, Jean 45
policy goal, autonomous learner 2
political autonomy 52
positive discipline 99
poststructuralist perspective 9, 78, 193–196
practices: classroom 1, 3, 8, 13, 107, 134, 201, 210, 217; differentiation 192; disciplinary 94, 99–100; discursive 194; educational 10–11, 28, 61, 97, 178, 192, 209; feedback 12; language 71; metacognitive 64; Montessori-inspired 36; pedagogical 9, 14–15, 42, 50, 64, 76, 94, 110, 126, 131, 214; reflective 126–131, 137–138; regulation 198–201;

social 12–13, 193–194; teaching 1, 14, 54, 84, 101, 125, 127, 178, 197, 212–213, 217
productive model 42
progressive education 6–9
project week 135–138
publicization 62–64
pupils: commitment of students 37–38; confronting 115–117; getting pupils to take responsibility for their learning 107–124; mastering school knowledge 168–171; interviewing 153–155; near absence of support for 32–33; supporting student activity 36–37

qualitative differentiation 34–36
quantitative differentiation 34–36

Rabenstein, K. 128
Rademacher, S. 128
Rayou, Patrick 141
reader's text 148–149
Reckwitz, A. 194
reflexive educational theory 127
reflexive modernity 126–128
Reformpädagogik 6
Reh, S. 128
remedial teacher *(Heilpädagogin)* 85
researcher, curriculum and 51–53
resource persons 114
responsibility, pupils 107–108; confronting pupils 115–117; learning arrangements as *dispositifs* 108–110; lower secondary school autonomy 110–111; offering choices 112–115; recourse to parents 119–121; thwarted autonomy 117–119
Rey, Jeanne 91
Richard-Bossez, Ariane 25
Rousseau, J.-J. 4, 6
Röstigraben 11

Schmid, Yannick 206
school order, maintaining 66–68
Selbständigkeit 2
self-directed learning 7–8, 107, 134, 206, 216–217; practices of 129–131; reflections on 212–214
self-government 142
self-organized learning environment 8
self-reflection 125–126; as central imperative in reflexive modernity 126–128; project week 135–138

semi-autonomous workshops 68
self-agency 93
socialization, term 13
"Souvenir de la nuit du 4" (Hugo) 150–152
special education classes 177–178; changing landscape 180–182; facade of autonomy 182–185; irony of autonomy 185–188; theoretical framework/methodology 180; Vaud canton, school system 178–180
special educational needs 9–10
Steinberg, Mario 206
structuralist theory 193–194
student errors, conceptions of 64–66
subject-related knowledge 148–149
Swiss National Science Foundation 11

Taylorian skills 166
technology of the self, concept 93–96, 98–100; *see also* governmentality
therapeutic surveillance 99
Thévenot, L. 214
third culture kids 102
thwarted autonomy 117–119
Topaze effect 31
topic, finding: academic subjects 161–163; cultural affinities 160–161; heterodox appropriation 163–164; socially and academically differentiated postures 164–165
Travaux Personnels Encadrés (TPE): finding topics 160–165; overview of 158–160; work during sessions 165–171

UN Convention on the Rights of Persons with Disabilities 197
United Nations 95
United Nations Refugee Agency 95

Vaquero, Stéphane 158
Vaud, Canton of 178–180, 182–185
vulnerability, concept 5
Vygotskij, Lev 142

Weidmann, Laura 75
work during sessions, TPE: co-construction 165–168
workshop-grouping *see* autonomous workshops
workshops 111
World Health Organization 95